Gerard Mai

Gerard Manley Hopkins was among the most innovative writers of the Victorian period. Experimental and idiosyncratic, his work remains important for any student of nineteenth-century literature and culture.

This guide to Hopkins's life and work offers:

- a detailed account of Hopkins's life and creative development
- an extensive introduction to Hopkins's poems, their critical history and the many interpretations of his work
- cross-references between sections of the guide, in order to suggest links between texts, contexts and criticism
- suggestions for further reading.

Part of the *Routledge Guides to Literature* series, this volume is essential reading for all those beginning detailed study of Hopkins and seeking not only a guide to the poems, but a way through the wealth of contextual and critical material that surrounds them.

Angus Easson is Emeritus Professor of English, University of Salford, UK.

Routledge Guides To Literature

Editorial Advisory Board: Richard Bradford (University of Ulster at Coleraine), Shirley Chew (University of Leeds), Mick Gidley (University of Leeds), Jan Jedrzejewski (University of Ulster at Coleraine), Ed Larrissy (University of Leeds), Duncan Wu (St Catherine's College, University of Oxford)

Routledge Guides to Literature offer clear introductions to the most widely studied authors and texts. Each book engages with texts, contexts and criticism, highlighting the range of critical views and contextual factors that need to be taken into consideration in advanced studies of literary works. The series encourages informed but independent readings of texts by ranging as widely as possible across the contextual and critical issues relevant to the works examined, rather than presenting a single interpretation. Alongside general guides to texts and authors, the series includes 'Sourcebooks', which allow access to reprinted contextual and critical materials as well as annotated extracts of primary text.

Already available:*

Geoffrey Chaucer by Gillian Rudd
Ben Jonson by James Loxley
William Shakespeare's The Merchant of Venice: A Sourcebook edited by
    S. P. Cerasano
William Shakespeare's King Lear: A Sourcebook edited by Grace Ioppolo
William Shakespeare's Othello: A Sourcebook edited by Andrew Hadfield
William Shakespeare's Macbeth: A Sourcebook edited by Alexander Leggatt
William Shakespeare's Hamlet: A Sourcebook edited by Sean McEvoy
William Shakespeare's Twelfth Night: A Sourcebook edited by Sonia Massai
John Milton by Richard Bradford
John Milton's Paradise Lost: A Sourcebook edited by Margaret Kean
Alexander Pope by Paul Baines
Jonathan Swift's Gulliver's Travels: A Sourcebook edited by Roger D. Lund
Mary Wollstonecraft's A Vindication of the Rights of Woman: A Sourcebook edited
    by Adriana Craciun
Jane Austen by Robert P. Irvine
Jane Austen's Emma: A Sourcebook edited by Paula Byrne
Jane Austen's Pride and Prejudice: A Sourcebook edited by Robert Morrison
Byron, by Caroline Franklin
Mary Shelley's Frankenstein: A Sourcebook edited by Timothy Morton
The Poems of John Keats: A Sourcebook edited by John Strachan
The Poems of Gerard Manley Hopkins: A Sourcebook Edited by Alice Jenkins
Charles Dickens's David Copperfield: A Sourcebook edited by Richard J. Dunn
Charles Dickens's Bleak House: A Sourcebook edited by Janice M. Allan

---

*   Some titles in this series were first published in the Routledge Literary Sourcebooks series, edited by Duncan Wu, or the Complete Critical Guide to Literature series, edited by Jan Jedrzejewski and Richard Bradford.

Gerard Manley Hopkins

Angus Easson

Routledge
Taylor & Francis Group

LONDON AND NEW YORK

First edition published 2011
by Routledge
2 Park Square, Milton Park, Abingdon, Oxon OX14 4RN

Simultaneously published in the USA and Canada
by Routledge
270 Madison Avenue, New York, NY 10016

Routledge is an imprint of the Taylor & Francis Group, an informa business

© 2011 Angus Easson

Typeset in Series Design by Taylor & Francis Books
Printed and bound in Great Britain by TJ International Ltd, Padstow, Cornwall

British Library Cataloguing in Publication Data
A catalogue record for this book is available from the British Library

Library of Congress Cataloging in Publication Data
A catalog record for this title has been submitted

ISBN 13: 978-0-415-27323-7 (hbk)
ISBN 13: 978-0-415-27324-4 (pbk)
ISBN 13: 978-0-203-83518-0 (ebk)

For Bernard

Contents

Acknowledgements

My thanks to Jan Jedrzejewski, who invited me to contribute to this series and was willing to allow me to write on the author of my choice. My thanks too to Emma Nugent at Routledge, who has supported and encouraged me, particularly in the later stages of finishing and preparing the manuscript. My thanks to Jackie Dias, my copy editor, and to Stacey Carter, my production editor, who has steered me through to publication.

Abbreviations and referencing

Throughout the text, references to the poetry are from *Gerard Manley Hopkins: The Major Works*, ed. Catherine Phillips (Oxford: Oxford University Press, 2002), by line number of the poem. References to editorial matter in this edition are abbreviated as *P*.

Other abbreviations are:

J *The Journals and Papers of Gerard Manley Hopkins*, ed. Humphry House and Graham Storey (London: Oxford University Press, 1959).

L, 1 *The Letters of Gerard Manley Hopkins to Robert Bridges*, ed. Claude Colleer Abbott (London: Oxford University Press, 1935, rev. 1955).

L, 2 *The Correspondence of Gerard Manley Hopkins and Richard Watson Dixon*, ed. Claude Colleer Abbott (London: Oxford University Press, 1935, rev. 1955).

L, 3 *Further Letters of Gerard Manley Hopkins*, ed. Claude Colleer Abbott (London: Oxford University Press, 1938, rev. 1956).

S *The Sermons and Devotional Writings of Gerard Manley Hopkins*, ed. Christopher Devlin (London: Oxford University Press, 1959).

All references to the Bible are from the Authorised Version, ed. Robert Carroll and Stephen Prickett (Oxford: Oxford University Press, 1997), the translation with which Hopkins would be familiar before his conversion.

For all other references the Harvard system is used, giving work and page number, e.g. (Thomas 1969: 15). Full details of items cited (by author's name and date of publication) can be found in the Bibliography.

Cross-referencing between sections is one of the features of the series. Cross-references to relevant page numbers appear in bold type and square brackets, e.g. [28].

Introduction

Gerard Manley Hopkins is a rewarding and, if we are to get the best of him, a demanding poet.

It is possible to read him with much pleasure without having a detailed knowledge of his life, of his beliefs, and of the technical means by which he expressed his ideas and feelings. Hopkins, though, becomes a greater and more rewarding artist, the better we know and understand his love and study of nature, his doctrinal beliefs, and his technical innovations. In closely observing and recording nature, in prose as well as poetry, Hopkins developed a language to describe what he perceived – terms such as 'inscape' and 'instress' [**pp. 27; 63**]. He developed a poetic language and a new rhythm, which he named Sprung Rhythm [**pp. 68–9**]. And intimately and necessarily involved with his view of nature and his poetic innovation, are Hopkins's doctrinal beliefs. It is not only that he became a Catholic, a Jesuit, and a priest. He was also deeply devoted to Mary as Mother of God, above all through the doctrine of the Immaculate Conception [**p. 78**], and he was deeply moved by the idea that the Incarnation itself, Christ coming as man to share humanity and to suffer, was part of a grand scheme of salvation, preceding the creation of the world [**p. 134**]. So all nature, as God's creation, is to be explored, delighted in, and a means to perceive God in his creation and through it the beatific vision of God in his glory. It is not necessary to be a Catholic or even a Christian to enjoy Hopkins, but it is essential in reading the poetry to have an understanding of his beliefs.

This study, designed to explore and illuminate these issues and others, is progressive and cumulative. It begins with the life and contexts, passes to the work, both poetry and prose, and then surveys a range (necessarily only a selection) of critical responses to Hopkins, picking up and developing key issues, the often clashing voices here enforcing the need to develop our own readings and responses.

In reading this study it is vital to have a complete and convenient edition of the poetry, including fragments and unfinished work, in chronological order. Catherine Phillips's edition [**p. xv**] includes all the poetry and a useful selection of prose. It should be to hand to explore the poetry and to test this study's claims in Part II and those of the critics in Part III. Anyone wishing to read at least some of the poetry before beginning this study might start with the first poems of mature production: might plunge into 'The Wreck of the *Deutschland*' and the sonnets that immediately followed; or 'The Wreck' and a selection that includes 'Felix Randal', 'Spring and Fall', 'Spelt from Sibyl's Leaves', 'That Nature Is a Heraclitean Fire', and 'St Alphonsus Rodriguez'; or as an intriguing alternative, early poems, including 'The Escorial', 'A Vision of the Mermaids', 'The Alchemist in the City', 'Floris in Italy', 'The Nightingale', and then 'The Wreck'.

The reader of Hopkins needs to have a serious (not solemn) interest and delight in poetry. As a reader of Hopkins since 'A' Level, many years ago, I hope that this study will aid that interest and pleasure in the supreme poetic voice of Gerard Manley Hopkins.

1

Life and contexts

Introduction

Gerard Manley Hopkins was acclaimed in the twentieth century as amongst the greatest modern poets: his language and his poetic experiments spoke to a time, after the First World War, that rejected Victorian attitudes, Victorian poetry and Victorian poetic language. Yet, paradoxically, Hopkins had died in 1889, over a decade before the Victorian age ended and he was in many respects a true Victorian. In his life he was known as a promising student who became a Catholic and a Jesuit priest who, as he himself was all too aware, seemed to have achieved little and to have served God to little purpose, a man virtually unknown as a poet, his work unpublished until thirty years after his death. His poetic language and forms, his integration of nature, that great Romantic force, with the strict doctrines of Catholicism, made a new poetry, unlike that of Tennyson, Browning or Matthew Arnold. Hopkins indeed was compared to Walt Whitman, whose loose rhythms sought, like Hopkins's experiments, to forge new poetic forms. Accepting the comparison with the American poet, Hopkins also saw himself as startlingly like the man – a pity, he remarked, since Whitman was 'a very great scoundrel' (*L*, 1.155). That wry recognition of the ruffian in his own nature hints at Hopkins's sense of humour and a vein of self-deprecation in a man who saw himself clearly (not always quite liking what he saw). Outwardly, Hopkins's life is not obviously eventful, yet each phase proved deeply significant for his poetry, not least the long interval (1868–75) when he renounced poetic creation.

Three aspects in particular intertwine: friendship; conversion and priesthood; aesthetic theories and poetic achievement. Friendship helped on his conversion, gave him critical support in his poetry, and developed an emotional life that found poetic expression. Conversion led to Catholicism and the Society of Jesus; to the tension between God and poetic creativity; and in the poetry itself both to the reconciliation of God with Nature and to an anguished sense of exclusion from God. Aesthetic theories and poetic development produced the astonishing representations of Nature and of God in Nature and the daring experiments in language and rhythm that baffled those of his contemporaries who ever knew them and caused this Victorian to be proclaimed a Modern in the twentieth century and to sustain him as a truly great poet in the twenty-first.

Early years 1844–63

Gerard Manley Hopkins was born 28 July 1844 in Stratford, East London. His father, Manley Hopkins, was in marine insurance; his mother, Catherine, had married Manley Hopkins in 1843 and Gerard was the first of nine children. Eight years later, the family moved to Oak Hill Park, Hampstead (the house was destroyed in 1961). His family offered Gerard material and emotional comfort, stability, interests in music and drawing, and a firm grounding in religion. The family were High Church Anglicans, whose beliefs and worship were based on the Oxford or Tractarian Movement of the mid-nineteenth century [**p. 10**], which had rediscovered the truth of Catholic doctrines. Such doctrines were linked to ceremonial and ritual in church. High Anglicans also insisted upon the validity of Anglican orders, that is, that their ministers were endowed in unbroken line of succession from St Peter and the Apostles with the powers of the priest. This very closeness to the Catholic Church often led to extreme hostility, with accusations against those who became Catholics that they were 'perverts' to Romanism (the 'Roman' Catholic Church, so designated to identify it with the Pope of Rome and his claim to supreme and exclusive authority). This doctrinal security made Hopkins's conversion easier, when the time came, but also increased the bitterness and sense of alienation for him and his family when he made his decision.

At first, though, Hopkins's life was on the surface an ordinary middle-class one. After tuition and private school, from 1854 he went to Sir Roger Cholmley's School, Highgate, where despite the incompetence of the headmaster, Dyne, a witless flogger, he got on well with other boys, was nicknamed 'Skin' (*L*, 3.394), and followed the usual kind of curriculum – the Classics, emphasis being laid on translation to and from Latin and Greek and the writing of verse in those languages; mathematics; and a modern language – Hopkins read and spoke French fluently. Amongst his masters, briefly, was

Richard Watson Dixon, ten years his senior, already a poet, whose poetry Hopkins came to admire greatly and with whom, from 1878, he was to maintain a friendship through correspondence. Later, Dixon remembered 'a pale young boy, very light and active, with a very meditative & intellectual face' (*L*, 2.4) – Hopkins's own description (1887) adds hazel eyes and lightish brown hair. While active in games, he was already thoughtful, with an inward streak, curious about his own nature and that of others, what he described as the 'taste of myself ... incommunicable by any means to another man (as when I was a child I used to ask myself: What must it be to be someone else?)' (*S*, 123). If he could not enter readily into other natures, his meditations were to lead into the world's mystery and the darker side of his own nature.

At Highgate school he showed an obstinacy, developed as determination, that was to be evident even at his lowest ebb. Hopkins bet another boy that he could abstain from all liquid. His tongue and lips black, he won the bet, only for the headmaster to intervene, beat both boys, and require Hopkins to return his winnings. Hopkins protested unavailingly: he had won, even if he were to be punished, while the other boy lost nothing. The strength of will demonstrated by liquid deprivation was seen by others: a fellow Jesuit recalled Hopkins as having 'a strong manly will of his own', adding that if 'somewhat eccentric in his views and ways', these ways were pleasing and many of them original (*J*, 421). And if Hopkins's 'eccentricity' could put him at odds with his superiors, the strength of will carried him crucially his own way. At times, Hopkins's self-assessment could be harsher than that of others: he is a scoundrel like Whitman or feels himself a blackguard (*L*, 1.139). Yet here and in his moments of blackness brought on by morbid self-scrutiny, it is important to recognise the edge of humour in such judgements or, with the late Retreat notes, their private nature. Certainly, such strength of character, obstinacy even, was necessary when he had to face his family at his conversion, to face the choices of priesthood and entry to the Jesuits, to face for the rest of his life the consequences of these decisions.

Outside school, Hopkins developed his interests in drawing, music, and language. Music developed his interest in rhythm and stress, while his Aunt Maria took him out sketching on Hampstead Heath. Though never a distinctive artist, the influence of Hampstead's artistic communities and even more of John Ruskin, the great if eccentric critic of art and architecture, made him observe natural forms in detail. Under Ruskin's insistence that we should 'go to Nature in all singleness of heart ... having no other thoughts but how best to penetrate her meaning ... rejecting nothing, selecting nothing, and scorning nothing' (Ruskin 1897: 448), Hopkins looked intensely and strove in his Journals to capture the particularity of things, by which their essence might be known. Ruskin's command did not deny beauty even amidst the ordinary and the excluded, so that later Hopkins, while a Jesuit novice at Roehampton, noted how the 'slate slabs of the urinals even are frosted in graceful sprays' (*J*, 196). Ruskin's beauty was not merely a general impression, which cast its eye aside from the sordid, but an intent scrutiny, and Hopkins followed him, though he was to perceive a very different power or charge within nature. Ruskin too helped point Hopkins towards a technical vocabulary with which to describe with precision what he saw. Directed by Ruskin's fascination with Gothic architecture, Hopkins consulted glossaries of architectural terms and found words that he used later – bay, boss, canopy, crest, cusp – for his own purposes (White 1992: 21).

Hopkins at school was already writing poetry. He won a school prize in 1860 for the subject set, 'The Escorial' [**pp. 44–5**], on Philip II of Spain's great palace. Hopkins drew on his architectural interests, siding with Ruskin and 'Gothic grace' against the 'monstrous' regularity of the palace, while he adopted conventional anti-Catholic and anti-Spanish prejudices, against 'those who strove God's gospel to confound'. While a highly finished piece for a teenager, two other poems can be placed more readily in Hopkins's poetic development. 'A Vision of the Mermaids' [**pp. 45–6**] was written out below a circular drawing (*J*, plate 3) and is exuberant in its sensory detail – 'spikes of light | Spear'd open lustrous gashes, crimson-white' – as the poet observes mermaids sporting, diving so that 'the argent bubbles stream'd | Airwards, disturb'd'. More restrained, more aware of language's ability when spare, is 'Winter with the Gulf Stream' [**pp. 46–7**], notable also for being Hopkins's only poem published in popular form before his death: it appeared in *Once a Week*, a magazine of fiction and poetry, in February 1863.

University 1863–67

In January 1863, Hopkins won a place at Oxford (White, 1992: 35, 39–41) and in April (academic years were not so set as now), he went up to Balliol College. On moving to Oxford, Hopkins of course did not put his family behind him and he reported eagerly back to his mother on his rooms in College, a bedroom and a sitting room in the roof (later more convenient ones on the ground floor), and set out the routine of his day, later declaring 'I am almost too happy' (*L*, 3.69, 82, 79). But other influences began to work upon him as he grew up and grew away from the family and here at Oxford he was to make the greatest decision of his life, followed by three other crucial decisions – he decided, though not without doubts and not until 1866, to become a Catholic. He then successively settled on the priesthood and on entry to the Jesuits, coupling these with a decision to abandon poetry.

Oxford when Hopkins arrived was an ancient city dominated by the University. Twentieth-century industry, notably cars at Cowley, transformed it, even while dividing Town and Gown, city and university going their own, often diverse, ways. In the nineteenth century, however, the townspeople, though liable to insult or rowdyism from the undergraduates – described vividly in Thomas Hughes's *Tom Brown at Oxford* (1861, ch.XI) – were largely dependent on the University through trade and services. Oxford, meaning the University, saw itself as a bastion of the Anglican Church and a powerhouse of ideas on religion, politics and social issues, in serious journals and magazines influential far beyond their circulation figures. Oxford, however strange and old-fashioned it may seem now and to many, particularly outsiders, perceived itself then as a power in the modern world, insignificant though that power might prove once you were beyond its influence.

The University in the 1860s was enjoying a period of comparative stability after the excitement and shake-up of the Oxford Movement. On the educational side, much was still to be reformed – female students were not admitted until the late 1870s, while in 1863 the University had only recently admitted Dissenters (including Catholics), though individual colleges were not required to follow this lead – fortunately for Hopkins, as it turned out, Balliol had. Fellows of colleges were clergymen of the Church of England and the curriculum was restricted – Classics (including philosophy), theology, and mathematics covered most studies. Yet the educational reorganisation earlier in the century had brought a new concern to teach, while many students showed a new seriousness. Oxford was now not simply a place for a young man to spend a few years sowing his wild oats, making friends and useful acquaintances, playing games or rowing, drinking, and fighting the town roughs. True, such students still existed into the 1860s. Cuthbert Bede's hero in *The Adventures of Verdant Green* (1853), an innocent, attends a friend's 'wine' evening, becomes thoroughly drunk, sings a song, makes an incoherent speech, and is found next morning lying on his carpet 'embracing the coal-skuttle' (Pt.I, ch.VIII). Thomas Hughes's *Tom Brown at Oxford*, set in the early 1840s, has wine evenings and betting, but also a new seriousness, in study and in the purpose of life.

Oxford was a religious foundation and although the grip of the Church of England was being loosened, its religious life was coloured by the Oxford Movement, sparked in the 1830s by a group of people concerned with England's ignorance of Anglicanism. John Keble had voiced the alarm of many when he spoke of 'National Apostacy', of the Church being controlled by politicians who did not believe in her doctrines or teaching, and betrayed by its members through indifference. Keble, and with him others, notably John Henry Newman, began publishing a series of pamphlets or tracts (hence the alternative title of the Tractarian Movement), which looked at the articles of belief of the Church of England, retrieving their historical origins and giving a new spiritual and mystical meaning to them, that contrasted with the social dullness of Anglican preaching and automatic church attendance: 'As they listened, men became strangely aware of the marvels of glory and awfulness amid which human life is passed' (Vidler 1974: 51). Newman in 1841 published Tract XC, the last as it proved, examining the 39 Articles, the basis of belief and discipline in the Church of England, of which students entering Oxford had then still to declare their acceptance, Articles that seemed clearly to reject Catholicism and Roman (Papal) authority. Rather than finding a reforming Calvinistic doctrine in the Articles, Newman argued that far from condemning, they allowed many Catholic practices and means of grace (Vidler 1974: 53–54).

Yet a puzzle remained. If the Church of England, in accepting Catholic doctrines, was indeed a part of the Universal or Catholic Church, how did one stand with regard to the Pope's authority, as a direct descendant of St Peter, to whom Jesus had given the power of supreme head on earth? After lengthy examination of the origins and development of Catholic doctrine, Newman embraced logical necessity and in 1845 became a Catholic. The Oxford Movement consolidated itself in the Church of England in Oxford and beyond in a revival of 'Catholic' doctrine and practices (altars, mass, candles, incense, veneration of Our Lady and the Saints, taken to extremes in ritualism's 'bells and smells'), and in an emphasis upon social work and reform, allied with a new urgency to bring the Church to the people in industrialised England. By the 1860s, its novelty gone, the Oxford Movement's achievements were familiar to Hopkins before he arrived at University and he, like others, came increasingly at Oxford to accept 'the idea of the Church as a sacred mystery, a holy fellowship, and in particular the seriousness' of its 'sacramental ordinances' (Vidler 1974: 158). But the end of his journey was to take Hopkins out of the 'middle way' (the *via media*) that the Church of England claimed to be.

Hopkins in 1863 was one of ninety or so undergraduates at Balliol, a college with an already established reputation for intellectual – and athletic – seriousness. He attended lectures in the college, where the set classical texts, Latin and Greek, were gone through, with translation and commentary (on linguistic matters, generally, rather than critical discussion). More important, more stimulating, were the weekly essays, alternately written in English and Latin, for his tutor. Hopkins's tutor was Benjamin Jowett, later Master of Balliol and the translator of Plato, but already remarkable in Oxford for his learning and suspect for his liberal theological views. To Hopkins he was a strange mixture, since 'when you can get him to talk he is amusing, but when the opposite, it is terribly embarrassing' (L, 3.73). Successfully passing his preliminary examinations in 1864, Hopkins went on to study classical literature, ancient history, and philosophy. Throughout his life, the Classics were important to Hopkins; he taught them and he thought of writing on Homer, on the Greek lyric metres and, importantly for his own poetic ideas, on the counterpointing, the interplay, between overt and covert meanings in the imagery of the choruses in Greek drama. Beyond comments in his letters, nothing of this was written, but the philosophical basis of his study, the meaning and, further, the rhythms of poetry, led him to think about the subtle interrelationship of language and thought – an undergraduate essay explores the crucial nature of rhythm and how sound can parallel meaning (J, 84–85). Language was no mere fancy decoration. Since to 'every word ... belongs a passion or prepossession or enthusiasm' (J, 125), the poet must strive to startle the reader with a clarity and precision that make that particular passion a revelation.

To Hopkins at Oxford, the natural world became increasingly a preoccupation, not simply because it seemed, as to the Romantics, to possess a power, but increasingly because that power was God's. If Jesus shared the world with us by becoming man, then the world, created by God, is to be celebrated, in all its concreteness. This discovery developed from the sensory and sensual delight Hopkins found in nature, his sight trained by his drawing and by Ruskin's 'great principle', that 'art should be made, not by learning from general ideas or words, but by looking at natural objects' (White 1992: 75), intensity of gaze and accuracy of observation, whether recorded visually or in words, leading to a quest for meaning. In Ruskin's case this led away from God to social issues; in Hopkins's, it led to a keener realisation of the indwelling power of God.

The surviving Journals show first and foremost the struggle, often triumphant, to record. Hopkins's acute vision seems to catch things almost invisible in their fleetingness to ordinary sight. Descriptions show Hopkins writing poetically – 'Moonlight hanging or dropping on treetops like blue cobweb' (*J*, 23) – or striving for precision – 'Shapes of frozen snow-drifts. Parallel ribs. Delightful curves. Saddles, lips, leaves' (*J*, 53). The shift of perception in the first from 'hanging' to 'dropping' is typical of Hopkins's poetic technique of redefining and refining meaning, while the second brings out Hopkins's emotional response to nature ('delightful') and his exploration of language's potential in the little list. Apart from the fascination with language shown by the Oxford Journal, the capturing of the visual in the verbal, Hopkins continued to write poetry. Despite his later attempt to destroy what he had written on renouncing poetry when entering the Jesuits, some 75 completed poems and fragments survive from 1864 to 1868. Hopkins experiments with forms and subjects, in epigrams or a sketch for a drama based on Ajax's madness after being refused the armour of Achilles (*J*, 17–18) or lines jotted down as hints or material. Several of the completed poems are concerned with the contemplative individual contrasted against the active world, whether the nun in 'Heaven-Haven' or the Alchemist of 'The Alchemist in the City' [**pp. 51–2; 55–6**], while a religious interest colours others.

These religious themes are symptomatic, for while study and leisure at Oxford, reading, canoeing or walking into the countryside, breakfasts and evening parties and debates, took up his time, Hopkins also developed his religious nature. Committed to the Church of England, coming from a closely-knit Christian family which had absorbed the doctrines of the Oxford Movement, in the Oxford where the memory of Newman was still strong though the man had been gone from Oxford and Anglicanism for twenty years, Hopkins began to attend Sunday evening meetings, where H.P. Liddon, a charismatic figure, explored the meaning of Christianity and the Church, and offered the chance of discussion and fellowship.

Hopkins was introduced to Liddon's Sunday evenings by friends and new friendships were a part of Hopkins's university life. Friends were made within the college and then increasingly and crucially outside it. A number of Hopkins's university friendships, important at the time, were naturally transitory; others survived, through correspondence, all his life, however seemingly unmatched each was to the other. Alexander Baillie, for example, a sceptic, wrote after Hopkins's death that 'All my intellectual growth, and a very large proportion of the happiness of those Oxford days, I owe to his companionship' (*J*, 296).

Two friends were to have an enduring effect on Hopkins, one lifelong, one necessarily transitory. These were Robert Bridges (1844–1930) and Digby Mackworth Dolben (1848–67). Bridges trained as a doctor, but after qualifying he abandoned medicine and concentrated on poetry (he became Poet Laureate in 1913). At Oxford, Bridges had High Church sympathies and possibly met Hopkins through Liddon's Sunday evenings: later, growing sceptical, he became scornful of Catholicism, though not holding his beliefs against Hopkins. A break in their correspondence (1871–74), which possibly indicates a break in friendship, was bridged and they exchanged poems, offering detailed comments, and Bridges met Hopkins in London on a number of occasions, in 1878 noting that 'we have sweet laughter, and pleasant chats. ... His poetry is magnificent but "caviare to the general"' (Phillips 1992: 91). Bridges, though, increasingly concerned to write in quantitative metres (based on the length of vowels, as in Greek and Latin poetry, rather than the normal English stress patterns), became less and less sympathetic to Hopkins's poetry. A month after Hopkins's death, lamenting that 'dear Gerard' was 'overworked, unhappy & would never have done anything great', Bridges, a man who had seen virtually all Hopkins's mature poetic production, put the knife in by adding how much worse his untimely death would have been 'had his promise or performance been more splendid. He seems to have been entirely lost & destroyed by those Jesuits' (Phillips 1992: 143). It was into these hands that Hopkins's poetic reputation would fall and however Bridges revised his estimate, he clearly saw no urgent reason or need to publish Hopkins's work and so the first collected edition only appeared in 1918.

It was Bridges who in February 1865 introduced Hopkins to a distant cousin, Digby Mackworth Dolben. Only one meeting, but an immediate sense of influence. Hopkins was smitten by Dolben's physical beauty and by his personality. It is difficult now to recapture the charm and magnetism that Dolben undoubtedly possessed: much of his behaviour was adolescent, carried to extremes. Already deeply religious, he was also a show-off. He had joined an Anglican order of Benedictine monks while still at school and in 1866 walked through Birmingham barefoot and in monk's habit (J, 325), at a time when Catholic ecclesiastical dress in the streets was still forbidden by law. Dolben was close to becoming a Catholic – had deferred his reception into the Church at the wish of his parents – when he was drowned while bathing in June 1867. It was a shock to Hopkins. He had written to Dolben letters 'without end', without 'a whiff of answer' (L, 1.1). Now to Bridges he wrote, 'there can very seldom have happened the loss of so much beauty (in body and mind and life) and of the promise of still more'. A little later, Hopkins was capable of steadier judgement, adding that there was 'a great want of strength in Dolben – more, of sense' (L, 1.16–17, 18). Yet Dolben seems to have deeply influenced Hopkins: years later, in 1873, he received 'as I think a great mercy about Dolben' (*J*, 236), presumably a conviction of Dolben's salvation.

'Smitten' was the word used earlier, and Hopkins was immensely attracted to Dolben, both by his religious life, at a time when himself close to conversion, and clearly also by his physical beauty. Hopkins was always possessed by physical beauty, whether of nature or humanity: one of his greatest self-mortifications was to deny himself the pleasures of sight. A penance prevented him seeing much for half a year (*J*, 190) and an earlier giving up of beauty 'until I had [God's] leave for it' is perhaps significantly linked to the arrival of a letter from Dolben, 'for which Glory to God' (*J*, 71). He insisted though upon the (traditional) physical beauty of Jesus (*S*, 35) and Christ's humanity fully justifies admiring the flesh as much as landscape or natural forms. Physical beauty was not a guarantee of moral or spiritual grace, though Hopkins declared (1879), 'I think ... no one can admire beauty of the body more than I do, and it is of course a comfort to find beauty in a friend or a friend in beauty'. But, he added, 'this kind of beauty is dangerous' (*L*, 1.95). Hopkins's feeling for Dolben, who he only saw once, was strongly charged and sexually charged. Hopkins wrote openly to Bridges about a man seen in Oxford: 'His face was fascinating me last term: I generally have one fascination or another on' (*L*, 1.8). Hopkins's attraction to men – and it is almost entirely to men – is understandable partly as 'crushes', particularly in the male ambience of school and Oxford, both homosocial societies, where friendship brings and binds men together. Such relationships include the sexual, but not therefore necessarily the physical expression of sex. Homosocial bonding, a common characteristic among men, does not necessarily lead to sexual or emotional exclusivity. Later, on entering the priesthood, Hopkins took a vow of chastity (that is, celibacy, sexual abstinence) and there is no evidence, not even a hint, to suggest he ever broke that vow (nor indeed that he ever in his life had sexual intercourse). The attraction to Dolben and Hopkins's later poetry do both suggest a strong homoeroticism – the love of man for man, a commitment beyond social bonding or even friendship. There is the beauty of the Bugler Boy, the 'lovely manly mould' of the *Eurydice*'s drowned sailor, and the broken roughness of Felix Randal [**pp. 102; 90; 102–3**]. Yet the sailor and Felix have an asexual poignancy. They are dead, rather than being objects of desire, their manhood broken. Beauty, attraction, desire and love are wonderfully interwoven in Hopkins's personality and art.

By modern definition, though, Hopkins was homosexual. Yet to say that may mislead rather than help, since that single term now covers a wide and varied range of possibilities, while convention then was, for example, both more accepting of physical contact in male friendship and yet criminalised certain sexual acts. Homosexuality was Hopkins's nature, not his practice. All his principal attractions were to men, though he had no difficulty in associating with women in his family and social circle and beyond in parish life. He writes about women: the Virgin Mary, obviously, and St Dorothea, and Margaret in 'Spring and Fall' (an intensely unsexual representation of beauty and loss) [**pp. 93–4; 50; 103–4**]. The intense concern, though, when not about nature and God and self, is men, yet no poem is a homosexual poem, just as Hopkins did not live out a 'homosexual life-style'. He recognised sexual temptations when preparing for confession (White 1992: 120), but avoided any overt physical expression. While leading a homosocial life as a Jesuit priest, a teacher at Stonyhurst, a professor at University College, Dublin, there are no signs of particular attachment to other priests, to students, or to members of his congregations beyond friendship. Nor did those who know him note anything irregular about his behaviour, though comments were made upon his oddity – in poetic language, by Bridges; in branches of his study, by his superiors; in eccentricities, by his acquaintance. Indeed, Henry Marchant stressed that Hopkins was certainly not effeminate: 'He had a certain *natural* grace of carriage that was pleasing and attractive but he was quite unconscious of the fact', adding that 'He spoke out pretty straight what he thought; once he said to me "I admire you and I despise you". I quite understood why. It gave no offence' (*J*, 421).

Catholicism

Hopkins at Oxford was thinking seriously and thinking seriously about his relationship to God, to Christ, and to the Church. Of this trinity, he was convinced of God's existence, except for a sickening moment in the summer of 1865, when, at odds with himself and others, he recorded in his Journal, 'Loss of faith in God' (White 1992: 120). He recovered his faith, but the loss was symptomatic of a struggle he went through: once recovered, he never doubted again. Of Christ, he had been brought up a Christian, so the beliefs he absorbed in his family, and from Liddon at Oxford, only confirmed him in the truth of Christ as saviour, of Jesus as man and God, of Jesus's real presence in the eucharist under the form of bread and wine – the doctrine of transubstantiation, that during the mass the priest not only commemorates the Last Supper, but that at the moment of saying 'This is My Body' and 'This is My Blood', the bread and wine become Jesus's flesh and blood. The Church was the stumbling block. Whereas Newman and others in the Oxford Movement had to start from the Calvinist foundations of Anglicanism and trace out, as though archaeologists, what the early Church believed and how that could be reconciled to the Church of England, Hopkins was already convinced of the doctrines of the Catholic Church. But was the Anglican Church truly part of the one Church, the preferred theory of the High Anglicans, a branch of the Church, possessing still its continuity and living nature, guaranteed by Jesus handing authority to St Peter? What if it were separate from that Church, no true part of it? In the end, Newman could see no way but one: the Catholic Church, the Pope at its head, was the only true Church and the Church of England was a heretical, illegal body, judged by the Catholic Church and rightly condemned. Hopkins's road was shorter and less difficult than Newman's, who had delayed and suffered, mentally and physically, while he tried to find the truth. Hopkins duly came to see the false position of the Church of England's claim to be a branch of the Catholic Church. On 17 July 1866, he noted in his Journal, 'I saw clearly the impossibility of staying in the Church of England' (*J*, 146). With a mood on him and no comfortable companion to his fellow students, he confided to one 'his fixed intention of going over to Rome'. The friend noted laconically, 'I did not attempt to argue with him' (*L*, 3.397).

This decision had grown on Hopkins for over a year, from shortly after his brief loss of faith. In September 1866 he noted that 'the silent conviction' that *he* was to become a Catholic, had been present for about a year, 'as strongly, in spite of my resistance to it ... as if I had already determined it' (*L*, 3.27). Now he felt the need for advice. It was to Newman he turned, not for advice about becoming a Catholic – that was fixed – but about 'my immediate duty' (*L*, 3.22). Should he become a Catholic at once or should he consider his family, break the news to them, then complete his degree, before taking the final step? Yet if he died before being received into the Church, would he be granted salvation? For Hopkins this was an intensely serious and painful question (*L*, 3.92). Conversion meant cutting himself off, spiritually at least, possibly socially as well, from his family, who would see it as abandoning Protestant truth. Afterwards, he could joke about it to Bridges (*L*, 1.10), but the joke roughly covered the pain. Newman in Birmingham was kind to him when they met in September and on 21 October 1866 Hopkins was received by Newman into the Catholic Church.

It was not easy to leave the Church of England. Newman himself, devoted as he had been to the Anglican way, walked with a friend shortly before his conversion, clinging to his hand, unable to speak, weeping, 'like a man suffering in extremest agony' (Faber 1954: 421).

Hopkins had no such ties over half a lifetime, of love and devotion to a Church which Newman, in his thought, writings and feelings, had given back to itself, but the immediate effect on his family and so on himself, was terrible. It is difficult quite to understand how hostile, how prejudiced, educated, apparently sensible people still were to Romanism as it was sneeringly termed, to 'Papistical practices', characterised as blind obedience, idol worship, false doctrine. Though only a draft of his father's letter to him survives, so we cannot be sure of the exact words sent, Hopkins's response about it to Newman – 'I cannot read [it] twice. If you will pray for [my parents] and me just now I shall be deeply thankful' (L, 3.29) – shows it was close to what was finally sent. The agony of the father, as though his son were dead, is painful still: 'O Gerard my darling boy are you indeed gone from me?' (L, 3.97). His father's attempt to dissuade Gerard was met by that determination – obstinacy, perhaps – so critically part of Hopkins's character. It is indicative though of how far parts of the Church of England had moved since the earlier part of the century, borne on by the Oxford Movement, that Hopkins's father could urge that his son had everything necessary in the Anglican communion – doctrine, valid priestly orders, ceremony. Whatever else Hopkins was entering the Catholic Church for, though, it was not ritualism: robes, candles, incense, the ceremony of the mass – these all could be had, and more, in the Church of England. Such forms, though, meant nothing to Hopkins without the truth of substance, of God, Christ, and the Catholic Church, founded by Jesus, with the successors of St Peter at its head. Indeed, many Catholic churches at this time were poor and shabby, poky by contrast with the decorative innovations of the Church of England. Rather, it was something 'deep down' he sought and found. It was the truth of transubstantiation that mattered, for religion without it was 'sombre, dangerous, illogical, with that it is – not to speak of its grand consistency and certainty – *loveable*' (L, 3.17). That truth though lay in the Catholic Church, not in the Anglican, and combining feeling with thought, reading the Bible with a conviction of God's command, Hopkins became and remained a Catholic.

Now Hopkins's determination – or obstinacy – stood him in good stead. Things had changed at Oxford since the turmoil of the Oxford Movement and Newman's 'perversion' to Romanism. High Anglicanism was accepted in Oxford and Catholics themselves were admitted by a number of colleges. Yet Newman, to whom Hopkins had turned, whom he remembered with affection throughout the rest of his life, was regarded with deep suspicion and those who went over to Rome might be insulted or cold-shouldered. Newman had been mocked in J.A. Froude's autobiographical novel, *The Nemesis of Faith* (1849) and now, fifteen years later, Francis Chavasse, afterwards Bishop of Liverpool, reacted to the news of Hopkins's conversion and to his 'wan face' glimpsed in Oxford, by declaring that for the first time 'the reality of a perversion came home with stunning violence to my heart' (Phillips 1992: 39).

And yet once away from Oxford, such attitudes dissolved. Oxford proved, however it remained in Hopkins's affections, a smaller, more parochial place than its inhabitants believed. Newman lived in a larger world at Birmingham, looking out across England to Europe and Rome, and Hopkins became in some measure part of that larger world, where 'perversion' and Romanism mattered little, though he found other constrictions placed on him. Newman gave Hopkins wise advice at the time of his conversion: for the first Christmas after his conversion, 'if you can be at home with comfort, home is the best place for you. ... Show your friends at home that your becoming a Catholic has not unsettled you in the plain duty that lies before you' (*L*, 3.405). And if there was pain and a sense of separation, nonetheless, Hopkins's family came to accept his conversion with time. Hopkins observed with some surprise the kind and contented way his parents took his entry to the Jesuits in 1868 (*L*, 3.51) and noted that he 'found things pleasanter than they have ever been since my conversion, which is a great comfort' (*L*, 3.56).

And despite all the hostility and irrationality of men like Froude and Chavasse – and even with them, the intensity of feeling indicates what they believed was at stake, the very institutions of England and the salvation of the individual – there is no evidence, during his remaining time at Oxford or at any time after, that Hopkins was the victim of anti-Catholic prejudice or felt himself to be so, however much being a Catholic, priest, and Jesuit might at times isolate him.

After Oxford: Catholicism and vocation 1867–68

Awarded a first class degree in Classics and Philosophy in 1867, Hopkins had to decide what to do with his life. That he was now a Catholic determined his spiritual life. Catholicism was a way of life, a discipline, a relationship with authority. But what profession should, indeed now could, he adopt? If he had not become a Catholic, he might have become a College Fellow and tutor at Oxford or an Anglican clergyman or even, like his father, gone into business. The priesthood was of course possible, if he felt he had a vocation, yet nothing in the published journals and letters suggests Hopkins had previously thought of becoming a clergyman.

As a stop-gap, essentially, he turned to Newman and accepted a post (1867–68) at the Oratory School in Birmingham. The routine was very different from Oxford. Up at a quarter past six, with 'a melancholy punctuality', he followed a timetable of mass, preparation, classes, games, meals. He scarcely had any time to himself, squeezing in letters to friends on a Sunday afternoon (L, 3.43). By the beginning of 1868 he was considering whether he had a vocation, seeing the priesthood as the 'happiest and best way', if adding rather ominously 'it practically is the only one' (L, 3.231). Even then, there were decisions to be made: would he be a secular priest, that is, work in a parish under direction of a bishop, but not bound by vows or rules beyond those of the priesthood, or would he join an order, bound by particular rules and obligations, whether an enclosed order of monks or one that operated in the world for particular purposes, like the Jesuits. The Oratorians, Newman's own order, seem not to have been an option (J, 534, 537). Founded in Rome in the sixteenth century, the Oratorians were priests united not by vows but by a common purpose in preaching, teaching, administration of the sacraments, and prayer (Chadwick 1972: 255). Indeed, Newman himself, once Hopkins had made his own decisions, said he saw, from the moment he came to the Oratory, that Hopkins had no vocation with the Oratorians (L, 3.408). The clarity of Newman's statement is puzzling, though probably he felt Hopkins cut out neither for preaching nor for work amongst youth, whatever his competence as teacher. Newman also probably felt that Hopkins needed a discipline and control that the loose association of the Oratorians could not provide. In May 1868, Hopkins resolved to become a priest and to enter an order, though 'still doubtful' between St Benedict and St Ignatius (J, 165), that is, between a monastery and the Society of Jesus. Benedictine monks are devoted to work and prayer, but their enclosed life of sustained contemplation would not have suited Hopkins. It is perhaps not surprising that he should urge, when some years a Jesuit, that ordinary worldly duties were a form of prayer, that to 'lift up the hands in prayer gives God glory, but a man with a dungfork in his hand, a woman with a sloppail, give him glory too' (S, 241). More certain is that close self-examination confronted Hopkins with horrors that might have overwhelmed him in the perpetual scrutiny of a contemplative order – during a retreat in 1883, 'an old and terribly afflicting thought and disgust' seized him and he had to seek help (S, 253).

At the end of April 1868, Hopkins went to Manresa House in West London, headquarters of the Society of Jesus in England, to discover whether he had a vocation. Here he made three resolutions: on 5 May, that he would be a priest (J, 165); by 14 May, that he would be a Jesuit (*L*, 3.408); and on 11 May that he would give up poetry, since it would 'interfere with my state and vocation' (*J*, 537–39; *L*, 1.24). Told of the first two resolutions, Newman insisted that priesthood and the Jesuits were 'the very thing' for him. He also urged Hopkins not to call '"the Jesuit discipline hard", it will bring you to heaven' (*L*, 3.408). As for Hopkins's third resolution, he burnt all his verse that was to hand and, except for three or four pieces for special occasions, wrote no poetry until December 1875, though a good deal of the early poetry, in copies, in letters and journals, did in fact survive this 'Slaughter of the innocents' (*J*, 165). Hopkins's belief that his poetry was incompatible with his vocation puzzled people who knew of it. Yet if Hopkins himself called the Jesuit discipline 'hard', perhaps his very character, determined, even obstinate, needing discipline and control, might also find in the order the parallel discipline needed for poetic creation. As Hopkins himself observed years later to a fellow Catholic poet, Coventry Patmore, 'Fineness, proportion, of feature comes from a moulding force which succeeds in asserting itself over the resistance of cumbersome or restraining matter' (*L*, 3.306). As a Jesuit, perhaps because a Jesuit, Hopkins was a very different poet when in 1875 he began to write again.

And so, on 7 September 1868, after an extended holiday in Switzerland, having said goodbye to family and friends, Hopkins again entered Manresa House, now to begin his noviciate, the training of a priest and Jesuit.

The Society of Jesus

Despite Newman's conviction that the Jesuits were 'the very thing' for him, Hopkins's decision to join the Society of Jesus puzzled people. His brother Lionel couldn't see why Gerard could not become 'an ordinary Catholic' like other converts (*J*, 310). Even Alfred Thomas, himself a Jesuit, in his admirable study, *Hopkins the Jesuit*, concludes that the question why Hopkins became a Jesuit 'still remains unanswered' (Thomas 1969: 10). At the simplest, the Jesuits offered a sense of order and purpose, both valuable to Hopkins, however much he felt later that he achieved nothing, was 'time's eunuch' ('Justus Quidem Tu Es, Domine', 13). The Jesuits offered not a life of meditation (however important directed contemplation was), much less brooding, but an involvement with society: 'we cultivate the commonplace outwardly' (*L*, 2.96). Yet their spiritual life stressed an emotional engagement with the facts of God's mercy and Christ's sacrifice, evoked through concrete images drawn from natural creation. Such things gave the poet, a poet in denial in 1868, material experience and means, already directed by Ruskin's precepts, to realise those discoveries in poetic form.

The Jesuits, founded in the sixteenth century, were a part of the Church Militant, an army for God, fighting not with the sword, but by preaching, education, service to the Church and to the world in which the Church had its being. Founded by St Ignatius Loyola (c.1491–1556; Attwater 1965; Chadwick 1972: 255–62), the Society's organisation reflected Ignatius's own earlier military life. A soldier, severely wounded in 1521, he sought a religious way of life, spending a year in contemplation, prayer, self-correction, near Barcelona, at Manresa (hence, Manresa House in West London), later gathering around him a group of men who in 1534 formed the core of the Society. From the first, the Jesuits' relationship to Church and State caused frictions; their very success, in growth and purpose, made them objects of suspicion and hatred as well as praised and applauded. They were obedient directly to the Pope and therefore not to any bishop or nation. Within the Church, the local authorities objected to them and within states, even Catholic ones, they were believed to meddle politically. Their first great successes were in the Counter-Reformation of the sixteenth century and increasingly they became known as educators, missionaries, founders of orphanages. Yet suspicion remained. In the United Kingdom, the Catholic Emancipation Act of 1829 specifically forbade the presence of Jesuits and though the clause was in abeyance – the Jesuits were openly established, had churches (Farm Street in London, for example, and St Francis Xavier in Liverpool), and schools (notably Stonyhurst in Lancashire) – yet preliminary vows were taken individually rather than openly as a precaution against the Act (Thomas 1969: 26). Hopkins was aware of all this history: the 'secret' of making his vow enforced it, while he noted in May 1868, perhaps humorously, that 'Cardinal d'Andrea being dead the *Times* Italian correspondent hints he was poisoned by the ... Jesuits' (*J*, 165).

The Jesuits were regarded as exotic, alien, even by people not hostile to Catholicism. Hopkins had chosen an Order that set him apart, yet he never found any problem with the Jesuits, never, even at his lowest, thought of leaving them, still less of leaving the Church. Other converts of his generation simply lived their lives as Catholics, some became secular priests, a few reverted to Anglicanism. Hopkins was not unaware of those who felt that Catholicism and more particularly the Jesuits offered an impossible set of beliefs, acceptable only to hypocrites or dupes. It pained him that as late as

1882 Robert Bridges should speak as though Christian things had no significance 'for me and you were only waiting with a certain disgust till I too should be disgusted with myself enough to throw off the mask' (L, 1.148). Even more extreme was a friend's judgement after Hopkins's death, representative enough of an attitude to the Jesuits in particular. Hopkins, the friend declared with a confidence unbased in fact, had made 'a grievous mistake' in joining the Jesuits, 'for on further acquaintance his whole soul must have revolted against a system which has killed many and many a noble soul' (L, 3.396). It is not clear, after twenty years in the Order, how much 'further acquaintance' was needed for Hopkins to be undeceived, but the comment, from a generally sympathetic witness, indicates how Hopkins might be seen by others to have isolated and alienated himself from himself by choosing the Jesuits.

More importantly for Hopkins, the Jesuits were an order where emotion and intellect were both stressed, under control of a discipline which if at times seemingly harsh was qualified both by the tenderness of its founder – Ignatius, who had himself fasted and curbed the flesh, none the less insisted that no penance should be beyond the strength of the individual (Chadwick 1972: 260) – and by an attachment to the physical world, the manifestation of God's love for his creation, however it might be 'bleared, smeared with toil' ('God's Grandeur', 6). St Ignatius had produced the *Spiritual Exercises* (Loyola 1996: 279–358) as a guide, by which one person is directed by another, in meditation and the use of the senses towards self-examination and the desire for union with God. At a simple level, Hopkins shows this 'technique' in his notes on the *Exercises*: 'The second point is to consider how God dwells in creatures: in the elements giving them being; in the plants giving them growth; in the animals giving them sensation; in men giving them understanding' (S, 193). The parallel with poetic discipline is obvious, and the *Exercises* had prompted poetic achievement from the seventeenth century. From things – the windhover, the star-light night – or from his self – 'I wake and feel the fell of dark' – Hopkins develops the concreteness of situations and through their particularity, their 'haecceitas' or 'thisness' (what makes the thing or state this and no other), the force of God, like an electrical charge, is sparked off. 'The world is charged with the grandeur of God' and Hopkins returned to this physical image in writing of Ignatius's *Exercises*: 'All things therefore are charged with love, are charged with God and if we know how to touch them give off sparks and take fire, yield drops and flow, ring and tell of him' (S, 195).

In September 1868, though, his foot was as yet only on the threshold of this venture.

Religious training 1868–77

The Jesuit training is long and demanding. Hopkins began as a novice for two years at Manresa House, Roehampton. The noviciate was designed to discover whether he and the Jesuits were suited: not all those who entered with him stayed the course. The routine stressed devotion, order, and obedience. The day began at 5.30 in the morning and ended at 10 at night. Each novice had a cubicle, which he had to keep tidy (a shock, surely, for young men accustomed to women of the family or servants performing such tasks: Hopkins in later life was thought eccentric merely for sewing on buttons and doing his own laundry). Later the novices also helped the lay brothers in kitchen duties. Prayer, meditation, mass, instruction on the rules of the Society, intermingled with meals and recreation, made up the day (Thomas 1969: 24–28). The noviciate was both ordinary and outwardly monotonous. Hopkins could go out occasionally and friends visited him; he also was sent to local churches to gain experience by instructing children in their catechism. In the grounds of Manresa House and out on Wimbledon Common and elsewhere he observed and noted the intricacies of natural phenomena: 'the crisp flat darkness of the woods against the sun and the smoky bloom they have opposite it' (*J*, 190). He had hoped to find violets to send his mother, but failing them, enclosed a duck's feather that she kept with the letter (*L*, 3.111). Other notes and letters record worn clothes, electric sparks from a pullover, someone's use of the word *whisket* for basket, friends, and odd incidents. On 8 September 1870, he took his vows, of poverty, chastity, and obedience. Then, his Oxford degree excusing him from the two year instruction in Latin and rhetoric (the Juniorate), he went to Stonyhurst in Lancashire, part school, part Jesuit college, to begin the three years of the Philosophate.

Hopkins was at St Mary's College, Stonyhurst, for three years (1870–73) and studied philosophy, through lectures, reading, discussion and debate (Thomas 1969: 87–128). Though separate institutions, the college and school had links. The novices were free at times to go walking and swimming, Hopkins recording little incidents, the rescue of a kitten (*J*, 217), and the changes of nature, a lunar halo, where halo and moon rhythmically echoed each other: 'it fell in on the nether left hand side to rhyme the moon itself' (*J*, 218). At times, he felt intensely the destruction of nature as in April 1873 when an ash tree was felled: 'looking out and seeing it maimed there came at that moment a great pang and I wished to die and not to see the inscapes of the world destroyed any more' (*J*, 230). The emotion seems extreme, and at times Hopkins is prone to tears, brought on by the concentration of meditation or religious retreat: it is not the tree he suffers with, so much, as the destruction of God's creation. It was also during this time that he first came across the writings of the great medieval philosopher and teacher, Duns Scotus, in whose ideas he found support and confirmation of his own about the essential identity of natural objects, their 'thisness', 'haecceitas' in Scotus's technical Latin term. This discovery was perhaps to be a problem for Hopkins later, but in the density and obscurity of Scotus's writing, Hopkins found an individual mind to whom he responded with delight.

After Stonyhurst, the Order put Hopkins's abilities to use for a year. In 1873 he returned to Roehampton and Manresa House and here he taught those who, having survived the noviciate, passed to the Juniorate, those years of study from which Hopkins as a graduate had been excused. He taught the Juniors Latin and rhetoric – essentially literary studies of Latin and Greek writers. Hopkins's surviving lecture notes (*J*, 267ff) show a concern not only for classical poetic forms and metres but also for rhythm and rhyme in English poetry, not openly revolutionary, yet evidence of his thinking about poetic technique. Latin and Greek verse demands for its metrical structure the counting of syllables and quantity – vowel length – as its base, while English poetry normally counts syllables (ten syllables in standard blank verse – iambic pentameter – or eight in octosyllabics), but is organised on the basis of stress: the iamb is an unstressed syllable followed by a stressed. And even in regular iambic pentameter (Shakespeare's blank verse, for example) there is irregularity allowed in English for variety and special effects of surprise or emphasis, achieved through variations of stress. Hopkins's interest already lies though in rhythm without count of syllables, the patterns that underlie Old English and much Middle English poetry, while he also explores the idea of 'counterpointing', a term from music, where the ear expects one level of stress and is given another, producing variously frustration, delight, or astonishment.

As Alfred Thomas's account makes clear, while under discipline and obedience, without money of their own, the Jesuits, even in periods of training, were never an enclosed order, like monks who have given up the world. With permission or at command they go about outside. While at Manresa, Hopkins visited museums and galleries, as well as churches, and friends and family could visit him. It was in January 1874, after a gap of more than two years, that he renewed his friendship with Bridges. The friendship lasted, yet the poetic difference between the friends is clear in a little incident, which though it happened some years later, is relevant to Hopkins's thinking about English poetry in the mid-1870s. Bridges visited Hopkins at Manresa in 1882 and they had a comically trivial misunderstanding about peaches. Bridges wanted to give Hopkins one (White 1992: 335) and Hopkins refused it from fear of sensual pleasure. The incident, no more than the occasional misunderstanding any friendship is liable to, takes on poetic significance when we compare what Bridges, with his theories of syllabic verse, made of it in *The Testament of Beauty*, his poetic autobiography, against the supple strength of Hopkins's use of *his* theories of stress and syllables in verse structures. Bridges remembers how the

> friend of my heart refused a peach at my hands,
> he being then a housecarl in Loyola's menie,
> 'twas that he fear'd the savor of it, and when he waived
> his scruple to my banter, 'twas to avoid offence.
>
> (Bridges 1929: 150)

Bridges's crippled metre, outlandish vocabulary, uneasy shifts of tone, and archaism, are things Hopkins was rejecting in his poetic thinking of the mid-1870s. And if the peach reminds us that Hopkins was always conscious of the dangers of the flesh, yet it was necessarily through the senses that he approached God and he not only observed nature acutely but responds, as in 1874, when, as 'we drove home the stars came out thick: I leant back to look at them and my heart opening more than usual praised our Lord to and in whom all that beauty comes home' (*J*, 254).

Now, having himself prepared novices by teaching, Hopkins's own training for the priesthood began its final stage, theological studies (the Theologate), at St Beuno's College, North Wales, a time which was amongst the happiest of his life and which saw the return to poetry. After an astonishing masterpiece, poems celebrating Christ's splendour in the natural world were to pour out. He arrived in August and found everyone 'very kind and hospitable' (*J*, 257). Hopkins was at St Beuno's for three years (1874–77), though he might have expected to stay for four and afterwards have been given an increasingly important role in higher education in the Order. The three years were a time of great happiness, poetically fruitful, and yet by 1877 there is a sense of the problems that were to dog Hopkins for the rest of his days. What were his duties to be and how might his talents be put to use (in the words of the Order's motto) To the Greater Glory of God? They were questions that puzzled both Hopkins and the Jesuits.

The routine of his days was soon established (Thomas 1969: 150ff) and he studied moral and dogmatic theology, canon law, church history, Hebrew, all as preparations for the priesthood. Thursdays, recreation day, he was free to go out into the countryside, with sandwiches but no money – the Jesuits were vowed to poverty: money was provided for travel and expenses only as necessary, for holidays, travel, visits to the dentist. Yet Hopkins, awarded a first class degree at Oxford, achieved only a low pass at the end of his first year (White 1992: 240) and he was barred at the end of his third year from a fourth and final year of study. Why? Clearly, this was not lack of intelligence. It may be, as Alfred Thomas suggests, that Hopkins's enthusiasm for Duns Scotus led him to a different theological tradition – not heretical, but quite out of the current mainstream – from that of St Thomas Aquinas, whose systematised theology was transmitted amongst the Jesuits by a standard text-book (Thomas 1969: 182–83). For Hopkins, Duns Scotus helped him understand his own perceptions and emotions: in 1872 he noted that 'when I took in any inscape of the sky or sea I thought of Scotus' (*J*, 221) and later, he recalled when he 'used to read [Scotus] with delight' (*L*, 3.349), though few modern readers, professional philosophers or theologians, would agree to delight, however important or interesting Scotus might be.

Wales also was a delight for Hopkins. It brought him back, here in the 'lovable West', to poetry. He delighted in the people: 'I warm to them – and in different degrees to all the Celts' (*L*, 3.127), though he was to be sorely tried on that in Liverpool and yet more in Dublin. Apart from the people (too often Hopkins is treated as though he had no interest in people), the landscape was beautiful and Hopkins set himself to learn Welsh. It is during this time that the Journals break off (1875; *J*, 263) while telling of an encounter by his Welsh teacher with fairies. He also visited Mary's Well and more importantly in October 1874 St Winefred's Well, a place of pilgrimage unbroken since the Middle Ages, which duly prompted Hopkins to write a never-completed drama. His involvement in the Welsh language and in philology renewed his fascination with words and in music, metre, and rhythm, while his intensive criticism of Bridges's poetry prepared him for his own, as he forged a poetic language akin, for all its unfamiliarities, to modern speech, not least in his objections to 'thee' and 'thou', to 'canst' and obsolete or affected forms. When 'The Wreck of the *Deutschland*' opens with 'Thou mastering me God', Hopkins uses the pronoun emphatically and precisely to express the relationship between God and his Creation. He was increasingly concerned with the sprightliness and emphasis of speech, disciplined by rhythm and rhyme. A persistent fascination with language led to exploration of the resources of meanings and of likenesses in sound. The sermons and religious writings show this fascination too, whether in a precision of vocabulary: 'cleaves' (*S*, 151, 154), or the opening up of a word's variety (*S*, 187): 'strain' may mean 'striving', and also mean 'kind' or 'variety', and mean 'trying too hard' or 'trying only to be frustrated'. Hopkins's linguistic awareness takes up the potential, like the slack of a rope, even while disciplined by the demands of emotion and reason – it is no empty wordplay, but a significant counterpointing of stress and sound with meaning. His very development of 'Sprung Rhythm' [pp. 68–9] – which puzzled Bridges who, for all his experiments with quantitative verse, seems to have had a defective ear – is a desire for rhythms that reflect and reproduce the emphases of speech. For Hopkins words and rhythm sought to convey the essential being of things, their inscape, and the living power that was their instress, the vitality that kept in being what they were. As he renewed poetic language, rejecting his predecessors and older contemporaries, so Hopkins insisted upon the need for renewal of response: 'Unless you refresh the mind from time to time you cannot always remember or believe how deep the inscape in things is' (*J*, 205). And, because he is not 'simply' a nature poet, because he is above all and always a religious poet, Hopkins's poetic resources are directed still to the indwelling presence of God in nature, a sacramental perception, that through nature we can gain God's grace, that power of God that helps us towards salvation, as the sacraments – above all, but not alone, the eucharist – do also. Just as the communicant receives God under the outward form of bread and wine, so the external elements of nature are the outward form of God's indwelling power and grace.

Hopkins, unknowingly perhaps, had been preparing himself technically, preparing himself imaginatively by absorbing and responding and dwelling upon his experience, ever since he abandoned poetry in 1868, and the creative explosion of 1875 and 1876 was detonated by an item in *The Times* early in December 1875, reporting the wreck off the mouth of the Thames of the *Deutschland*, a German ship 'America outward bound' from Hamburg (Street 1992). Amongst the passengers drowned were five nuns, expelled from Germany. Since 1870, Bismarck, the German Chancellor, had sought to suppress the opposition Catholic Centre party, invoking a 'Kulturkampf', a 'cultural struggle', of the nation against Catholicism (Street 1992: 18–22; White 1992: 250–52). In Prussia, the Falk Laws of 1873 sought to bring the Catholic Church under State control and all religious orders were dissolved: the nuns, expelled, were making their way to America. Seizing on a remark by his superior that some commemoration of the nuns might be appropriate, Hopkins set to work and produced his longest – and greatest – poem, 'The Wreck of the *Deutschland*' [pp. 64–78]. 'The Wreck' is a celebration (a curious word, but true) of the nuns' death in the crisis of the storm, seen in parallel to his own conversion, a meditation also on God's ways and a dramatic reconstruction of the nuns' ordeal. The 'mastering' God, who gathered Hopkins into the safety of the Church, had reached out to the nuns in the 'buck and flood of the waves' and through them had touched Hopkins afresh.

Hopkins: Modern or Victorian?

After a gap of nearly seven years, during which he had written no poetry, believing poetry incompatible with his priestly vocation, Hopkins became a poet again. Hopkins was a Victorian – he was born five years after Victoria's accession and the Queen reigned another twelve years after his death. But Hopkins can be seen as modern and in more than one sense. The question whether Hopkins is a Modern is discussed in Part III. It is useful, though, given what he achieved as a poet, to think about him as modern in his own time, an era categorised as the High Victorian Age. It has already been suggested [p. 9] that Hopkins's Oxford was modern and Hopkins was obviously modern in response to things of his age. He was aware, as an intelligent layman, of science and was sensible (as educated Catholics are) on Darwinism (L, 3.128): it was not for him contradictory to Christianity. Hopkins also naturally draws on scientific imagery, part of the common currency of the age. Electricity, for example, inspired 'the world is charged with the grandeur of God': 'touch' the object and it discharges God's glory (but does not lose it). Or again, he turns to an industrial process for illustration: 'You have seen a glassblower breathe on a flame; at once it darts out into a jet taper as a lance-head and as piercing too' (S, 242).

Poetically, like other Victorians, Hopkins shared a Romantic inheritance – that poetic language should be drawn from current language, that poetry should mirror and reflect upon the natural world, that poetry be aware of the ordinary, even primitive, and yet be capable of finding the heroic in ordinary people ('Felix Randal') and the mysterious in ordinary experience (a caged skylark; a lantern out of doors). Drawn to Keats in the youthful splendour of 'A Vision of the Mermaids', it was to Wordsworth that Hopkins later turned. For while Wordsworth clearly was no Christian in his greatest poetry, he was one of those men who had 'seen something' (L, 2.147) and it was that 'something', inflected religiously, that Hopkins too sought to express. The earlier Victorian poets, Tennyson, Browning, Matthew Arnold, direct inheritors and contenders with the Romantics, had developed new poetic languages – a higher selective speech in Tennyson, a dramatic range down to curses and grunts in Browning – and embraced, instead of Romantic self-forged systems, ideas of uncertainty or (an alternative, not an opposition) of Christian belief, so wandering as Arnold expressed it, between 'two worlds, one dead, | The other powerless to be born' ('The Grande Chartreuse', ll.85–86) or else standing upon Tennyson's 'Believing where we cannot prove' ('Prologue', *In Memoriam*). The Victorian period is a long one: Tennyson, Browning and Arnold were all well established by Hopkins's youth and while Hopkins shared his age's enthusiasm for Tennyson, he early began 'to *doubt* Tennyson' (*L*, 3.215), as though Tennyson were a god and Hopkins a believer – the tone is humorous, yet aware of the older poet's status. He tired of Tennyson's later frigid language (*L*, 3.216–19) and never reconciled himself to Browning, who he felt had all the gifts except the essential one of a poet. For Hopkins, Browning like Charles Kingsley was coarsely assertive, never imaginatively subtle as a poet should be, like 'a man bouncing up from table with his mouth full of bread and cheese and saying that he meant to stand no blasted non-sense' (*L*, 2.74). Between 1868 and the end of 1875 Hopkins abandoned the established forms of the earlier Victorian poets. He evolved and then triumphantly used a distinct poetic language and forged 'Sprung Rhythm' [**pp. 68–9**]. Hopkins's aesthetic determination to harness these technical resources to the representation and praise of God in Nature and in his own spiritual life make him a new kind of poet, drawing on established Catholic beliefs as no Romantic poet did, accepting those beliefs (as most other Victorian poets did not), and proving the greatest of all Catholic poets in his century – the rest, Newman, Patmore, Francis Thompson, Alice Meynell, coming nowhere. Hopkins, virtually unknown in his own time, was entirely modern, having worked out an individual poetic, new both in his own age and in the twentieth century when it came eventually to read him, a poet who would, as Wordsworth declared any original poet must, 'create the taste by which he is to be relished'.

'The Wreck' and its consequences 1876–77

'The Wreck of the *Deutschland*' could have been written by no one else, but Hopkins was denied the opportunity in his lifetime to 'create the taste by which he [was] to be relished'. If he was held to be strange, different, eccentric, then poetically at least, it was by having no sizable readership that might respond to him through criticism and discovery. Despite early efforts at publication of 'The Wreck', it did not appear in print for another forty-five years. The dam though had burst and Hopkins no longer felt he should not write poetry nor did he now need the express wish of his superiors to write, though he might still regard poetry as subordinate to other duties, to be written and worked over (he revised carefully and thoroughly) only when he had time. 'The Wreck' was the first of forty-nine poems Hopkins completed before his death (there are also about twenty fragments, some substantial) and the Welsh landscape inspired the first great flush – among them 'God's Grandeur', 'The Starlight Night', 'The Sea and the Skylark', and 'The Windhover' [pp. 81–6]. Again, while drawn from his experience, we should be cautious of seeing these poems as simply biographical evidence – Norman White offers a skewed version of both life and poetry when he says of the 1877 poems, 'Hopkins's knowledge of the joys of nature in its uncorrupted freedom serves to throw into relief his misanthropy and loneliness' (White 1992: 288). True, Hopkins places himself in some, by no means all, as an isolated figure – in 'The Lantern Out of Doors' or 'The Windhover' – yet this is crucial to the poetic structure, the figure acting as a channel through which we pass from the natural scene to God's presence. While Hopkins was isolated in later life, even in Dublin he had friends and correspondents. In all this there is no suggestion that at any time he was a misanthrope.

Ministry 1877–81

Hopkins's time at St Beuno's was particularly happy, and yet not free from problems, of course. He had not done well at the end of his first year of studies and, all but failing at the end of the third, was not recommended for a final year, which might have led effectively to a position as an 'academic' in the Order. The problem was not, surely, lack of ability. Yet there were signs at St Beuno's of going his own way: he had an independence and, as some of his correspondents noted, a certainty of judgement that might give rise to friction or difference of opinion. This in part led him to be called 'eccentric' (a solution by label) and though we have little evidence, clearly his superiors were puzzled by him and by what use he could be put to in the Order. In his teaching and from 1878 in his parish work as priest, Hopkins was entirely conscientious and often effective, but he was not really cut out for either. Increasingly he shows signs of exhaustion and dryness. As a priest, he was sent to a number of parishes, very different in their natures, yet they did not really suit, neither he to them nor they to him, though they gave him poetic material and inspiration and prompted him in sermons to work out his ideas.

Yet if his life to the casual observer was to seem wasted, Hopkins noted as consolation during an 1881 retreat the words of a fellow priest, that the hidden life of Jesus at Nazareth 'is the great help to faith for us who must live more or less an obscure, constrained, and unsuccessful life' (*S*, 176). Since Christ was the hero, even his obscurity might be a model. Whether this consolation worked for Hopkins in Dublin is less certain, yet one of his last poems, when he was in more cheerful mood, celebrates St Alphonsus Rodriguez [pp. 119–20], a lay brother of the Society and hall porter for forty years, whose career was crowded with 'conquest', even through those 'years and years' of 'world without event | That in Majorca Alfonso watched the door'. Heroic virtue, the quality of the saint, need not lie in battle and strife and bright activity. If Hopkins was not a saint, Alfonso yet still might be an inspiration.

In September 1877, after nine years of preparation, Hopkins was ordained priest. Thereafter, whenever possible, he said mass daily (*L*, 2.58) and administered the sacraments as part of his priestly and parochial duties. In the event, his first post as priest was not attached to a parish church, but at a school, Mount St Mary's College at Spinkhill, effectively a suburb of Sheffield. Here he first seriously came in contact with the modern urban experience, at a time when there was a renewed urgency in the need for social activity. The misery of the poor led him to reflect, he said later, on the 'hollowness of this century's civilisation' (*L*, 2.97). At St Mary's, he taught, examined, did occasional mission work, and preached. He found 'his muse sullen'. Without feeling he could not create: feeling is the source of Hopkins's poetry, wonderfully transformed in the creation. To Bridges a little later he wrote, 'Feeling, love in particular, is the great moving power and spring of verse and the only person that I am in love with seldom, especially now, stirs my heart sensibly and when he does I cannot always "make capital" of it' (*L*, 1.66).

The comment about poverty and civilisation just quoted was in a letter to R.W. Dixon, Anglican priest and poet, historian of the English Reformation (Sambrook 1962). In June 1878, Hopkins, transferred to London, leaving Spinkhill, opened a correspondence with Dixon, who had taught him briefly at Highgate. Hopkins had long admired Dixon's poetry, had learnt it off by heart in Oxford, had copied it out when he entered the Jesuits, in case he had to give up the book. Dixon was much struck by Hopkins's praise and as a fellow clergyman he had a sense of delicacy (*L*, 2.5), so that Hopkins could say things to him that he would not say to Bridges, say, for instance, that 'The only just judge, the only just literary critic, is Christ, who prizes, is proud of, and admires ... the gifts of his own making' (*L*, 2.8). While Dixon was puzzled that Hopkins had burnt his early poetry, as a poet-priest himself asking, 'Surely one vocation cannot destroy another'? (L, 2.90), and while he never subjected Hopkins's poetry to the close scrutiny Bridges offered, he was appreciative even when not fully understanding, detecting, as Bridges could not, the echo of a new rhythm in 'The Wreck' (L, 2.14; 42–43). Dixon was important as a friend and a support in ways Bridges could not be and the two poet-priests' correspondence gives valuable light on Hopkins.

The church of the Immaculate Conception, Farm Street, in London's Mayfair, was fashionable, with a well-to-do-congregation. Here Hopkins began to preach, a skill which his studies had sought to develop by speaking and trial sermons. Twenty-six of his sermons survive, not all complete, written down so that they could be used again. It is not easy to be sure what Hopkins was like as a preacher, but it may be thought he was generally too detailed and 'subtle' for a large or an ordinary congregation. He had some personal difficulties, as any speaker may, noting in November 1879 that the 'first 6 paragraphs of this I delivered confusedly' (S, 43), and recording with a wry humour other failures: he thought he saw his listeners in tears, whereas, being a hot day, they were wiping away sweat (S, 81). Much depends on personality – Hopkins was not comfortable with the large gesture, the rhetorical cry. He was a speaker rather than an actor and depended also upon his audience. And when the audience was his fellow Jesuits, the effect could be farcical, though the fault not necessarily entirely his. In a retreat address at St Beuno's, given during a meal, not in church, at the end of a long day of prayer and concentration, talking of the Feeding of the Five Thousand and likening the Sea of Galilee to the Vale of Clwyd, something, some incongruity, some chance reaction of a listener, triggered off the rest and the whole dining room went into gales of laughter, the repetition of certain phrases making them, as Hopkins noted of the performance, 'roll more than ever' (S, 233). This was exceptional, though Hopkins was thought not always to be judicious: once, we are told, he compared the Church to 'a milk cow and the tits to the seven sacraments' (J, 421). It is unlikely either the congregation or his fellow priests fully appreciated this, nor perhaps his parishioners, effective though it is, if he had declared to them, 'I see you living before me, with the mind's eye, brethren, I see your corpses: those same bodies that sit there before me are rows of corpses that will be' (S, 245).

From Farm Street, Hopkins went to Oxford in October 1878. Perhaps, as has been suggested (S, 3), the Order hoped Hopkins would settle there, in a congenial and familiar atmosphere, bring Town and Gown together, and find an outlet for his undoubted talents. To be a parish priest in a Jesuit church was very different, though, from being a member of the University. Many of the people he had known in Oxford were gone or meant nothing to him now nor he to them; while the townspeople were polite but distant. The Muse, though, returned and in 1879 he wrote a fine set of poems, including 'Binsey Poplars', 'Duns Scotus' Oxford', 'The Candle Indoors', and 'The Bugler's First Communion' [**pp. 91–2; 94–5; 102**]. Then after only a year, he was moved (October 1879) to his happiest ministry, in the northern industrial town of Bedford Leigh (now, more commonly, Leigh). Here he liked the people and they responded to him, unlike Oxford, where 'I was fond of my people, but they had not as a body the charming and cheering heartiness of these Lancashire Catholics, which is so deeply comforting' (*L*, 1.97). It was only to be an interlude, for after a mere three months he was again moved, January 1880, to the vast and vastly popular church of St Francis Xavier, Liverpool. The squalor of Liverpool ('this horrible place'; *L*, 1.126) was a shock after Bedford Leigh's settled urban population, the parish work being 'very wearying to mind and body ... There is merit in it but little Muse' (*L*, 2.33). As his duties pressed on him, he snatched what moments he could, writing a letter (May 1880) while waiting in the confessional for the next penitent (*L*, 3.244). Even amidst this grinding round there were experiences to be grateful for: in Feburary 1881 he anointed a lad who had typhus, ready for death, who then recovered (*L*, 1.123–24), while the death-bed of one man, perhaps several, brought him to write 'Felix Randal' [**pp. 102–3**], a poem recognising, as Hopkins did elsewhere, the value of work and the glory that may flash from darkness. Like Felix at work, 'Smiting on an anvil ... gives God some glory' (*S*, 240).

The writing of a letter in a confessional, while waiting for the next penitent, hints at Hopkins's parish duties. They included obvious religious duties – saying mass, hearing confessions, baptising, marrying, visiting the sick and dying, administering the last rites. He was also drawn into the working class of the urban areas where he worked and into their underworlds too. He cared for and visited men like Felix Randal, or 'my man in Wm. Henry Street' (*S*, 247), and gives hints of people and scenes, the illicit and criminal, where he went as priest: 'Alas, brethren, to what filthy places have I not myself carried the Lord of Glory! and worse than filthy places, dens of shame' (*S*, 249) – the reference suggests brothels – and such experiences may have contributed the disturbing examples in writing on the *Spiritual Exercises*: of a woman consenting to be violated by accepting narcotics and a man taking cantharides (a sexual stimulant) (*S*, 143). To be a parish priest was not to lead a sheltered existence and Hopkins was brought face to face with sickness and suffering and, however sustained by his faith, worn down by them.

Amidst all this, at Liverpool, came a failure, almost comical, dealt with sensibly by those most immediately concerned, yet symptomatic of the Order's problems in finding the best role for Hopkins. St Francis Xavier was popular as a preaching church and famous for its evening sermons, to which people came from all over the city and Merseyside. The size of the church invited an expansive and dramatic rhetoric and while this was not Hopkins's style, he was called on (January 1880) to give the evening sermons. He announced a series, to begin with the Fall of God's First Kingdom. This was, innocently enough, meant to be on the Fall of Man, but if the title was intended as provocative, it worked better than expected, for if God is eternal and supreme, how could *his* kingdom be subject to decay or dissolution? As Hopkins noted in his sermon-book, 'I was not allowed to take this title and on the printed bills [posters] it was covered by a blank slip pasted over' (S, 62). The command was that Hopkins must submit all future sermons to his superior before they were delivered, though the superior did not take the matter too seriously: when the next sermon was given him, he showed his trust in Hopkins by declining to read it.

After Liverpool, Hopkins was two months (August–October 1881) in Glasgow and so ended four years as parish priest, in which he had never been less than conscientious, never complained, however over-worked or frustrated at times, yet clearly not cut out for such work. And again the question arose, what should the Order do with him? Surely he had talents that might be better used elsewhere. An idea was beginning to emerge, exaggerated and essentially unfair, that he was eccentric. He was undoubtedly individualistic and would, under obedience, go his own way.

The final phase 1881–89

During his four years as parish priest, Hopkins had written some eighteen poems and as Christopher Devlin suggests (S, 109), Hopkins's interest shifted from the presence of God's design in inanimate nature, the delight in beauty and recognition of Christ's presence, of the dauphin or chevalier of 'The Windhover', to the working out of that design, in the minds and wills of men. So not only does Christ shine forth through creation, but the salvation of man may be worked out, without natural beauty, even with initial resistance to that design, as in 'Felix Randal', or the innocent may be disturbed by premonitions not fully understood, yet which Margaret, in the masterly 'Spring and Fall' [pp. 103–4], will understand when, not simply mourning the decay autumn brings, she realises it is Margaret she mourns for. In his final years, Hopkins almost abandons the nature of landscape, flowers and trees, the beauty of physical form. Nature now has a sterner aspect as God's design, however difficult or incomprehensible, is dramatically enacted within Hopkins or others, over a psychological landscape [pp. 107–14]. This change runs along with his changing experience once he ceased to be a parish priest.

The immediate cause of Hopkins ceasing to be a parish priest, was the need to spend a year (1881–82), as all Jesuits must, on the Tertianship, for which he went back to Roehampton and Manresa House. It was a period of preparation before taking his final vows, a point that puzzled his friend Dixon who assumed (rightly) that Hopkins had already taken his vows on entering the Jesuits. As Hopkins explained, while he was to renew his vows, the Tertianship's chief purpose was a renewal of that 'fervour which may have cooled through application to study and contact with the world' (L, 2.75; Thomas 1969: ch. 6). With this return to prayer, meditation, group discussion, away from parish demands, Hopkins wrote the bulk of his Devotional Writings [pp. 87–8], especially during the Long Retreat of November–December 1881. This Manresa year was relieved by outings, by meetings with friends and family, and by a mission in Cumberland (April 1882), like a Revival, says Hopkins, but without the hysteria or heresy, adding, perhaps slightly surprisingly, given his difficulties as preacher, that 'it had the effect of bringing me out and making me speak very plainly and strongly (I enjoyed that, for I dearly like calling a spade a spade)' (L, 1.143). To speak out, to use the rhythms of speech, lies at the heart of Hopkins's poetic belief. Then, as though his superiors were still not sure, he was off to Stonyhurst again (1882–84), though not now to the college but the school itself, to teach Classics.

After two years came the opportunity that offered Hopkins and his Superiors a solution to his future, though it was to prove, if a solution, a galling and at times bitter one, even if it wrung out of Hopkins some of his finest poetry. Newman had been first rector of a Catholic University in Dublin (Lyons 1973: 94–95). This fell into decay and, taken over by the Jesuits, was being revived in the 1880s. The post of Professor of Greek, to which he was now elected, sounded splendid enough and suited to Hopkins's academic background and interest. An immediate problem was the intense national tensions in Ireland at this time, taken up at all levels and not least by the Irish Province of the Jesuits and the electors of the professor. The appointment, then, was part of a political struggle in which Hopkins uncomfortably found himself, between, on one hand, nationalist or Home Rule interests and, on the other, English domination (White 1992: 357–63; Lyons 1973: 141–201). Hopkins, though, remarkably, elected, was seen as an outsider, an alien, and not unnaturally felt himself to be so. People were not hostile to him, but often indifferent. The appointment was permanent and Norman White comments that 'the place where he was doomed to stay was the least congenial' (White 1992: 367).

Excellent though his overall account is, White's 'doomed' is melodramatic, coloured by the hindsight of Hopkins's early death. If Hopkins at times faced the prospect of living out his life in Dublin, yet that was not certain – 'permanent' appointments need not be for ever, especially if one is in a religious order. Hopkins was an adult, committed to the Order and to the service it thought best for him, and despite depression and bouts of ill health, he could hold on to a fellow priest's wise advice, that 'a great part of life to the holiest of men consists in the well performance ... of ordinary duties' (S, 253). Again, the almost trivial nature of Hopkins's last illness, the unexpectedness of his death, should warn us against giving the significant shape of tragedy to events that have no such meaning.

Certainly, Hopkins had an intensely dark period in 1885 when God seemed to have deserted him, a desertion the more terrible because he never ceased to believe in God. The danger is to take the 'Terrible' Sonnets [pp. 107–4] of that time as directly and merely autobiographical. Clearly they draw, however shaped for the reader, upon a period of spiritual aridity and bitterness. Yet, after this, particularly towards the end of his life, Hopkins seems more cheerful in his letters, he renews his interest in languages, even thinks of possible books to write. Because he died there of typhus, Hopkins did indeed live out the rest of his life in Dublin. But he was not yet 45 and there was no 'doomed' inevitability in this, however uncongenial Ireland, Dublin, and the National University might be.

Uncongeniality to distaste was certainly much of what Hopkins experienced. In the university Hopkins had few friends, his colleagues offering neither much companionship nor intellectual sympathy. Academic resources were minimal and his duties were not so much professing Greek as teaching at a fairly elementary level and being grossly overburdened by tedious examining and marking (L, 3.251). Outside the University, Hopkins found some friends (White 1992: 410–11) and he met the poet Katherine Tynan, in whom he found an affinity (L, 1.245; 3.372). He was further alienated within the University politically, since as he noted in 1884, of the College as of the country in general, 'what is Ireland but an open or secret war of fierce enmities of every sort?' (L, 3.163). He could not be indifferent, though by tendency a Conservative and against Gladstone's Home Rule proposals: 'the grief of mind I go through over politics ... in

Ireland about Ireland and about England, is such that I can neither express it nor bear to speak of it' (L, 3.170). Though believing that Home Rule was inevitable – it might not placate Ireland, but Ireland would be far worse without it (L, 3.181) – he was driven at times to be more consciously English, as in 'The Soldier' [**pp. 115–6**]. And all the time he was dogged by the sense that he was not doing what he might, though ideas did come to him about the Greek Lyric Ode, about Homer's Art. He mused on Odysseus and the hero's return home to wife and kingdom in Homer's supreme poem, but where were the fruits of his intellectual voyage, where were *his* Penelope and Ithaca?

For us the Dublin achievement lies in the 'Terrible' Sonnets of 1885 [**pp. 107–14**] – 'Carrion Comfort', 'No Worst', 'I Wake and Feel the Fell' among them – and the poems of 1887–89 which, founded in his scrutiny of his times and himself, show a renewed energy and affirmation of God's purpose [**pp. 117–22**].

'The war within'

Wrong though it is to trace a tragic trajectory in Hopkins's final years, when the evidence points to a period of recovery and acceptance in the last three, the situation in Ireland, Dublin, and the University College was deeply dispiriting. In 1885 Hopkins writes of 'that coffin of weakness and dejection in which I live' (L, 1.214–15), and at this time his letters give a sense of darkness and struggle, so that even poetry was the product of agony: 'I have after a long silence written two sonnets … if ever anything was written in blood one of these was' (L, 1.219). He felt himself, knowing he was a poet, unachieved. In a phrase that reappears in 'Justus Quidem Tu Es, Domine' [**p. 120**], he declared 'it kills me to be time's eunuch and never to beget' (L, 1.222). Yet even the most pessimistic or desperate poetry at this time (1885–86) has a compressed energy that enacts the struggle towards a life in the love of God and achieves a poetic grandeur. Later, even himself as 'eunuch' can be an offering to God, as from 1887 he copes with self and situation, so that if he is a eunuch, 'it is for the kingdom of heaven's sake' (L, 1.270), his very obscurity and labour to no apparent end drawing strength perhaps from his fellow priest's observation that Jesus's hidden life at Nazareth 'is the great help to faith for us who must live more or less an obscure, constrained, and unsuccessful life' (S, 176). And both in the 'Terrible' Sonnets and in himself there is the continuing conviction of his belief. God might seem to withdraw himself, but that did not mean that he ceased to exist. For Hopkins, what other people like Bridges called dogma, was a living truth (*L*, 1.187–88) and in January 1889, a few months before his death, Hopkins noted that 'I do not waver in my allegiance, I never have since my conversion … The question is how I advance the side I serve on' (*S*, 261; misdated by Hopkins 1888). Hopkins's later mood was not unalloyed gloom and it is vital to read within contexts and beyond the obvious phrases. The 1889 Retreat notes, for example, begin with expressions of darkness and pessimism. Yet after the Ignatian concretisation of the inconvenient and painful journey to Bethlehem, Hopkins presses on in outbursts of delight and enthusiasm to the Epiphany and Flight into Egypt, Jesus's baptism, and the miracle of Cana (*S*, 263–71).

After 1885–86, there is evidence of recovery. His friendships with Bridges and Dixon continued, while Coventry Patmore, a Catholic poet, became a regular correspondent. The relationship with Bridges was still a strange one. Bridges clearly was in many ways congenial, companionable, a poet whom Hopkins (to an unreasonable extent) admired and who responded, up to a fairly limited point, to Hopkins's genius. An unpublished poet is scarcely encouraged if his chief critic stigmatises his poetry as repulsive. Dixon might be a lesser critic, but he was more admiring, even where he did not understand, while Hopkins stirred Coventry Patmore to renewed creation. And although Patmore wrote to Bridges that Hopkins's poetry was 'veins of pure gold imbedded in masses of unpracticable quartz', he added that his 'genius is … unmistakeable' (*L*, 3.353 fn). Friendships and criticism, even Bridges's rebarbative comments, helped Hopkins through these later years and all the evidence suggests that he was more cheerful, however exhausted, by 1887. Friendship, visits to family, all helped, while the darkness of the final poems is a very different darkness from that of the 'Terrible' Sonnets, a dark of social and political tensions that turns outward, after the agonised self-scrutiny, to 'Tom's Garland' and 'Harry Ploughman', while other late poems ('That Nature is a Heraclitean Fire', 'St Alphonsus Rodriguez') are triumphant apprehensions of nature and spiritual purpose.

'Glory is the flame': typhoid and death

Hopkins paid his last visit to his family in 1887 (they had moved from Highgate to Haslemere, Surrey) – though with no idea of its being his last. Teaching and, even more, examining, was wearing work, and while his spirits were good, Hopkins's physical state worsened. In the past he had had the usual kinds of illness and two successful minor operations, and had at times felt pulled down, though even when at his lowest, he still observed wonderfully his own condition: 'being unwell I was quite downcast: nature in all her parcels and faculties gaped and fell apart ... like a clod cleaving and holding only by strings of root' (*J*, 236; 1873). In May 1889 he contracted what was first identified as rheumatic fever, then as typhoid, a condition associated with poor sanitation and dangerous to those weakened by harsh conditions of labour and poor diet. Yet no one else at University College was struck down and the drains seemed efficient. Until near the end, his recovery was possible. He became so weak, though, that he had to dictate letters. His parents were at last sent for (he had long been reconciled to his father) and arrived shortly before he died. Given the last rites, Hopkins died early in the afternoon of 8 June 1889, aged 44, and was buried in Glasnevin cemetery, Dublin. His name appears on a Jesuit memorial there and he is commemorated in a memorial window at St Bartholomew's, Haslemere, by a plaque at Manresa House, and an inscription in Westminster Abbey.

Hopkins would now be virtually unknown, if he had not been a poet, except from Jesuit records and a footnote in Dixon's History of the Reformation. Even Hopkins in his lifetime had some desire to be known as a poet, since to produce works of art 'is of little use unless what we produce is known' (*L*, 1.231; 1886). He was, though, deeply ambiguous even about being read, since 'use' was, for Hopkins as a Catholic poet, the glorification and revelation of God and what if his poetry should work adversely? On a retreat, he noted that 'today I earnestly asked our Lord to watch over my compositions, not to preserve them from being lost or coming to nothing ... but they might not do me harm through the enmity or imprudence of any man' (*S*, 253–54). He had felt strongly a conflict between religious and poetic vocations when he destroyed his early poetry, yet even when he felt after writing 'The Wreck' that he could write again, there was a problem of publication. As a youth he had had a poem in *Once a Week*; his 'Silver Jubilee' poem for the Bishop of Shrewsbury was gathered with others; poems were circulated amongst his friends, sent to his mother, and offered to possible publishers. Who were his lifetime readers after he entered the Order? His mother, Robert Bridges, R.W. Dixon, Coventry Patmore, a few Jesuits. It was, unfortunately, Bridges who was the guardian and editor of Hopkins's poetry. Bridges felt the poems too strange, too eccentric, to be published, at least immediately. He 'prepared' the public, without obvious effect, by a trickle over a quarter of a century. Only in 1918 was the first collected edition produced, stressing obscurity and difficulty, not least in approaching 'The Wreck', where

Bridges, in a phrase whose brilliance and inaccuracy has made it notorious, declares the poem 'a great dragon folded in the gate to forbid all entrance' [p. 132]. Fortunately early readers and reviewers were not to be put off from a poetic voice they embraced as a Modernist. Hopkins was 'made' into a twentieth-century poet, and only comparatively recently has been fully assessed as a Victorian. Gradually, as the letters, the journals, and the devotional writings were published and new editions of the poetry appeared, Hopkins became available and as his work became more familiar so the critical heritage, traced in Part III, has moved from explication to a fuller understanding of a great poet in his time and in his influence in the twentieth century.

FURTHER READING

The current standard biography is White (1992); this is supported by Thomas (1969) on Hopkins's Jesuit training. These should be supplemented by the Letters, Journals, and Sermons. Part III surveys earlier biographies [pp. 142–9]; three others that may be useful are Bergonzi (1977), Martin (1991), and Roberts (1994). On Hopkins's friendships, for Bridges, see Phillips (1992); for Dixon, Sambrook (1962); for Patmore, Hudson (1949). Dolben's poems were edited, with a memoir, by Bridges (Dolben 1915). For John Ruskin, the most important influence on Hopkins's ways of seeing and imagining, there are the biography by Hilton (1985; 2000); a useful brief introduction by Bell (1963); and an important study by Hewison (1976). The Victorian Church, and in particular the Oxford Movement, Science and Religion, and Roman Catholics, is covered by Chadwick (1966 & 1970).

2

Work

Introduction

Hopkins's poetic reputation necessarily rests on the poetry of his maturity: the astonishing 'The Wreck of the *Deutschland*' (1875), the fifty completed poems and those unfinished, some substantial pieces, notable even as torsos. Until recently editions have printed the finished poems and only then the unfinished, as though the latter could be relegated to an appendix for the curious few. But the most fragmentary lines, even from Hopkins's student days, can be illuminating or give delight, while to read him complete, shows a poet striving, experimenting, developing, sometimes failing, in fascinating ways. Hence this study's choice of Catherine Phillips's edition (Oxford, 2002), which gives the poetry complete in chronological order. In reading this Part, have Phillips's edition to hand.

The first section of this Part deals with the surviving poetry up to 1868, when Hopkins determined to give up poetry [**p. 20**] and destroyed it all – or more precisely, all that was to hand. Much though did survive, in copies sent to family and friends, and in the Journals. What does survive reveals a significant minor poet as well as a writer seeking to find a voice.

The break in composition (1868–75) is a convenient point at which to consider the Journals (1862–75) as separate literary productions. These Journals end while Hopkins was at St Beuno's College [**pp. 25–6**], shortly before the poetic outburst, beginning with 'The Wreck', that deals with the wonder of nature and the power and glory of God. Again, the ending of Hopkins's novitiate in 1878 and his early priesthood offer a convenient point to discuss the sermons and other devotional writings. The rest of the mature poetry is then explored, and the letters dealt with last, since they provide a retrospect of friendship and point forward to the critical responses explored in Part III.

The early poetry to 1868: introduction

To read through the early poetry complete, reveals a very different poet from that of standard selections, which rarely offer more than 'Heaven-Haven' and 'The Habit of Perfection', washed-out precursors of the mature religious poetry. This early poetic production shows a poet aware of contemporary poetry and of new voices like Dante Gabriel Rossetti and his sister Christina, constantly experimental, often witty, sometimes playful. If in 1868 Hopkins was still a minor poet, he had forged an individual voice, while the disciplines of Jesuit meditation and teaching fed the hidden but potent poetic impulses that again found expression in 1875.

On a count, some 130 poems and fragments survive from Hopkins's years as schoolboy and as Oxford student. Of these, some twenty-five are complete, the others uncompleted or fragmentary experiments and sketches, often no more than jottings of the moment. Hopkins obviously would never have considered publishing such fragments in his lifetime, but they feed into the Romantic and Victorian fascination with the sketch, valuable because more spontaneous, more directly in touch with the inspiration of the moment, giving the reader access to poetic process and intensity. So brief are many of these, that it is impossible to discuss every one nor always helpful to take them in chronological order. The translations, to and from Latin and Greek, that Hopkins produced throughout his life, are largely ignored here: Phillips, however, provides details of sources and translations of original compositions, the most interesting of which is 'Inundatio Oxonian', describing the flooding of college meadows.

The early poetry: schooldays 1854–63

'THE ESCORIAL' (1860)

The first of Hopkins's surviving poems, 'The Escorial', which won a prize at Highgate School, the set subject being Philip II's great palace outside Madrid, is written in elaborate stanzas (nine lines, using three interlaced rhymes), competently handled. Like other prize poems in the nineteenth century – Tennyson's 'Timbuctoo' (1829); Matthew Arnold's 'Alaric at Rome' (1840) – it offers a grandiose subject, which encourages evocation of the past and of the exotic. The material, naturally enough, is drawn from books, particularly

The Reign of Philip the Second (1859), by the American historian,
W.H. Prescott, which may have prompted the competition's subject.
Hopkins's handling reflects Victorian fascination with the 'horrors'
of Spain and Catholicism – the Inquisition, suppression, gloom. Part
palace, part monastery, the Escorial was also to be the king's tomb,
each locus in turn providing a focus of the poet's meditation. The
palace, dedicated to St Lawrence, is laid out on a gridiron pattern,
the object on which traditionally the saint suffered martyrdom.
Philip neatly, as a witty conceit, raised a building modelled on the
very object of the saint's martyrdom, while Hopkins 'neatly' com-
pares Lawrence on his gridiron to a ship, though a 'wreck that
flames not billows beat' (22), a detail in which some prescience of
the storms in 'The Wreck' and 'The Loss of the *Eurydice*' might be
detected, though such imagery is not in itself startlingly original.
Philip and the monks, branded as gloomy fanatics, sought to con-
found true (Protestant) religion, the palace being 'the proudest home |
Of those who strove God's gospel to confound | With barren rigour
and a frigid gloom' (6–8), the king's fanaticism being treated ironi-
cally, his view of the Dutch dissenters set against the nineteenth-
century conviction of reformed religion's victory. Modern knowledge
of Spanish policy's failure in the Netherlands in turn allows Hopkins
to review, in a temporal perspective, Spain's historical decline,
beginning with a Keatsian passage, reminiscent of 'The Eve of
St Agnes', as the forces of nature batter and invade the palace:

> The driving storm at hour of vespers beat
> Upon the mould'ring terraces amain ...
> Afar in corridors with pain'd strain
> Doors slamm'd to the blasts continuously ...
>
> (101–2; 105–6)

Spain's decline is paralleled with the palace's degradation and mir-
rored in the dynastic political quarrels that dragged Spain down
through much of the nineteenth century.

Of its time 'The Escorial' may be, conventional on Spain, monks
and even Gothic architecture, where Hopkins, with Ruskin [pp. 7–8],
prefers 'Gothic grace', but the poem shows competence and some-
thing more for a sixteen-year-old in its technical ability and in its
spatial and temporal panoramic range.

'A VISION OF THE MERMAIDS' (1862)

'A Vision', which Hopkins wrote out carefully below an ink drawing
(*J*, plate 3), is deeply indebted to Keats in its riotous indulgence in

sensory accumulation, and like some of Keats's early works, shows Hopkins flexing his poetic muscles. Keats is responsible for its fantastical situation and its sumptuous, often-compounded adjectives ('lustrous gashes, crimson-white' (8)), while its expert use of couplets, run on, echoes Keats's *Endymion*. Yet the poem, besides revelling in the resources of language, is also fascinated by effects of light, the way the eye behaves, that are distinctly Hopkins's own: 'spikes of light' open 'gashes' (7–8), but the physiological detail suggests experiment and observation, for

> Where the eye fix'd, fled the encrimsoning spot,
> And gathering, floated where the gaze was not ...
>
> (9–10)

Sensations are mixed as the setting sun, an 'orb'd rose', a visual image exuding perfume, produces breath or breeze, takes on human characteristics ('lips'; 'gasp'd'), and ends in overwhelming light and dark ('splendour and eclipse', 20–23).

The poem is not just a virtuoso sunset, for out of the sea come six or seven mermaids, who if decently clad, give sensual splendour, in colour and exotic invocations of Tyrian dye (imperial purple) and Pompeian wall-painting. Occasionally Hopkins stumbles – for example, in 'jacinthine thing' (65), where 'thing', lacking precision or sensual appeal, makes us pause to ask 'what *thing*?' The mermaids and the Nereids, sea nymphs, sport, while the poet watches, an unheeded observer, unlike the figure of the poet in Hopkins's later poems, with his important dramatic role in 'The Wreck', as a channel of revelation. The vision fades, dusk comes on and with it, the right Keatsian note of melancholy, 'I watch but see those Mermaids now no more' (143).

'WINTER WITH THE GULF STREAM' (1863)

'Winter with the Gulf Stream', the only poem published in any widely distributed form during Hopkins's lifetime, appeared in the family magazine *Once a Week*. It was significantly revised by Hopkins in 1871, the version in *P*; the discussion here is based on the original (*L*, 3.437). The poem again shows Hopkins experimenting, using terza rima, the poetic form of Dante in *The Divine Comedy* and extraordinarily difficult to handle in English, where rhymes come less easily than in Italian. In the initial three lines two rhymes (aba) are used, the second (b) then being rhymed alternately with a new rhyme in the next three lines, and so on until the end, where a couplet rhyming on the central line of the previous triplet emphasises closure.

It is an evening piece, contemplating the sun setting on a winter landscape, yet one (again, Hopkins's scientific interest) where the full ferocity of snow is kept at bay by the effect of the Gulf Stream. Essentially lyrical description, it is more controlled, more immediately apprehensible, than in 'A Vision'. The observer of the scene, present from the beginning, only specifically enters at line 19 of 32, and if his observation does not significantly shape or change what is seen, he offers a 'figure in the landscape', by whom we stand and contemplate.

The opening repetition, 'The boughs, the boughs are bare enough', may echo Tennyson's 'Tithonus' (1860) ('The woods decay, the woods decay and fall'), but its emphasis is not on the dramatic voice of Tennyson's monologue, but on the naked trees, while 'enough' is qualified by what is missing, since 'earth has not yet felt the snow' (2). The scene is tranquil, fixed in frost, though the implied observer offers the contrast of imagined rain, when the 'clogg'd brook' would run with 'choking sound' (9). The moon rising through black branches is contrasted with the setting sun and the poet's voice takes us beyond description to the imaginative world of the mythological river Pactolus, its bed rich in gold, the light of the sun 'running' like water, until it sinks 'engulf'd' (32), water, sea, and sun drawn together in a single metaphor. There are oddities, yet in ease of rhythm and rhyme, in precision and originality of description, *Once a Week* rightly saw this as an original and successful poem.

The early poetry: university student 1863–68

The best way to read Hopkins's early poetry is straight through, chronologically, but in discussing it, it is helpful to take the finished poems and substantial fragments roughly in groups by genre – religious; dramatic; personal (in mood, rather than necessarily purely personal to Hopkins); natural and symbolic; and responses to other poetry and poets—whether romantic ballads or more particularly Dante Gabriel Rossetti and his sister Christina.

RELIGIOUS POETRY

Hopkins's poetry from 1875 is very largely religious, showing a natural continuity of involvement in religious thought and feeling, however transformed by conversion and Jesuit discipline, from his undergraduate days. It is possible to distinguish amongst the early religious verse written until the renunciation of 1868, the dramatic; devotional; biblical; and the personal (involving himself or imagined religious figures such as the nun in 'Heaven-Haven'). The characteristics of this poetry show themselves in subject matter and form, its material taken from Christian doctrine, the Bible, and the life of Jesus and the saints, and its imagery including allegory, symbolism, and paradox (often witty, in the manner of the seventeenth-century devotional poet, George Herbert). Many of these poems explore spirituality and personal devotion, whether to the achievement of grace or to a sense of desertion by God or barrenness in the self. Individual examples of each kind of poem are discussed below, but it is also useful first briefly to illustrate the characteristics found again and again.

The witty conclusion of 'New Readings', for example, unites Christ's warning that 'By their fruits ye shall know them', since thistles will not produce grapes, with the paradox that out of the crown of thorns (metaphorically) comes 'wine', Christ's blood in his passion and perpetually on the altar at the sacrifice of the mass. Elsewhere, in 'Easter Communion', the passion of Christ, itself brutal, calls up in Hopkins disturbingly brutal images – 'You striped in secret with breath-taking whips' (3) – images that shock, but which, in 'The Wreck of the *Deutschland*', where meaning controls means, are modified to focus on relationship rather than pain – 'I did say yes | O at lightning and lashed rod' (9–10). The experiences that Hopkins describes later in the 'Terrible' Sonnets [pp. 107–14], the sense of his own unworthiness and of God's withdrawal from him, are already experiences he knows, even if not yet expressed with the dynamic sense of immediacy later achieved.

It is not clear whether any of these poems directly reflect Hopkins's process of conversion to Catholicism, though 'The Half-Way House' may be one, as perhaps also 'Let Me Be to Thee', full of premonitions as well as a notable achievement in itself. A sonnet, Hopkins's preferred later (highly modified) form, its structure, related to musical terms, shows observation and linguistic individuality in the bird or bat ('with tender and air-crisping wings', 2), circling as he would desire to circle before God, the single note of bird or bat being then in the sestet (the last six lines) developed in an image of musical terms, his 'cadence' finding its 'dominant', Love. Hence he calls God Love and himself Lover ('to call Thee Love and Love', 14). If the poem works at the level of image rather than the dramatic revelation of 'The Windhover' [pp. 84–6], yet, in its technical assurance and a handling of the sonnet, without the cramping or farcing out that can arise in fixed forms, it shows Hopkins an accomplished religious poet.

'PILATE' (1864) – 'SOLILOQUY OF ONE OF THE SPIES' (1864)

These two poems, both incomplete, though subjected to revision at various times, are soliloquies. The first is in the style of Browning's dramatic monologues, revealing a character who has undergone a strange and disturbing experience. Pilate, a historical character, vividly recalls his reactions to the judgement and crucifixion of Christ. The second, in which one of the spies sent by Moses to report on the promised land of Canaan (Numbers 13 & 14) yearns to return to the 'fleshpots' of Egypt, is more strongly allied to Tennyson in, for example, 'The Lotos Eaters'.

'Pilate', written in a seven-line stanza, the closing couplet emphatically shutting up each stanza, is dramatic in Pilate's representation of his fate and his suffering, though the images are often more effective than the actions they describe – in stanza 3, the image of the 'freezing runnel' (14), with its sense of cold and constriction, fine in itself, hardly clarifies how life is 'more thin' or in what sense it was 'fat' before. The subsequent history of Pilate, Roman governor of Palestine, who allowed Jesus to be condemned and crucified, is found in Eusebius's Church History (Eusebius 1989: 43) and in legends: variously he commits suicide, is executed, or sent into exile. Hopkins opts for exile, in a place where the extreme contrasts of winter cold and summer heat might daunt any man, a climate and landscape reminiscent of Dante's *Inferno*.

Yet however severe these extremes, Pilate's guilt scarcely allows him to notice them. Only once a year, on the anniversary of that judgement, does life revisit him and 'I try the Christus o'er again' (53). His only hope is that one day he may expiate by acting out his own crucifixion – Hopkins shows a certain morbid fascination in how a man may crucify himself, a morbidity found occasionally elsewhere in a dwelling on detail of physical suffering. The soliloquy is a character study of a weak yet sensitive man, uncoloured by the ironies that Browning brings by a supposed reader ('An Epistle of Karshish') or listener ('My Last Duchess'). Indeed, Pilate's voice is simply internalised: he has no audience except himself for the still nagging, as yet incomplete, metamorphosis one false decision brought upon him.

ST DOROTHEA (1864–1868)

Hopkins has been accused of not writing about women, and yet he shows a fascination not only, and properly, in Mary as mother of Jesus, a figure of devotion, but also in certain saints, in particular martyrs and virgins, while he was to find his great subject in the death of the five nuns of the *Deutschland*. If the student Hopkins tends to prize the retiring virgin (as in 'Heaven-Haven' [**pp. 51–2**]) over the heroic sufferer, he already exhibits an interest in those women who face the turmoil and perturbation of the world, so wonderfully encompassed in 'The Wreck' and 'Spring and Fall'.

Four poems deals with St Dorothea. Why Hopkins was particularly struck by Dorothea is not clear, though his idea of writing a poem linked to a painting was a popular one from the mid-nineteenth century. Dante Gabriel Rossetti wrote poems to be (mentally) attached to Renaissance works of art (Giorgione's *The Tempest*, for example) and developed the conceit further by writing poems to go with paintings of his own, often inscribed on specially elaborated frames – such paintings Hopkins is likely to have seen at galleries he went to in London. The relationship of image and word is emphasised, even when no such picture actually existed, and Hopkins, particularly in the first version ('For a Picture of Saint Dorothea', 1864: *P*, 48) plays with the relation between picture and looker (who also 'hears' Dorothea's account of what her picture shows), even suggesting at the end that it is indeed all a device, that no such picture really exists ('We see | Nor fruits, nor flowers, nor Dorothy', 23–24), not because the canvas is imaginary but because Dorothy has been taken away to heaven.

In the legend, Dorothea, martyred (*c*.300) during the reign of Diocletian, was mocked by a young man, to whom an angel appeared, at the moment of her execution, with roses and apples: he was converted and executed in turn. Dorothea is traditionally shown with a woven basket containing flowers (not always roses) and fruit. Hopkins, in 'For a Picture' (1864), imagines two voices, of Dorothea and of the viewer – her fate is bitter, but the flowers brought in exchange to convince Theophilus, the young doubter, are sweet – they are lilies, suggesting chastity, rather than the more sensual roses, and the fruit is a quince, the flowers and fruits' miraculous nature enforced because the 'world is wintering' (12). Yet, gazing, the viewer not only sees, but first doubts, then begins to intervene and interpret: 'Had she a quince in hand? Yet gaze: | Rather it is the sizing moon' (19–20). The stability of the picture begins to break up, and as Dorothy's status as martyr is confirmed by her execution, her image fades and the picture passes from static to dynamic in her transition to heaven.

The other versions ('A basket-broad' (1865); 'Lines for a Picture of St Dorothea' (undated); and 'S. Dorothea' (?1867–68)) show Hopkins elaborating the legend and experimenting (not entirely successfully) with stress patterns. The care and elaboration shown over three or four years of writing and revising these poems suggest Hopkins's involvement with the subject, faith's triumph through objects of beauty, and how teasingly he could not get it right and yet wanted to.

'BARNFLOOR AND WINEPRESS'

'Barnfloor and Winepress', published in the Oxford *Union Review* (1865), is a finished poem that expertly explores the doctrine of

Christ's sacrifice and his gift – out of the barnfloor, where grain for bread is threshed from the wheat heads, and out of the winepress – of the bread and wine that in the perpetual sacrifice of the mass become Christ's saving flesh and blood. It draws on the traditional interpretation of the Old Testament as foreshadowing the fulfilment of God's promises in the New, the details of the Old – here, the harvest of bread and wine – allegorically standing for the flesh and blood of Jesus. Taking the Bible's common images of agriculture, Hopkins presents Christ's passion and death, which led to his 'harvest' in the Resurrection and the hope of salvation, as a process of threshing and pressing, of binding and blood-letting. 'Scourged' (6) not only represents the threshing process but picks up, in a kind of pun that links harvest and passion, Old Testament and New, the scourging of Jesus at the order of Pilate. Then, the tombstone is likened to a millstone which revolves to grind flour, as the tombstone was rolled away at the Resurrection and Christ is the 'heavenly Bread' (8). The first stanza formally represents threshing, the second winepressing, and we (the reader, the Christian) are drawn into the meaning by the final image of grafting, the taking of cuttings that are inserted into trees to produce new fruit: here Christ is the tree, and the tree is also his cross, as symbol of his suffering and sacrifice.

'HEAVEN-HAVEN' (1864) – 'THE HABIT OF PERFECTION' (1866)

The last of this religious group includes two poems often chosen in anthologies to represent Hopkins's early poems. Their popularity, partly because they are finished, partly because they are felt to indicate Hopkins's early religious impulse, can be misleading if taken as typical of the early poetry, much less of the confrontations and physical particularity of the mature poetry.

The first, 'Heaven-Haven', subtitled 'a nun takes the veil', reflects the language of Tennyson: 'Where falls not hail, or rain, or any snow' ('Morte d'Arthur', 260); 'Where springs not fail' ('Heaven-Haven', 2). It also shows the Victorian fascination with the nun in life and art: Catholic nuns had assisted Florence Nightingale during the Crimean War in the 1850s, several orders of sisterhood and nuns were founded within the Church of England, while Charles Alston Collins's painting, *Convent Thoughts* (1850–51; Ashmolean Museum, Oxford), shows a nun struck into contemplation of the Passion as she gazes at a passion flower. A mood picture, rather than a dramatic renunciation, the stress in 'Heaven-Haven' is upon a safe harbour (haven), while the effect of the imagery is to praise a cloistered and fugitive virtue, rather than positive entry into a life of prayer ('out of the swing of the sea', 8). Glancing ahead to 'The Wreck of the *Deutschland*', there in contrast Hopkins sees no immediate refuge for the nuns – expelled from convent and in the hurlyburly of storm and the struggle of death.

'The Habit of Perfection', subtitled 'The Novice', is a sequence rejecting in turn each of the physical senses, in the hope of divine faculties—eyes, for example, are to be 'double dark' and to 'find the uncreated light' (9–10). It is effective enough, not quite the retreat of 'Heaven-Haven', rather a desire for spiritual over physical powers, though the language at times is too self-conscious, in its compounded adjectives ('lovely-dumb', 5). If the religious interest of 'Heaven-Haven' and 'The Habit' suggest devotional continuity with the later poetry, to read 'The Nightingale' [**p. 60**], composed during the same two days as 'The Habit of Perfection', can only enforce the importance of reading the early poetry whole: the accomplished integration of place and feeling in 'The Nightingale', a deeply felt, entirely dramatically projected, exploration of a woman, making it amongst the greatest of the early poems and evidence of how variously talented Hopkins was as a poet.

DRAMATIC POETRY

In being drawn to the dramatic, Hopkins was very much of his age. Both Romantics and Victorians were fascinated by the stage and the prospect of reputation and money that it gave, though often repelled by the low ebb of dramatic values in a practical theatre of melodrama and spectacle. The nineteenth century revived interest in the drama of Shakespeare's contemporaries, above all the tragedies of John Webster and John Ford. Such Jacobean plays, exploring the darker ways of the psyche, of love (and lust), incest, torture and murder, encouraged nineteenth-century poets to dramatic imitations, often grotesque and terrifying, to exploit sexuality and violence under the guise of the older literature, when, unlike the 'modern age', such subjects were allowed – so Shelley wrote *The Cenci* (1819), centring on the rape of Beatrice by her father, who in revenge prompts his murder. Most poets, though, chose to write 'closet' dramas, poems in dramatic form to be realised on the stage of the imagination: early successes of this kind are Thomas Lovell Beddoes's *Death's Jest Book* (1825–28) and Tennyson's grimly jokey and exuberant *The Devil and the Lady* (1823–24). Many of these dramas are fragmentary, choosing to intensify dramatic moments or to expand mood through lyric description or songs, with the concentration of the sketch. The dramatic possibilities were further developed by Browning in the dramatic monologue, where a single speaker is imagined revealing himself, often with unconscious irony in response to situation and dramatic listener, whose presence is supplied by the reader through opening 'stage directions' or hints and variations of voice.

Hopkins, still impressionable, naturally followed fashion. Despite his later declared dislike for Browning ('all the gifts but the one needful' (*L*, 2.75)), both 'Pilate' [**pp. 48–9**] and 'The Soliloquy of the Spy' owe something to the dramatic monologue, and he responds with exuberance to the possibilities in situation and language, if not subject, given him by imitation of the Jacobean dramatists.

DRAMATIC POETRY: *FLORIS IN ITALY*

Three poetic scenes of *Floris in Italy* (1864) survive, and two prose scenes in the Journals, while other fragments seem associated with the situation and its 'medieval' setting. In the fragment, 'I am like a slip of comet', the speaker dramatically extends the image of herself as a comet, obscure, a wanderer, who grows in power approaching the masculine power of the sun (scientifically correct: a comet's tail extends as it approaches the sun) and 'sucks the light' (11) in an appropriately Jacobean allusion 'as full as Gideon's fleece' (11), a reference to the miraculous dew that drenched the fleece while all else was dry (Judges 6: 37–38).

The main fragment of *Floris*, sixty-six lines of blank verse, deliberately imitates seventeenth-century English in structure and style. Giulia, passionately in love with Floris, who has transferred his affections to her cousin, determines to flee, disguised as a boy, and takes her leave of the sleeping Floris. Reminiscences from Shakespeare's romantic disguisings, especially of Julia in *The Two Gentlemen of Verona*, and from Iachimo's cataloguing of the sleeping Imogen in *Cymbeline*, if not deliberate, are hints from a pool of reference available to the reader. The farewell, during which Giulia contemplates both the sleeping Floris and her own predicament, alternates between moods, deliberately if wryly comic at the beginning as Giulia displays her male clothes and false moustache, tearful yet resolved as she dwells on her continuing love and her conviction that her cousin's love will not match what she could offer Floris. The flow and shift of response within the situation shows Hopkins's ability, despite his early declaration that he could not enter into other people [**p. 7**], to empathise with another, and again calls in question the too easy claim that Hopkins did not write about women. The images are poetic, Giulia invoking sleep, for example, to bind Floris while she takes a ring from his finger ('Ply fold on fold across his dangerous eyes', 18), yet they also show a heightening of Hopkins's own observation rather than a mere imitation of the stylistic quirks of the Jacobeans, so Sleep's imagined blindfold is to be easy, 'light | As the laid gossamers of Michaelmas | Whose silver skins lie level and thick in field' (19–21). A night piece, the passage of time, the need for haste in departing at the end, leads to Giulia's subtle play on 'gone' (53) – gone physically, 'Warn'd by the bright procession of the stars' (54), but also lost, indeed dead, to Floris.

PEOPLE AND PERSONALITIES

A group of poems written between April 1865 and January 1866, not specifically religious, is cast variously in forms that while dramatic, offering voices not Hopkins's own, explore feeling rather than unfold a story. 'The Beginning of the End', three sonnets, not only show Hopkins's technical delight in what was to be his main poetic form, but also his exploration, in 'a neglected lover's address to his mistress' (P, 319), of three stages of the pains of heterosexual love. At the first stage lies the paradox of love's intensity, vastly 'higher even yet' in its *less* than is the 'treble-fervent *more* of other men' (12–13), the witty contrast in some measure qualified as true feeling by the preceding gasp of pain in 'ah!' (11). As love lost is traced, the final line of the third sonnet crowds in stress (and an extra syllable) to produce the inertia of disappointment, the lover comparing his feeling of loss to that a boy feels 'when the poet he pores upon | Grows less and less sweet to him, and knows no cause' (13–14). Another empathetic exploration is 'Mothers Are Doubtless', where Hopkins recognises the loss a mother feels at the death of a child, an intensity the childless cannot know. Yet there is a Wordsworthian perception here that the mother is a fuller person for the very intensity of her grief. A child speaks the six lines of 'In the Staring Darkness', while the four lines of 'The Stars Were Packed So Close' might be the words of a disembodied voice or of a character in ecstatic contemplation or emotional crisis. The massed starlight overwhelms the night's darkness, enclosing like fencing ('hurdles') the 'liberties' (4) of air – a restraint compensated for by the glory of light. The fragment also shows Hopkins visualising the immensity of sky and space as fields and farmland and domestic space, a vision developed in 'The Starlight Night' and 'The Candle Out of Doors' [pp. 81–2; 83–4]. Three poems of this period deserve detailed attention.

PEOPLE AND PERSONALITIES: 'WHERE ART THOU FRIEND' (1865)

This poem, a sonnet, is organised by rhyme as two four-line quatrains and a sestet. There is no break in the argument between octave and sestet (the rhymes indeed tighten the structure) and if the parentheses in the sestet which emphasise the contrast between Hopkins's weakness and God's power lose the reader, the conclusion is on a rhyme ('thee') that returns us to the first line and the poem's opening desperate question, since 'thee' refers to the Friend whom 'I shall never see'. The argument of the poem is presented dramatically, Hopkins crying out in present distress ('Where art thou ... ?') and exclaiming ('Oh!'), while the vacillation between parenthesis and parenthesis, between God and self, are all features of the dramatic processes of the mature poetry.

The sonnet has been linked to Hopkins's attraction to Digby Dolben [pp. 13–4] and indeed its concern that the 'friend' will never be seen now (in 'the age that is', 3) or in the future (in life or after death) might hint at Hopkins's fear (touched on also in 'Henry Purcell' [pp. 101–2]), that non-Catholics, as heretics, might be damned. If that interpretation is correct, then he as a convert and Dolben, dead before joining the Church, are separated by that death and might not to be united after death. Such a view, held then, might find support in Hopkins's later reference to a 'great grace' received about Dolben (J, 236). Yet one can doubt whether Hopkins does indeed express such an unorthodox doctrine of salvation here and a closer reading, of what is undoubtedly a convoluted argument, seems to challenge this account. At the opening Hopkins, who did meet Dolben, if only once, refers to the friend 'whom I shall never see', not 'never see again', and then adds that if he imagines ('conceives') what the friend is like, he 'must conceive amiss' (2) – because he has never met him and never will. Is the friend then the imagined reader, Hopkins's audience, you and me? Or might the friend be taken as an ideal companion or partner, no more to be found than ideals ever are in a real world? Certainly there is a strong religious element, that ties in with Hopkins's own conversion and his sense of God's loving yet transcendental nature, a love confirmed in Christ who, unlike Hopkins himself, foreknows and therefore cannot conceive amiss of the friend.

PEOPLE AND PERSONALITIES: 'THE ALCHEMIST IN THE CITY' (1865)

If the persona of 'Where Art Thou Friend' might seem close to Hopkins himself, the Alchemist here is clearly separate from the poet, an imagined character, who from his perspective, a high window, surveys and stands apart from the inhabitants of the city (features of which clearly reflect Oxford's colleges and towers). While not immortal (the Alchemist wishes for the longevity of those, like Methuselah in the Bible, who lived before Noah's flood, in the 'prediluvian age', 10), he stands apart from the flow of time found in clouds, seasons, the 'making and the melting crowds' (3). Yet if he seems superior in his high vantage point, it is others who achieve things, 'happy promises fulfill'd' (8), while he proves to be the prisoner of a futile obsession.

The paradox here is a recognisable, poetic one, found in Keats's empty village of the Grecian Urn Ode, eternal but frozen. While Hopkins's paradox is not so stunningly constructed, his Alchemist's schemes seem doomed to unfulfillment, the gold is 'not to be discover'd' (14), while his knowledge ('lore') 'holds no promise of success' (34). The poem is written around contrasts: of time present and lengthened out; of people engaged in temporal activities against an individual who observes; of achievement and disappointment. The Alchemist is close to being 'time's eunuch', that bitter phrase Hopkins was to use later of himself [p. 37], unachieving despite his gifts, though here no God offers the Alchemist an alternative way. Yet the Alchemist imagines a further polarity – between the city and the wilderness, away from man's achievements to a nature which is 'houseless' yet sweet (35) and where he might be free from the demands of his own science ('lore') and so

> pierce the yellow waxen light
> With free long looking, ere I die.
>
> (43–44)

Freed from the city, he might also be free from his projects, and in rejecting find happiness – though the poem only offers this as a desire and not an action.

PEOPLE AND PERSONALITIES: 'THE EARTH AND HEAVEN' (1866)

Like 'The Alchemist', this poem begins with a fixed observer, though the perspective is not from city buildings, but an egotistical confidence of the self's all-inclusive nature, for while 'All else may whirl or dive or fly' (8), he is (apparently) the supremely confident centre of the universe:

> I am the midst of every zone
> And justify the East and West ...
>
> (3–4)

Yet in seeking to establish his confident fixity, the persona describes the transitory yet beautiful ease of the natural world, in swallow and in cloud which passes into rain and in runlet from the millbrook. So while the structure of polarity between the speaker's fixity and the external world's mutability seems to scorn the impermanence of bird and vapour, the particularity of nature, set against the general-isations of his 'mastery', enforces delight and achievement however passing. The swallow

> drops upon the wind again;
> His little pennon is unfurled.
> In motion is no weight or pain,
> Nor permanence in the solid world.
>
> (13–16)

And the speaker reveals he too has desired (the past tense suggests a wish now hopeless), 'desired to pass' (28), like swallow and cloud, and be part of the flow of time. The 'lovely ease' of description and argument reveal an assured mastery before Hopkins's renunciation of poetry.

EARLY POETRY: NATURE AND SYMBOLISM

From early on Hopkins was constantly observing and recording nature, yet while describing what he saw and developing techniques for seizing the shifting natural world, he also necessarily transformed what he grasped through the senses into significance by structure and selection. While much of the early poetry is fragmentary, abandoned, some fragments can be taken as complete moments of experience or insight – the strange perception, for example, of 'Late I fell in the ecstacy' or the symbolic yet undeterminable quest of 'I must hunt down the prize', where the images are more significant for us than the object, as the trail compels him to

> see the green seas roll
> Where waters set
> Towards those wastes where the ice-blocks tilt and fret
>
> (5–7)

– 'fret' showing that lively comprehension of two meanings so typi-cal of Hopkins, the physical rubbing and sensory irritation. In 'It was a hard thing', Hopkins, as in 'The earth and heaven', touches on the paradox of perception and our self-created universe, a philoso-phical concept inherited from the Romantic poets, as the rainbow shines, 'but only in the thought | Of him that looks' (2–3), while if the sun on water 'writes the text' (8), only the eye or thought 'reads' it. Later, Hopkins explored how God's creation, a living universe, was to be read to understand God's meaning. As Hopkins, striving for exactness, makes trials of his poetic resources, he uses images that later reappear with more significance – the 'min'd embers' (13) of the dying fire in 'Glimmer'd along the square-cut steep' will become the blue-bleak embers that 'fall, gall themselves, and gash gold-vermilion' ('The Windhover', 14) [pp. 84–6]. In all this, Hopkins is 'reading' nature, scrutinising both its distinctive 'thisness' (its *haeceitas* in Duns Scotus's technical term [pp. 62–3]) and its meaning beyond itself.

NATURE AND SYMBOLISM: 'SPRING AND DEATH' (?1863)

Hopkins used the musical term 'counterpointing', the simultaneous juxtaposition of notes, to describe both rhythmic effects and the interplay of meaning in poetry. 'Spring and Death' is an early example of such 'counterpointing' of meaning, with decay and death, loss and grief, present even amidst the luxuriance and vigorous life of Spring. The poem uses the familiar device of a dream to counterpoint the polar opposites of Death and Spring. The Spring landscape is overwhelming in its lushness ('A little sickness in the air | From too much fragrance everywhere', 3–4) and in it the figure of Death confronts us, his 'charnelhouse-grate ribs' reminiscent of both ghastly ship and Death in Coleridge's 'The Ancient Mariner', Hopkins adding the acutely imaginative overlaying of life with death, as the light passes through Death's ribs, so that 'with coffin-black he barr'd the green' (11). Spring, the new birth, is an incongruous setting for Death, yet the mutability of all earthly things, the progression of the seasons and of life, means that death is a constant underpresence, given concrete shape by Hopkins's dream-vision. Spring's renewal is disturbed by an awareness of mortality, that what flourishes must perish. The same counterpointed sense, of nature's fullness yet of the fallen condition of the world and of mankind, was to preoccupy Hopkins and finds fuller, more complex expression in the child's unconscious apprehension of death in 'Spring and Fall' [pp. 103–4].

EARLY POETRY: RESPONSES AND REFLECTIONS

Hopkins's inheritance from the Romantic poets and his admiration for Tennyson, as the greatest poet of his age – if later qualified by his 'doubt' (*L*, 3.215) – should not hide his affinity with other poets. Hopkins admired Edward Lear, though he never followed him. It was a medieval world of romantic love and spiritual crisis, found particularly in Dante Gabriel Rossetti and his sister Christina, that attracted Hopkins. 'Stephen and Barberie' (?1864–65) embodies the medieval ballad mood, alluding also, in Barberie's name and her desertion, to Desdemona's song of the abandoned maid, Barbary, in *Othello*. 'The Summer Malison' (1865), two stanzas of a curse ('malison'), imaginatively exploits superstition, as harvest, sailor, soldier, friends are all ill-wished.

RESPONSES AND REFLECTIONS: 'THE QUEEN'S CROWNING' (1864) – 'THE NIGHTINGALE' (1866)

Two poems in this group show how Hopkins absorbed Dante Gabriel Rossetti's style and how he went beyond it to his own expression of love. 'The Queen's Crowning' is written in the ballad stanza used by Dante Gabriel in his medieval romances and adopts the characteristic particularity and inverted word order that are part of the other poet's pictorial medievalising:

> They were wedded at midnight
>   By the shine of candles three ...
>   (1–2)

Love is stronger than death: William, a king's son, married Alice, a maid of low degree, and promises to return after two or three years abroad. On his return, now heir to the kingdom, William refuses to marry and is slaughtered by his brothers. Alice learns the old king's sons are to come hunting, yet William is not amongst them, but that night William's ghost comes to her –

> As she lay weeping at the night
>   She heard but knockings three.
> 'It is as cold as death without:
>   Open the door to me.'
>   (113–16)

William urges her to follow him, gives her 'kisses three', and

>   Down upon the ground fell she.
> She has gone with him to Paradise.
>   There shall her crowning be.
>   (154–56)

Even with occasional uncertainties, 'The Queen's Crowning' is a remarkably successful medieval revival ballad of the kind made popular in pictures and poems by the Pre-Raphaelite Brotherhood.

'The Nightingale' is a fully-achieved poem of love and loss, a lament, painful but wonderfully observed, prompted by an awareness unnaturally heightened by the protagonist's desire and grief. Sited within a woman's consciousness, except for the third person perspective of the final stanza, Frances relives her vigil after Luke has departed for the sea, when all her senses were aroused, so she could hear even 'The bats' wings lisping as they flew' (19). A rare delight, the nightingale's song proved bitter though, as it swamped out the object of her vigilance, so that, in unexpected contrast to the bird's song, the sweet sound of Luke's 'passing steps'

> I never heard
> For warbling of the warbling bird ...
>> (48–49)

Hopkins creates the nightingale's power of song at length, to make sense of everything being blotted out for Frances, except its song, which itself absorbs all other natural features:

> He might have strung
> A row of ripples in the brook,
> So forcibly he sung ...
>> (30–32)

The very pain that Frances felt at separation is transferred from Luke to the bird, and yet both pains exist simultaneously for the reader:

> I thought the air must cut and strain
> The windpipe when he sucked his breath
> And when he turned it back again
> The music must be death.
>> (36–39)

Luke and the nightingale, wonder and death, are linked and at the close, the tenses passing back from memory to a contemporary present, Frances sleeps as Luke drowns, the pair intricated at the moment of death –

> She pillowing low her lily neck
> Timed her sad visions with his wreck
>> (55–56)

– visions which, unlike William's ghost in 'The Queen's Coming', do not promise a supernatural union or even a glimpse of the wreck. 'The Nightingale' shows in 1866 the kind of poet Hopkins might have been if he had not entered the Jesuits, not renounced poetry. It was no mean achievement.

Journals

Hopkins kept a series of diaries or journals at least from 1862 until 1875, though not all survive. They cover his student days at Oxford and the earlier years of his training as a Jesuit, serving as a bridge of creativity over the poetic gap of 1868–75. Hopkins renounced poetry, but his imagination still worked on language, nature, and the perception of God, qualities that came together rather than came from nowhere with 'The Wreck of the *Deutschland*'.

The Journals are diaries in part, but not exclusively so – often they are verbal sketch books or accounts of things that struck him, like his Welsh teacher's encounter with fairies, the point at which the Journals break off in 1875. Even the diary entries were often written up after the event, so that something so important as his determination to become a Catholic is noted by Hopkins on 17 July 1866 as coming to him that night 'I believe but possibly the next' (*J*, 146). As with other people's diaries, the entries, depending on circumstances, pressure of time, and mood, may be reduced to appointments or the weather, or expanded into lengthy description.

The diary entries proper record the ordinary traffic of everyday life, at times jumbled or without discriminating significant and trivial. Early on, there is a joke about his brother Lionel (aged ten), who wanted a razor for his incipient moustache: rather, butter should be put on the lip, butter and moustache together 'to be licked off by the cat' (*J*, 21). The ordinary business of entering into lodgings at Oxford, daily life at the University – ratting with terriers and May Day celebrations—find their place, and while there are significant entries ('I confessed on Saturday, Lady Day' (*J*, 59) or 'A day of the great mercy of God' (*J*, 58)), that suggest spiritual progress, the acquisition of a 'Little book for sins' is jotted down in a list that includes 'Necktie. Boots to see after' (*J*, 60). Holidays are recorded, visits to art galleries and the dentist, a detailed account of the Swiss trip before he entered the Jesuits, while disconcertingly, quite apart from the shock of Dolben's death [**p. 13**], we glimpse the high number of deaths amongst Hopkins's contemporaries and connections.

Hopkins also used his Journals until 1865 for poetry, mostly fragments that attempt to seize a moment or perception, or show him experimenting with metre, rhyme, and imagery, where a description can open out beyond the inert comparison to a realisation of living colour, as the black shining 'bean' that is the dark centre of the eyes in the peacock's tail

>   plays its liquid jet
>   To win a look of violet.
>
>   ('The Peacock's Eye', 5–6; P, 25)

Yet also in them and alongside these, important for his future poetic development, are the prose attempts to describe and seize, to apprehend and so comprehend the world and its meaning, a world not random, but with laws ('I have now found the law of the oak leaves', *J*, 146) and all the evidence of God's goodness and purpose. The natural world is real, not an illusion or a mask, though God is within it and may be perceived through it. For Hopkins, unlike the Romantics, God is not simply a spirit resident in natural forms; he does not subscribe to Wordsworth's pantheism, but to a separate and all-comprehending power. In this exploration of nature, both before entering the Jesuits and after, he is concerned with pinning down the material world. Already in the Journals Hopkins is disciplining himself in ways of seeing and seeking a theory of perception and a language in which to describe it. There is a great precision in this prose and Hopkins draws on terms and ideas of representation from the visual arts and music. Rather than 'just looking', he is engrossed in the act of perception: 'The lines of the fields, level over level, are striking, like threads in a loom' (*J*, 23); while a description of the hills near Oxford (*J*, 133–34), in its detail of colour and recession, distinguishing different trees, uses painterly terms, the accuracy and acuteness of observation suggesting how he is training the eye, catching at the swallows, the colour of their upper parts and how they are reflected in the river. He can startle by the way he sees, not simply content with description: 'Sun seemed to make a bright liquid hole' (*J*, 134) or 'the moon outside was roughing the lake with silver and dinting and tooling it with sparkling holes' (*J*, 184).

In the Journals, Hopkins does not simply jot down what he sees, but strives to capture the specific nature, following in this the teaching of John Ruskin [00], in the process developing a technical language, taken over into his poetic theory, from his exploration and perception of the nature of things. He conceives of the 'thisness' of a thing (what makes it what it uniquely is and not something else), and in his later reading of the medieval philosopher, Duns Scotus [00], found confirmation of this idea and term in Scotus's Latin '*haecceitas*' ('thisness'). He adopted Scotus's ideas and vocabulary so readily not because Scotus was a revelation but, rather, a systematic expositor of what Hopkins had come to by long and careful scrutiny, a scrutiny in which emotion – joy, exultation – was also a crucial element. Scotus was a happy confirmation of Hopkins's own practice, so that as he records, after first reading Scotus (1872), 'when I took in any inscape of the sky or sea I thought of Scotus' (*J*, 221). In Hopkins's development of a technical language, some words only appear once in the Journals and had no further importance for him, but for the essential nature of an object or scene he used the term 'inscape', the object's internal shape and distinctness, both particularity and the word overlapping with 'thisness' ('*haecceitas*'). For the force that keeps the object in being, its dynamic power (metaphorically at least, a power like electricity, 'charging' the object), he coined 'instress' – such terms occur occasionally in the poetry (e.g. 'instress stressed': 'The Wreck of the *Deutschland*', 39). Perceiving the 'inscape' of object or scene, through the power of its 'instress', might come as a sudden revelation (an 'epiphany' – a 'showing forth'—though Hopkins never used this term), often the result of engagement in mind and feeling with the object, as in the climaxing moment of 'The Windhover': 'air, pride, plume, here | Buckle!' (9–10) [p. 85]. 'Instress', for Hopkins, is bound up with power and with God, the source of that power, bound up therefore also with God's glory and the revelation of God's nature and purpose. Creation is not corrupt, though man may foul it, as when the smoke of London rolls up the Thames valley (*J*, 256). Nature is wonderful both in itself and in its showing forth of God's splendour, as if 'from shook foil' ('God's Grandeur', 2). The descriptions of the Journals lead to the epiphanies of the nature poems, with their dramatic transformations and flashed-down understandings.

Later, describing the more technical side of rhythm and his poetics – his theory of art and of poetry in particular – Hopkins writes of Sprung Rhythm (the stress patterns of his mature poetry [**pp. 68–9**]), of counterpointing, of outriders (additional syllables to the verse line). It is important to know the terms, yet even better, in first reading Hopkins's poetry, is to take his advice, draw breath, and read it aloud or voiced internally. The voice will carry us through the dramatic revelations and conflicts.

Hopkins's technical terms, however important, are only a small part of his general interest in language, sustained through much of his life and vital for his poetry. As early as September 1863 (*J*, 4), he has a long note about 'horn', expanding on its meanings and associations, constantly aware of sound intertwined with meaning, a series of words associated by sound often proving to have significant semantic connection. He links '*Grind, gride, gird, grit, groat, grate, greet*' as a sequence (*J*, 5), where meaning is passed through sound shifts from an original root meaning. Such buildings of sound and meaning became a crucial feature of the poetry, where alliteration and other sound effects support the stress patterns and develop meaning. The surviving notes on Rhetoric (*J*, 267–90), lectures delivered to novices at Roehampton (*c*.1873–74), deal with issues of metre and language in more conventional terms, but touch on the essential principle of Sprung Rhythm – 'rhythm without count of syllables'. The notes are reminders that while Hopkins broke with standard English metre, he was formalising something that was not entirely unfamiliar to the Victorians.

While the Journals, especially from the 1868 renunciation of poetry, are important for our knowledge and understanding of Hopkins, they must be recognised as not primarily a spiritual or emotional record, so that qualities that mark the poetry, qualities implied in what has been written in this section, the link between nature and God, spiritual revelation, sacramental celebration, are not common features in them. True, the Journals do note experiences, usually separate from observation of the natural scene, where Hopkins is moved to tears. Yet it is startling even, after many of the descriptions of scenery or flowers or leaf, when he adds, describing the bluebell, 'I know the beauty of our Lord by it' (*J*, 199). He is disturbed by the destruction of an ash tree (*J*, 230 [**p. 23**]) and, when unwell, is thrown out of equilibrium, as 'nature in all her parcels and faculties gaped and fell apart ... like a clod cleaving' (*J*, 236). It is the mature poetry that intertwines an intense vision of Nature and God; in the Journals Hopkins retains rather a deep consciousness that unless 'you refresh the mind from time to time you cannot always remember or believe how deep the inscape in things is' (*J*, 205). If such moments of emotion or spiritual perception are rare in the record, yet the Journals show how his experience prepared Hopkins for the chance seed, the hint that something might be written about the death of the five nuns in the wreck of a German ship. There is a bridge over into that in a passage (1874) that links the beauty of a starlight night with the power and love of God:

> As we drove home the stars came out thick: I leant back to look at them and my heart opening more than usual praised our Lord to and in whom all that beauty comes home ...

> (*J*, 254)

Mature poetry: 'The Wreck of the *Deutschland*'

'THE WRECK': INTRODUCTION

For Hopkins in August 1874, the stars 'coming out thick', celebrated in that Journal entry, part of the beauty and consolation of nature, were yet also, as God's creation, partly gift and partly a path to God's power and majesty: 'my heart opening more than usual praised our Lord to and in whom all that beauty comes home'. And the stars and a beauty both lovable and leading to love lie at the heart of 'The Wreck of the *Deutschland*': as Hopkins declares, 'I kiss my hand | To the stars, lovely-asunder' (33–34). Belief may involve intellectual conviction, but a religious life is little without warmth of feeling and for Hopkins the heart is an essential part of our nature, for however treacherous it can be, leading us into folly and sin, inclining us to perverse desire, the heart also connects us through the impulses of love to God. That love begins in the beauty of the God-created material world and propels us on to glimpses of the beatific vision, of God in his glory. Such impulses to God through the bond between his heart and natural beauty, encapsulated in that Journal entry, run powerfully through the first poem of Hopkins's maturity, 'The Wreck of the *Deutschland*', a poem possibly his greatest, certainly his longest and his most complex. There were various promptings to the poem: it is firmly founded in an event of the material world; it springs out of Hopkins's wish to commemorate the shipwreck; and it came into being when Hopkins's superior hinted something should be written [**p. 27**], effectively absolving him of his resolution to abandon poetry.

'THE WRECK': STORM AND DUALITY

The *Deutschland* was wrecked in the early hours of 7 December 1875, the day before the feast of the Immaculate Conception, a celebration of the Virgin Mary that Hopkins draws on late in the poem. The nuns, expelled from Germany ('Deutschland') by Bismarck's 'Kulturkampf' [**p. 27**], the struggle of Prussian authority against Church authority, sailed for the United States in a ship named *Deutschland* and so the single name of country and ship is 'double a desperate name': the nuns, rejected by country, drown in the ship. This drawing together of two into one, a duality significantly rooted in the unity of a single word, is an important conceptual and structural clue to be followed as the poem unfolds. Surprising connections are found, even in what appear paradoxes, as in the very title itself which dedicates the poem to the 'happy' memory of the 'drowned' nuns. How can the drowned be happy? The poem explores and answers that question, amongst many others. Duality is one key at least to the poem. Duality, an opposition, lies in storm and wreck set against the peace of Hopkins's Welsh haven, yet the nuns and Hopkins are drawn together in their Catholicism (as well as their humanity). The first part of the poem depicts Hopkins's inner experience of storm and coming to God; the second part depicts the tall nun's external storm, leading back to a hope for salvation. God, too, is one, but the poem contrasts his power and his love. Yet power and love are joined too in Christ, the Second Person of the Trinity, man and God, loving but to come at the end as judge, the sufferer who is yet triumphant.

Hopkins structures 'The Wreck' around himself and the tall nun, both sufferers in storms and proofs of the hope, in the love and majesty of Christ, the Person of God to whom our shared humanity makes us feel closest, of salvation, out of the storm to a haven. The poem unleashes the power of nature in the physical and metaphorical experiences of the storm, physically in the peril of the sea (paralleling the perils of life) and metaphorically in the wrath of God which is a manifestation of his power.

Contrasts, dualities, lie within the poem, some arising out of a single word or idea, others oppositions that are resolved and reconciled – God's power and God's mercy; Hopkins's 'quiet' conversion and the struggle of the tall nun in her time of trial; the 'lovable west' of St Beuno's and the gale that makes a prey of ship and travellers. Hopkins's account of his conversion is paralleled to the nun's situation. And if not strictly converted, the nun takes part in an experience that creates her afresh – as is Hopkins in contemplating the wreck and the nun's death: 'Over again I feel thy finger and find thee' (8). Both he and she have experienced storm, in the midst of which they have found Christ.

'THE WRECK' AS ODE

The poetic form of 'The Wreck of the *Deutschland*' is an Ode, derived ultimately from classical forms, adapted into English poetry, notably, amongst the Romantics, by Wordsworth in 'Tintern Abbey', by Coleridge in 'Frost at Midnight', and by Keats in 'Ode to a Nightingale' and 'Ode on a Grecian Urn'. The formality of Classical odes is, in English, relaxed into shifting moods and responses to a situation or an object or an emotion, usually giving prominence to the poet as centre of consciousness, who responds, meditates, looks inwards and then outwards, questioning or exploring or rejoicing, the form allowing the poetic expression to rise to heights of drama or excitement and to return to calm inner reflection, the language more poetically formal or closer to ordinary speech as the situation requires, giving a sense of dramatic activity, of something unfolding, to the reader.

'THE WRECK': STRUCTURE AND STANZA

'The Wreck' is in two parts, of ten and twenty-five stanzas. The dual centres of interest are the poet (identifiable as Hopkins: the poem is clearly autobiographical) and the tall nun. While Part I is mainly about Hopkins and Part II mainly about the nun, both are linked. The poem develops through parallelism and echoing: Hopkins and the nun find their ways to Christ, the nun acting out that struggle and triumph, while Hopkins recreates his own progress and gazes as a puzzled, yet finally satisfied, spectator, as though watching the unfolding of a drama upon a stage – here the theatre of God's power and mercy. It is Christ in his double nature as God and Man who dominates the poem's religious perspective – indeed, it should be noted that it is Christ who is invoked in the poem by name, not Jesus, Hopkins steering clear of the pious sentimentality of his contemporaries. Christ suffers as man, but he is also the Pantocrator, ruler of the world, Messiah and Saviour, God on earth.

Within the two-part structure, only one stanza runs on to be completed in the next (stanzas 7–8) and there a fine dramatic suspension and fulfillment is achieved. Many of the stanzas are of course linked, but still each has a sense of completion. This closing up is enforced too by rhyme as, for example, in stanza 1:

> Thou mastering me
> God! giver of breath and bread;
> World's strand, sway of the sea;
> Lord of living and dead;
> Thou hast bound bones and veins in me, fastened me flesh,
> And after it almost unmade, what with dread,
> Thy doing: and dost thou touch me afresh?
> Over again I feel thy finger and find thee.
>
> (1–8)

Line one ends with 'me' and the first four lines dwell on 'me' in relationship to God, emphasised by the rhymes on 'bread', 'see', 'breath' – food, sight, and life itself; lines 5–8 begin with 'Thou' (God) in relationship to 'me' and the rhyme words are 'flesh', 'dread', 'afresh' – humanity in its frailty, recognition of God's might, and yet the perpetual possibility of renewed relationship with God. The last line refers back to God ('thee'), rhyming with 'me' in the first line, so that lines 1 and 8 are 'laced in' (a favourite technical term of Hopkins) by rhyme to stress the relationship of Hopkins and God ('me' and 'thee').

'THE WRECK' – A NEW RHYTHM: READING HOPKINS

Underlying the structure of parts and stanzas, Hopkins used a new rhythm, evolved over years of thinking about poetry and, in the years of poetic silence, from his rhetorical training and rhetorical teaching [pp. 24; 63–4]. Perhaps the very imposition of silence on himself and submission to Jesuit discipline [p. 20] was an advantage, since if Hopkins had continued on his earlier poetic path, he might have been a lesser, certainly a less technically innovative poet, and his technical innovation was crucial to his poetic expression. Hopkins was well aware of metrical structures, in classical languages and in English poetry. He saw no point in trying to apply the metrical basis of Greek and Latin – length, long and short, of syllables – to English poetry and instead found a new rhythm based on natural English stress and therefore on the English speaking voice.

Hopkins himself described to Dixon what he already heard in his head and sought to use in 'The Wreck':

> I had long had haunting my ear the echo of a new rhythm which now I realised on paper ... it consists in scanning by accents or stresses alone, without any account of the number of syllables ... I do not say the idea is altogether new; there are hints of it in music, in nursery rhymes and popular jingles ...
>
> (L, 2.14)

Hopkins called this Sprung Rhythm (see Gardner 1949: vol. 2, chs. III & IV). As he explained to Dixon and in his own Preface (P, 334–35), stress is the basis of English poetry and it remains so in Sprung Rhythm. But the differences are crucial. In English, for example, the most common poetic foot or unit is the iamb, two syllables, the first unstressed, the second stressed, usually represented on the page as x / (Leech 1969: ch. 7)

Hopkins does two things with stress that differentiate him from standard English poets. He prefers, first, like the common beat in music, to open each foot with a stressed rather than an unstressed syllable. His poems of 'standard' line lengths, particularly the sonnets, will tend to have five stresses to the line, but in stanzaic poetry like 'The Wreck', the stress varies from line to line (another feature adapted from the Ode), though every stanza (normally) has the same stress pattern. Second, Hopkins uses feet of one to four syllables, the first syllable being stressed, but he will add more unstressed (weak) syllables for special effects or needs. If a foot has only one syllable, then it must be stressed. And so while on the face of it his line endings may be unstressed (a falling rhythm), they can, by being a single syllable foot, which must be stressed, end in a stress. Take the opening lines of the poem:

> Thou mastering me
> God! giver of breath and bread ...

The first line has three stresses and three feet, opening with the stressed (musical) beat that Hopkins desired:

```
 /       / x x    /
Thou | mastering | me ...
```

The second line then has four stresses and four feet:

```
  /     / x x     /     x     /
God, | giver of | breath and | bread ...
```

Problems do arise, partly from the very nature of stress in English, which in reality is not a simple matter of choice between stressed and unstressed. But the important thing in Hopkins's poetry, taking us back to music and in particular song, is voice. To understand his rhythms, Hopkins asked that the reader take breath and read aloud (or voice to the self). Read his poetry aloud and it will come right. Stress and meaning are inextricably meshed: Hopkins always linked sound and meaning, since to 'every word ... belongs a passion or prepossession or enthusiasm' (*J*, 125; [p. 11]). 'The Wreck' should be read by a combination of ear and eye – ear for the rhythm and rhyme, eye for rhyme too and for line ending – to voice the poem is not to abandon the shapes on the printed page: in rhyme, sight and sound combine. The ear monitors stress, the eye stanza form and lineation, rhyme forming a link between the two senses, the whole poetic structure an interlacing of sound and sight into the total meaning of a single stanza and on through the poem's totality.

'THE WRECK': PART THE FIRST

'The Wreck' is an elegy and yet a celebration, commemorating both the nuns' death, as Milton had the young drowned poet Edward King in his elegy 'Lycidas', and the happiness of finding Christ in the terrible process of the storm. The subtitle gives a date and a completed action, while the body of the poem is dramatic, living through that event, as though enacted even while the poem is being read. The question also early arises how the poem is to proceed, since the first ten stanzas (Pt. I) deal not with the nuns, but with Hopkins himself. The elegy and the ode as poetic forms both offer models, since it is usual for the poet to link in with the subject – Milton on his own poetic fate, contemplating King's death in 'Lycidas', or Coleridge recalling his childhood as he watches by his sleeping son in 'Frost at Midnight'. Stanza one declares God's power, which gives 'breath', life itself, and 'bread', the means of sustaining life. God in his triune form is suggested: the power of the Father, the spirit of the Holy Ghost in 'breath', and the gift of bread from Christ, in the bread of life in the Eucharist, distributed at the Last Supper and perpetually renewed in the sacrifice of the mass. The poem's structural duality already underlies 'breath' (the breath of life and the breath that sustains us in life), and 'bread' (food that keeps us alive in body, but is also the living body of Christ that can give eternal life). Hopkins has been made by God and 'dread' recognises his might, beyond anything human, yet Hopkins is *not* unmade by him, *not* killed by that power, even if 'almost unmade', and as he did in the past, so Hopkins is again brought to recognise God's power, in the wreck, as 'Over again I feel thy finger' (8), an enforcement of God's physical relationship with the human both in the act of making and in the Son's taking on himself man's physical nature.

Stanzas two and three explore the process of Hopkins originally finding God. They are not necessarily an autobiographical transcription of his conversion, rather a representation of its drama, in the various elements of terror and desire for refuge, pre-echoes, as it were, of the wreck's terror, where ship and passengers desire a safe harbour or haven. God the Father's authoritative presence may be in the 'frown of his face' (17), but Christ also is involved ('O Christ, O God', 12), while the Holy Spirit, often represented as a dove, is echoed as Hopkins sees his self (heart) as a carrier pigeon, instinctively 'homing'. Dramatically, Hopkins enforces the sense of reaching out, of experiencing, even in the act of writing, an action yet (again) incomplete: 'where, where was a, where was a place' (19), the stumbling repetition of the words striving not to explain, but to represent or act out a mystery, the language and meaning 'stretching out' as he reaches for some goal (place) of safety. Hopkins displays the power of his new rhythm in the imitative swoop –

And fled with a fling of the heart to the heart of the Host

(21)

– punning on 'heart' as the seat of love and 'heart' as core or deep centre. The Host is Christ, manifested in the physical Eucharist (the wafer of the mass is the host), with perhaps some echo of the 'heavenly host', the Church Triumphant, with Christ at its heart's core, while the Host is the core of Christian understanding and love. Though Christ in majesty, the universal ruler, the judge of living and dead, inspires dread, the Host is the source of love that speaks to the human heart, offering atonement for sin and salvation.

After the dramatic dash of his heart like the homing pigeon, his heart and the Holy Ghost linked in 'dovewinged', and in a turn characteristic of the Ode, stanza 4 is a new direction and an assessment after the turmoil of flight amidst the ardent flames. Hopkins, claiming that the heart has reached a new height or 'pitch' (*P*, 336, l.24 note), now explores that 'pitch' and his relationship to God. In a contrast between God's eternity and human time, Hopkins takes the hourglass, a common symbol, verbal and visual, of time and man's mortality. Yet typically of Hopkins, he also has a keenly apprehended perception of how an hourglass works, the movement of tiny grains, as seconds are tiny units, yet adding up to a life's span and to the span of all God's creation. In the pitch to which he has been raised by his heart's exultation and God's grace, God now tries him, sifts him, as sand sifts through the hourglass. Hopkins, in a second metaphor, of water in a well, represents his own stillness, out of the hurly-burly, after finding God. The well keeps its level ('pitch') even though water is taken from it – 'poise' suggests this unaltered surface as also Hopkins's own serenity, while pane is the reflective surface of the water. With 'vein' ('a vein | Of the gospel proffer', 31–32), the image opens out from water in the fells to a living flow of blood, so that organically Hopkins is linked in life to God, while blood reminds us that life comes through the sacrificial spilling of Christ's blood. That sacrifice and the salvation it offers is in the gospel, as Christ's gift: we can desire it, but Christ by becoming man offered it as a gift to those who would receive it – not grace which is given by God alone and may be withheld (as in Calvinistic doctrine), but the possibility, the 'proffer', of salvation to all.

With stanza 5, calm continues, but now another expression is found for that roping or linking that goes 'upward' from himself to God, drawing upon Nature, no longer in metaphor, but through its physical reality. The stars, so constantly a wonder to Hopkins, are lovely ('I kiss my hand | To the stars', 33–34), as is the sunset, and thunder, for this beauty of creation is a wonder and delight in all its aspects, and within creation is the presence of God's mystery. Not for Hopkins the hideous duality that would condemn physical nature outright or call it a barrier to union with God. That mystery is 'instressed, stressed' (39), both present and emphasised [**pp. 63; 180–1**], so that Hopkins greets God in greeting nature, in stars, thunder, sunset, and blesses God when he recognises, through nature, God's purpose and mystery – recognises the mystery, even if not understanding it (if he did, it would cease to be a mystery).

This mystery receives a new emphasis (against, the shift of per-spective) in stanzas 6–8. Christ, the Christian, and the nature of the Incarnation are explored, as Hopkins is led to understand God through his creation, that to which we are closest, and where we have some hope of understanding the instress, the inner power that keeps it in being. The created world links in also with the incarnate God, made flesh in Christ, the Son, who came to make the proffer. Stanza 7 is a series of paradoxes of the incarnation, with underlying images still of water or electrical current gathering for a discharge in the spark of revelation ('the discharge of it, there its swelling to be, | ... in high flood yet', 54–55). Christ is placed in history, in the tides of time that individual humans share, and the meaning of his acts then is in 'high flood' – full tide – still ('yet'). It needs to be, for the heart, the same heart as in stanza 3, is 'hard at bay' (56), under 'stress' (pressure resisted, at bay like a hunted animal) since intel-lectual conviction is not enough, to admit its love for God. Here there is a fine dramatic suspension and fulfillment: each stanza, so far, has ended on a completed sentence. Now comes a pause on the heart, driven to a stand at the stanza's end, 'hard at bay', so that the reader, however momentarily, is uncertain of success or failure until the 'leap' across into stanza 8 takes us from hesitation to certainty, for the heart 'Is out with it' (57). The heart is driven to admit, to accept, that it is Christ's suffering, the 'frightful sweat' (53), not his bliss (41), that forces the heart to admit and submit.

What to make, though, of the sloe-image that fills out stanza 8? In itself, it is clear: a sloe, pressed by the tongue, exploring it, until the ripe pulp bursts out of the skin, a slow process, suddenly completed, offers a taste experience which is overwhelming and which may (no judging sloes by ripeness) be either all sweet or all bitter. Yet, partly because of Hopkins's desire for poetic compression, there is some problem in applying the metaphor. The 'sour or sweet' surely link back to the 'best or worst | Word last!' (58–59). The heart finds itself, as with the sloe's taste, eventually filled, with joy or loathing, saying 'yes' ('best') or 'no' ('worst') to Christ and his 'proffer'.

While stanza 9 affirms the glory of God, it also recognises the heart as a rebel, separated by sin from God, that must be driven, if obstinate, to seek salvation. 'Wrecking' and 'storm' recall the 'hurtle of Hell' and anticipate the *Deutschland*'s wreck (already situated in the poem's title) and stanza 10 becomes a prayer for God to work his grace by force or by stealth, as though working at the forge with hammer and anvil or through the great infusing power of Spring. An example of each process is given in St Augustine (Austin) of Hippo (354–430; Attwater 1965), author of the autobiographical *Confessions*, and in St Paul of Tarsus. Any temptation felt (as I have often) to relate the duality of their experiences to the duality of the sloe – sweet *or* sour – should be resisted. Paul's conversion came 'at a crash' when a persecutor of Christians, as he was struck down and heard Christ's voice (Acts 9: 3–6), while Augustine's was long drawn out, with Christ as the master artist and healer with 'a lingering-out sweet skill'. Through such an experience go Hopkins and the nun, too, he perhaps like Augustine, she perhaps like Paul.

And so the first Part concludes with the affirmation of God's power, his mastery and his adorable nature, in both majesty and love, the last word 'King' linking back to the poem's first, 'Thou', while Hopkins himself has moved from 'me' at that opening to 'us all', a link across to Part II, where he is to explore the visionary glory of Part I, founded in his personal internal experience, on an external level with the storm and the nuns.

'THE WRECK': PART THE SECOND

At the opening of Part II, quite apart from the formal division, the shift is proclaimed by the voice of Death. This is King Death, with his scythe (the 'grim reaper'), for as man cometh up as the grass, so also he is cut down. Death comes to battle, with drum and bugle (storm anticipates the *Deutschland* again) and while his masque-like figure may remind us of the medieval Dance of Death, this undoubtedly is the modern world and violent death: by war; fire; wild animals (though 'fang' equally might be the catch of industrial machinery); and railways ('The flange and the rail', 82). Death is certain, but one of its terrors, as Hopkins noted, is not knowing when it may come, 'that *it may be sudden* and find us unprepared' (*S*, 247). We are wonderfully confident in ourselves, 'rooted in earth', yet out of earth springs the flower cut down by the scythe and the ground is ploughed by Death's 'blear' ploughshare.

After this dramatic prologue, the next three stanzas (12–14) move to the factual details of the *Deutschland* – its sailing, its crew and passengers – 'souls' they are called, a common term for human beings, but here it enforces Hopkins's concern for their eternal fate rather than that of their physical bodies. Yet in stanza 12, the activity of the poet's mind means the second half of the stanza follows up fact with questioning, just as stanza 13 opens factually ('Into the snows she sweeps, | Hurling the Haven behind', 97–98), yet the sea becomes Death's agent, 'the widow-making unchilding unfathering deeps', the deliberate omission of commas making the terms all one intensified quality of the sea. Then drawing still on *The Times*'s reports (Street 1992: 75–76, 85–86), the running aground is enacted through stress, taking full advantage of Sprung Rhythm –

> night drew her
> Dead to the Kentish Knock
>
> (107–8)

Where in standard English rhythm, the first syllable is normally (not invariably) unstressed, here it is a single foot, therefore stressed, so that the reader pauses after 'her', only to move on to another stress, another stop, on 'Dead'. 'Dead' is here 'exactly', as 'dead on' = 'spot on', yet draws to itself the power of Death, while nautical undertones, as in 'dead reckoning', are not only appropriate to a ship, but also suggest blindness, since a 'dead' reckoning calculates a ship's position without astronomical observation and the *Deutschland* proved indeed to be lost, both on its course and in its impending doom. The ship's fate is decided, it seems, in being drawn exactly here as though to some plan or design. Yet 'design' should not suggest that the storm is other than a natural phenomenon. It is not miraculous, out of the order of nature, but, the storm seizing on the nuns and the *Deutschland*, God uses the natural order.

The focus shifts again with stanza 15, from detail of the ship's grounding, to the allegorical figure of Hope, a counter to Death. Here Hope is a passive figure against Death's activity. Hope sees no hope; grey-haired, stricken with age and sorrow, she can only mourn, the passage of time being signalled by the starkly concrete 'twelve hours gone', where 'gone' suggests a pregnant woman, so many months gone, an expression here bitterly ironic for the outcome is not birth and new life. The ship's complement, crew and passengers, are caught up in the stanza's second section into hopelessness, yet cling to the shrouds, a precise technical term for the mast's ropes, which Hopkins, constantly alive to variety of meaning, exploits simultaneously as the wrappings of the dead.

As the ship's people are dying, so in stanzas 16–19 the focus is drawn to an individual (if futile) act of bravery and then to the contrasting, enduring figure of the 'tall nun', and so into Hopkins's comparison of himself with the nun and the exploration of her predicament and its resolution. The man who tries to go to the women's assistance is pitched to his death 'at a blow' (124), for all his skill and bravery. A 'dreadnought', he is fearless, like the class of fighting ships that bore that name – but here brave heart and male physical strength are to no avail. Then a woman's voice is heard –

> a lioness arose breasting the babble,
> A prophetess towered in the tumult, a virginal tongue told.
>
> (135–36)

Without denigration to the sailor of stanza 16, now, where a man cannot, a woman may cope, like the great figures of the Old Testament, above all the prophetess Deborah (Judges 4: 4ff), who led the Israelites and proclaimed God's victory in a song of triumph. Now (again, following the contrasting turns of the Ode), Hopkins dramatically responds to his heart, as though living the episode for the first time, that heart which is both 'unteachably after evil', yet also capable of 'uttering truth' (141), a reminder to the reader (Hopkins scarcely needed it) that unlike the Calvinistic belief in the heart's utter corruption, so that individuals are powerless to find their own salvation, the heart can lead us right as it is touched by a pain, 'an exquisite smart' (138), both intense and wonderful. Hopkins looks back, not explicitly, but we should remember, to his heart in Part I, stanzas 2 and 3, when his heart was 'carrier-witted'.

Stanzas 20 to 23 stand together. After identifying the nun, Hopkins muses, then more deeply meditates upon her fate and its significance, again turning to a dualism now deeply seated in oppositions of homeland and exile (Deutschland, the country and the ship), of truth and heresy (Catholic and Protestant). Yet if Germany's political dogma is wide of its good, Germany itself may be good, just as St Gertrude (c.1256–1302; Attwater 1965) and Martin Luther (1483–1546) come from the same town – she the great Catholic patron of Germany, he the heretical destroyer of God's Church – the 'beast of the wastewood', quoting Psalm 80:13 (the 'boar out of the wood', the 'beast of the field'), with allusion also perhaps to the waste wood in which Dante loses his way at the beginning of the *Inferno*. This stanza perhaps most strongly reflects the pre-ecumenical spirit of nineteenth-century England (Hopkins was anyway writing for a Jesuit audience), Hopkins most obviously Victorian in his attitudes, caught in the duality between established Protestantism and his own Catholicism.

The storm is again around the nuns, like a beast ('Surf, snow, river and earth | Gnashed', 164–65). But greater than any storm is God, all-encompassing, called 'Orion of light' (165), not just the name of the constellation and the mythological hunter, but an accepted symbol of God as the hunter of souls, a being 'of light' to bring salvation. God also brings revelation and judgement: his hands, 'unchancelling' (166), open the chancel, the screen that separates enclosed nuns from the lay congregation, to reveal but also to judge them, his hands poising and weighing.

Already Hopkins has identified symbolic value through the allusions to Luther as 'beast of the waste wood' and God as Orion. Now (stanza 22), prompted by the nuns being organized as Franciscans, he meditates on the significance of five – five nuns, five sufferers, five representatives of the five wounds of Christ, which St Francis, the original founder of the Franciscan order, received as the stigmata, the imprinting of Christ's wounds on his own hands and feet and in his side. Five, represented by the nuns, are the sign ('finding') and reflection ('sake') and a way of reading ('cipher') (169–70), and so of understanding the meaning of Christ's wounds and suffering. The mystery here, that demands 'deciphering', is picked up by 'word', our reading or understanding of Christ's sacrifice, which in turn echoes Christ as the Word made Flesh, come as man to suffer, as the nuns' suffering reflects and also shares with the suffering of Christ. St Francis was literally marked with the stigmata (stanza 23) and these 'daughters' of Francis are marked out, not literally, but effectively, as suffering as Francis suffered.

Again, there comes a change (stanza 24) as Hopkins, in safe haven, contrasts himself, 'Away in the loveable west' (185), with the nuns. As the poem moves back and forth, so this stanza, like stanza 1, for example, is divided between self and others, though all are bound up in the same concern of God's love and salvation. Hopkins seizes on the tall nun's cry, reported in *The Times*, 'O Christ, Christ, come quickly' (191) and is forced to consider what it means. Hopkins enfolds the cross (the instrument of suffering) and Christ about a single verb that identifies the two – 'The cross to her she calls Christ to her' (192) and the nun calls ('christens') her 'wild-worst', the storm and imminent death, as her 'Best', just as, the heart at bay, 'We lash with the best or worst' (58). But did she simply hope for rescue (as Christ's disciples did in the storm on the Sea of Galilee)? or did she want (a higher desire) to be a martyr, a sufferer in Christ's cause, and cried out for death to come more quickly, so the agony over ('the combating keen', 200), she could come to the comfort of Christ? Neither of these really makes sense, Hopkins suggests: she did not seek to be saved (as the disciples did), nor did she seek the relief of death, since it is the grind of ordinary existence that 'fathers that asking for ease' (211), while meditation upon the Passion is better done 'in prayer apart' than in the hurly-burly of storm and wreck. In the very midst of this exploration, stanza 26 is a lyrical interlude, at first sight strangely at odds with the storm and struggle, though clearly it might be linked to Hopkins in Wales, on his 'pastoral forehead'. It offers relief, yet also, following from the last line of stanza 25 ('The keener to come at the comfort for feeling the combating keen'), it is an extended metaphor of comparison, from lower to higher, as light gathers and Spring weather prevails, of delight in the comfort experienced by someone saved (by God) after suffering, the physical beauty of the 'moth-soft Milky Way' (206)

providing a hint, however inadequate, of what the sufferer will enjoy
('The treasure never eyesight got', 208).

Seeking to understand the meaning of the tall nun's experience,
Hopkins shifts from the confident dismissals of stanza 27 and
enters an immediately dramatic uncertainty that mimics his groping
to understand. The broken phrases imitate the gradual approach
to revelation. Brokenly, they represent what the poet perceived when
first confronted by the *Deutschland*'s wreck, as though lived through
at this very moment. A perception of what the nun's cry meant, in a
metaphor appropriate to the perils of the sea, looms up to Hopkins,
partly like a ship in the storm, partly like a great rock. Hopkins's
own emerging understanding is paralleled to the nun's perception,
as she is given it (by the poet) in a broken sentence like his own:
'Thing that she … ' (220) – where 'perceived' or 'realised' or 'sighted'
must be supplied by the reader who is drawn into the creative pro-
cess of poem and revelation. The difficulty of the quest for truth is
shown in a wonderfully characteristic list, attempting to define
Christ, to tell what thing he is (221): 'Ipse' (Latin for 'himself',
given in English as 'the only one'); Christ (his divinity); King
(his majesty); Head (the true origin of Christianity). Hopkins, the
nun, the reader are all human and the truth, the human truth, is a
broken truth, coming, as our frail human understanding must, in
fragments.

Echoes from earlier in the poem enter the attempt to define Christ,
as 'lord it with living and dead' (223) harks back to 'Lord of living
and dead' (4), not a simple repetition, though, since 'lord' shifts from
noun (4) to verb (223) as Christ acts ('Do, deal, lord it'), the violence
of action parallelling yet also challenging the storm: 'Let him ride,
her pride, in his triumph' (224), as though the nun were a horse to be
broken. The nun may indeed have had a vision of Christ, looming
up, so that one (but only one) completion of her sentence is 'Thing
that she [sees]' (220), as Hopkins, through nature, sees Christ in this
event, as St Francis saw Christ when he received the stigmata. The
nun does not want Christ to release her from suffering nor even the
glory of martyrdom. Rather, she wants Christ for himself, as she is
filled flush with the heart's love, as the sloe fills flush the sensation of
taste, and comes out with the 'best word'.

Hopkins, after this dramatic struggle, moves back to himself and
his judgement of the nun, 'a heart right' (225), who read the meaning
of God's power and God's love in that shocking night. She is a rock
like Peter (the name in Latin means rock: see Matthew 16:18),
though Hopkins may puzzle us by adding that in the gale ('blast') she
was 'Tarpeïan-fast' (232). The Tarpeian rock in Rome is by the
Capitol, the centre of Rome, and its common association is with

traitors, thrown from it by the Romans. Hopkins seems rather to see, with Milton, that rock as Rome's 'citadel | Impregnable' (*Paradise Regained*, IV, 49–50), rock and city now identified with the Catholic Church and the popes, St Peter's successors.

A quieter section (stanzas 30–31), moving to larger perspective than the nun and storm, muses on the significance of the Feast of the Immaculate Conception, 8 December (the wreck was over the night of 6–7 December). The doctrine of the Immaculate Conception, long debated but only finalised by the Church in 1854, is peculiarly significant for Hopkins, because it was championed by Duns Scotus [p. 24], 'Who fired France for Mary without spot' ('Duns Scotus's Oxford', 14), while the nuns, like Scotus, were Franciscans. Hopkins, in a sermon of 1879 (*S*, 43–46), explored this doctrine, which declares Mary, the mother of Jesus, alone of all human beings since the Fall, to have been born without sin, so that she might receive the Son, both man and God, in her body. Through Mary's purity (and her acceptance of the news that she was to be the mother of God – mirroring the nun's acceptance of Christ), mankind might be saved. The nun's salvation seems assured (so far as can be known), but what of the rest of the ship's complement? Yet even here, in a delicate bird-like reminiscence of the Holy Ghost, traditionally represented as a dove, descending on Mary, there is hope in 'lovely-felicitous Providence | Finger of a tender of, O of a feathery delicacy' (245–46). While a paradox that shipwreck is 'a harvest' (248), Mary is an intercessor with her son to save us.

So still using imagery of storm and the ark (in Biblical interpretation, Noah's ark, at one level, represents the Church, salvation of those aboard), Hopkins affirms God's power and mercy, 'sway of the sea' (3) now echoed in 'master of the tides' (249). God is mightier than Death, the presiding figure of Part II, who proves merely the way to God, 'throned behind | Death' (255–56). If God is power, then again (stanza 34), Christ, born of Mary, is mercy rather than fury, 'A released shower', life-giving rain, rather than 'a lightning of fire hard-hurled' (272).

The final stanza, gathering threads to a conclusion, is a prayer to the nun to intercede for England's return to Catholicism, an insistent reminder, not always to modern taste, of Hopkins's own Catholicism. The prayer is supported by images of sea and harbour, the roads (the safe waters near shore), the heaven-haven, and concludes with an extraordinary long line of fourteen syllables, only fulfilled at its final word – Hopkins stretching verbal and poetic resources to hark back to the poem's opening word ('Thou') in a noun ('Lord') that affirms God's presence and power, the object of our hearts and homes, love and worthy action.

Celebration, exultation – and taint: poems 1876–78

Released from his self-imposed abstention from poetry, released into poetic creation, Hopkins after 'The Wreck' poured out an astonishing series of poems, celebrating nature, exulting at God's grandeur and love, yet also only too well aware of man's fallen state and the associated blear, smear, on the natural world. Apart from occasional pieces and unfinished poems, Hopkins completed nine sonnets (the date of a tenth, 'As Kingfishers Catch Fire', is uncertain; it is discussed later [**p. 97**]), before ordination and departure from St Beuno's.

OCCASIONAL POEMS

As 'The Wreck' was in some sense an 'occasional' poem, prompted by a particular event, though transcending the particular moment, so other poems were prompted by occasions. The silver anniversary of the establishment of the diocese of Shrewsbury (and of its bishop, James Brown) prompted 'The Silver Jubilee' (1876), in four-line stanzas, the last line a refrain, which combines wit with compliment and celebration: if the bishop's hair is now white, it is 'silver' (16) only to celebrate the jubilee. 'Penmaen Pool' also is a public poem, meant for a Visitors' Book (White 1992: 265), and its 'voice' is public, an assertion of the delights of Penmaen against objectors who advance the claims of mountains, water, leisure activities, natural beauty elsewhere: all can be found at Penmaen. It is witty in its refutation of the implied objectors, but also sharply observant of that natural beauty, so that Cader Idris (the Giant's Stool) and at night Charles's Wain (the Plough) are reflected in the Pool, stars which

> For all they shine so, high in heaven,
> Shew brighter shaken in Penmaen Pool.
>
> (19–20)

Even wet weather (and Wales can be wet!) offers pleasure to the acute visitor: what is there to see when raining?

> Why, raindrop-roundels looped together
> That lace the face of Penmaen Pool.
>
> (27–28)

Though a poem for immediate impression, it shows Hopkins alert to language, in the internal rhyme of 'lace' and 'face' that places the lacing over the face of the pool and combines tactile with visual in 'Furred snows, charged tuft above tuft' (31).

SONNETS 1877

Ten other poems completed in Wales in 1877 represent an achieved process of response (to nature, to God), of meditation and of feeling, a poem's creation apparently simultaneous with our reading of it, a performance by Hopkins and ourselves, underlined by spoken and even non-verbal exclamations: 'ah!' 'ah well!' 'O!' 'oh!' These poems, except 'Pied Beauty', are all sonnets, Hopkins's preferred poetical form after 'The Wreck', using the Italian structure adopted into English by Milton [p. 78] and Wordsworth. The fourteen lines of the 'Miltonic' sonnet are divided eight lines (octave) and six (sestet), the structure of both parts emphasised by their rhyme, the sestet showing development or reversal from the octave. Further division is possible (emphasised by Hopkins through line spaces) of the octave into two quatrains and the sestet into two triplets. The metre is much of it regular English scansion, five iambs (unstressed and stressed syllable), the iambic pentameter, though with the possibility (common in English metrical practice) of a reversed foot at opening, stressed syllable followed by unstressed, a foot Hopkins called 'opened'.

SONNETS 1877: OBSERVATION AND GRACE

These sonnets are full of natural observation, precision of observation, and delight in the world. Even when they seem most simply 'nature poems', though, these poems insist on the sacramental power of nature, the granting of grace, first, by recognising in nature the creative power of God and, next, by joy and praise uniting oneself closer with God. Even 'Spring', apparently a celebration of the season, where weeds, generally condemned as useless, rooted out by gardeners and farmers, 'in wheels, shoot long and lovely and lush' (2), yet moves from the octave's unalloyed delight in 'juice and joy' to ask in the sestet what is all this and finds it 'A strain of the earth's sweet being in the beginning' (10), a moment when the innocence of first creation, before the Fall, may momentarily be captured. Here Hopkins offers the Ignatian particularity of detail, moving constantly into action and meaning. The thrush's song 'does so rinse and wring | The ear, it strikes like lightnings' (4–5). This cleansing (set against clouding and souring in the sestet) of 'rinse' and 'wring' (with the aural play between 'wring' – wet clothes; sharp physical action – and 'ring' – the bird's song amidst 'the echoing timber') takes us back to an innocent world. Yet Hopkins, rather than indulging passive delight, urges action – 'Have, get before it cloy' – and urges it, startlingly, not upon the responsive observer, who is moved by Spring, but rather upon Christ, urgently, almost it might be thought impudently. Though what is at stake here, salvation itself, does not bother about impudence, as Christ is urged to seize (parallel to the freshness of spring) the innocence of childhood.

Nature in Hopkins's poetry combines scientifically accurate observation and investigation with a religious sense of God's grandeur revealed, if sometimes only in glimpses, within and behind it. 'Hurrahing in Harvest' is a world of transient activity, time passing ('Summer ends now'), the corn stooks 'barbarous in beauty', 'barbarous' a word that is roughly insistent, while drawing in another sense, allied to 'barbarian': the heads are *bearded* with the grain, the heavy harvest itself beautiful. The perspective shifts, as gazing upward at the clouds, he progresses 'down' the heavenly furrow as a gleaner in the field would progress, eyes down, to search for heads of grain left by the reaper. So Hopkins picks up something out of God's bounteous harvest. The earthly harvest and God's power, strong and sweet, 'stallion stalwart, very-violet-sweet' (10), need the human participant to link them: when harvest and beholder once meet

> The heart rears wings bold and bolder
> And hurls for him, O half hurls earth for him off under his
> feet.
>
> (13–14)

Such dramatic shifting of perspective through the dynamics of the beholder's relationship to nature is crucial to 'The Starlight Night'. The disorientating experience of looking up at the night sky, if less common now in overlit urban areas, can still be achieved and for Hopkins was common, delightful, even disturbing, but also a way to God: 'I leant back to look' at the stars and 'my heart ... praised our Lord' (*J*, 254). As Hopkins urges us to look upwards – 'Look at the stars! look, look up at the skies' (1) – up becomes beyond, no longer on firm earth, the night sky becomes a new world of 'diamond delves' ('mines', from 'delf'), in a series of transparencies that recede further and further, up and up, through star folk, buildings, mines, eyes of elves, lawns grey with dew that sparkles in the sun (compare 'the skies were then clear and ashy and fresh with stars' (*J*, 201; quoted McChesney 1968: 57)). The octave ends as Hopkins exclaims over the sight 'Ah well! it is all a purchase, all is a prize.' The reader, after the exhilarating journey through a fresh world of experience, may well pause (as the closing of the octave demands) and wonder about 'purchase' and 'prize'. To seize on the beauty of the stars might be a prize, a possession, but where does purchase come in? Rather, the starry night is a prize, to be won, if we only will, by purchase. The sestet opens with the mundane voice of the auctioneer: 'Buy then! bid then!' And 'Bid what?' asks the reader of the auctioneer, slightly baffled, 'What should I bid?' Not money – rather, 'Prayer, patience, alms, vows' (9), the devotional and active elements of the Christian life. And as if the 'bid' has worked, the stars are again before us, like a 'May-mess' (a Hopkins coinage, a great mess or mass of spring blossom), and in a shift of perspective, the night becomes the dark walls of a barn, pierced with holes, through which the glory of heaven gleams as stars, the dark shutting out from human eyes the gathered harvest of the souls in heaven:

> This piece-bright paling shuts the spouse
> Christ home, Christ and his mother and all his hallows.
>
> (13–14)

Hopkins's deliberate displacing of 'home' from 'shuts' allows Christ himself to be the home we (should) seek: bid for the stars and we may also be part of the harvest gathered in the barn.

Yet if the beauty of the world lies in its variety, its piedness, 'All things counter, original, spare, strange' ('Pied Beauty', 9), it is all fathered forth by God, 'whose beauty is past change' (10). Creation, compared to God, is imperfect, though that imperfection may be a delight, and the natural world would be vacant without its beholder, man, who, exultant, may celebrate, yet tainted by sin may degrade the world. In 'The Sea and the Skylark', the first quatrain describes the sea, active in tide, and (the space between quatrains virtually replicating the urban gap between sea and open country) the second the lark, ascending to 'pour | And pelt music, till none's to spill nor spend' (7–8). These primal sounds, to his right hand and his left, Hopkins hears while in Rhyl, 'this shallow and frail town' (9), words which are firstly a physical description, hemmed in as Rhyl is by sea and railway, liable to storm and flood, then a moral rebuke set against sea and skylark, which shame the town. Sea and lark are bells that ring out (as bells ring out the old year) 'our sordid turbid time' (10), reminders of what man, supposedly 'life's pride and cared-for crown' (11), has lost. Rather than progressing on the evolutionary scale, as Tennyson would have mankind do (*In Memoriam*, lyric cxviii, ll.27–28), man seems to be moving down the evolutionary scale, draining fast 'towards man's first slime' (14). While Hopkins is in no way pessimistic or despairing in these sonnets, as he may seem later in the

'Terrible' Sonnets [pp. 107–14], he is aware, as man and priest, of humanity's fallen state and of its capacity to degrade the environment and its own nature.

'God's Grandeur' explores this terrible paradox, the spoliation of divine creation by God's highest created form, the octave representing the paradox of grandeur and degradation. The world, like some great electrical battery (the image scientifically derived), is 'charged with the grandeur of God' (1) – not passive, but ready to discharge for the viewer's benefit, to flame out, 'like shining from shook foil' (2). Yet man ignores this 'greatness' in the relentlessly repetitive treading down, so apparent in industrialised Britain, blearing, smearing, with toil: 'the soil | Is bare now, nor can foot feel, being shod' (7–8). The counterswing of the sestet, though, opens into renewal and hope in the eternal creation of the Holy Ghost. Nature is never spent: the image of nightfall reasserts the continual renewal in dawn, the perpetual springing of 'the dearest freshness' that lies 'deep down things' (10):

> And though the last lights off the black West went
> Oh, morning, at the brown brink eastwards, springs ...
>
> (11–12)

Hopkins, in the sestet, rescuing us from our own destructiveness, is not oblivious to man's self-degradation nor to the processes of industry, yet his faith, sustained by the perpetual greatness of nature, presents still an image of the Holy Spirit that is warm and bright, that broods over the world, to care for it, even while thinking and foreseeing.

Structurally, 'The Sea and the Skylark' contrasts octave and sestet, 'God's Grandeur' offers contrast within the octave and resolves it in the sestet. 'The Caged Skylark' pursues a parallel of subject matter through its course. The skylark (caged wild birds were common in the nineteenth century) and man's spirit are both prisoners: the 'dare-gale' bird 'scanted in a dull cage' (1); the spirit cramped in the body, a bone-house whose ribs enforce the cage image. The skylark needs rest, but it also needs liberty, 'his own nest, wild nest, no prison' (11). The spirit demands freedom – but in a parallel that seems to break down, moving as it does from natural to doctrinal, Hopkins invokes the final resurrection of body and soul, reconciled, when the body will no more vex the spirit than a rainbow 'footing' on meadow-down. 'The Lantern Out of Doors', rather than using the octave/sestet structure, shows something of the Ignatian method of meditation, starting from an observation of our material experience. The opening incident is generalised by 'Sometimes': this is a common sight, but Hopkins is involved, as we all are, with the common matter of life, just as in the sestet he picks up the 'homely' proverb, 'out of sight, out of mind', its meaning virtually worn out, only to turn it against itself into new vitality, for Christ 'minds', and no one indeed is ever out of sight of Christ. Yet the lantern that 'moves along the night' (1) is made particular by being one that 'interests our eyes' (2), unlike others that are merely casual. Object (lantern) leads to meditation: we need no direct link to spring to the obvious question, 'And who goes there?' (2) Where from and whither bound? The dark becomes a sea, for a voyager with 'his wading light'. The night travel of the first quatrain is paralleled in the second with life's journey – from literal journey to metaphorical. These men give off light as they pass and in the sestet Hopkins, in his humanity, declares his own limitation – however hard he tries, he cannot imagine what their end will be. The final triplet is a turn against his own limitations and a proper Ignatian ending, by bringing us to God, for 'Christ minds' and is our 'first, fast, last friend' (14).

SONNETS 1877: 'THE WINDHOVER' (1877)

The most daringly experimental of those sonnets that immediately followed 'The Wreck' is 'The Windhover', which Hopkins two years later called 'the best thing I ever wrote' (L, 1.85). A windhover is a kestrel, a small hawk (Sterry 2004: 88–89; photograph in Milward & Schoder 1975: opposite 48). Two things may immediately strike us: first, outspread physically on the page, the long flowing swoop of the lines represents the assured flight of the bird, the assured control of Hopkins 'capturing' the bird; second, its subtitle, 'to Christ our Lord', despite no direct reference to God within the poem. The subtitle, added in the corrected copy, has been a matter of critical dispute: is the poem about the bird and its mastery of the air, a poem dedicated to Christ as an offering by Hopkins; or is Christ the unstated parallel to the windhover and the poem an extended metaphor for his nature and power? Both interpretations are possible, yet given the constant religious attention of the other poems of this period, the second is here preferred, enforced as it is by a poetic language of chivalry, romance terms such as 'minion' (from the French, 'mignon', darling); 'chevalier'; above all 'dauphin', a prince, son of a French king and so forging a link to Christ, God the Son.

The poem also demonstrates Hopkins's delight in compounding, setting words together so that their different meanings interact, with a progressional sense of understanding and possibility. The windhover, the 'dapple-dawn-drawn' Falcon (2), is drawn to the sky by dawn, but the falcon's markings are 'dapple-dawn' and so dawn is both situational, the time when the falcon rises, and descriptive, the bird itself dappled like the dawn. Again, the same word repeated, shifts its meaning and our understanding – 'I caught this morning morning's minion' (1): Hopkins is specific about time ('this morning') and then makes the falcon conceptually the darling of the morning. The octave creates the bird's mastery of the air – he rides it, in control, hence the use later of 'chevalier', suggesting chivalric codes and sure control of horses, and from hovering aloft on the air currents revels in the downward sweep, using his wings for control as the rider the horse's reins, then (changing the activity) for the delighted movement of a skate on ice.

Hopkins comes in again as observer and again as in 'The Wreck', his heart 'in hiding' reacts impulsively, suddenly stirred at 'the achieve of, the mastery of the thing!' (8) Does 'thing' refer to the action, the mastery of movement (the whole 'thing' is wonderful) or does it refer to the bird, a natural object? While the first meaning may be primary in line 8, the opening of the sestet ('Brute beauty and valour and act') may insist that the bird *is* only a thing, a brute of creation, not a man: something below Hopkins and yet through it God shows his power. As in 'The Sea and the Skylark' or 'God's Grandeur', man has to learn from the natural world and in those poems the link is explicitly back to God. The windhover displays innate quality ('beauty'); innate power ('valour'); innate capacity ('act'), repeated in 'air, pride, plume' (9). The immediacy of Hopkins's perception is stressed by the exclamation 'oh', as these qualities 'here | Buckle'. They come together in an epiphany, a revelation, for the heart, as a buckle clicks into place and holds and completes (not, though, as it has been suggested, any sense of 'buckle' as crumpled [**pp. 138; 191**]: the bird has achieved, not failed in, this wonder). The image is both familiar to any belt user, yet also extends out into the chivalric language (of armour and sword belt), especially as at this instant

> the fire that breaks from thee then, a billion
> Times told lovelier, more dangerous, O my chevalier!
>
> (10–11)

Nature is not only lovely – its power may also threaten: the windhover is a bird of prey and the armoured knight is a killer, yet the fire is thrilling as God is both beautiful and terrifying, the God of 'The Wreck' who gave Hopkins life, fastened him flesh 'And after it almost unmade, what with dread, | Thy doing' (6–7). The final triplet seems to turn from the bird, yet reinforces the 'billion | Times told lovelier', since if ordinary things can shine and show gold-vermilion (the plough-share shining as it is driven by 'sheer plod' through the plough-land ('sillion'); the 'blue-bleak embers', 13–14), how much more the bird in assured flight and Christ in majesty. Revelation lies in the mundane, the routine of work and fireside, while beyond that lies the yet greater revelation of windhover and (by metaphoric implication and dedication) of Christ our Lord.

Sermons and Devotional Writings: 1879–89

SERMONS 1879–81

Hopkins was trained in speaking and practised preaching before being ordained. As a parish priest, for just over three years, July 1878 to September 1881, he would have given sermons regularly. Of these, twenty-six survive. The surviving sermons would not always be easy to follow, one would think, as spoken discourse, often detailed and subtly exploratory as they are, however amplified or explained in the pulpit. As talks or lectures in church, the sermons, as might be expected, variously explain doctrine (the Immaculate Conception: S, 43–46), commemorate the feasts of the Church (the Precious Blood: S, 13–15), explore gospel narratives and parables, and (commonly) apply these meanings to the lives of the congregation.

Hopkins's techniques show some individuality, though he was never a dramatic or self-centred preacher. He was aware of the need for familiar language and images. Considering the responses of those who heard Christ declare the second great commandment to be 'Love thy neighbour as thyself' (S, 87), Hopkins notes how the answer 'acted on them in opposite ways. For as the sun, we know, melts wax and bakes clay and as one man's meat is another man's poison, so Christ's answer' (S, 87). Elsewhere, the individual's potential for evil is compared to a watch wound up but kept from going (S, 44), while at Bedford Leigh, the miners would recognise themselves:

> those that work in the pit go where all is darker than night and work by candlelight and when they see the light of day again their work is over, as if day were night to them and night day, so then this life is dark, a pit, but we work in it …
>
> (S, 39)

The occasionally personal touches are subdued, though the use of 'sweetheart' provoked trouble at Liverpool (S, 89). Hopkins mentions cricket (S, 70) and, perhaps more characteristically yet also obscurely for his auditors, is proud that Duns Scotus (unnamed), 'the greatest of the divines and doctors of the Church' who supported the Immaculate Conception, 'came from England' (S, 45), a reminder of that English patriotism which occasionally surprises us.

In preaching, Hopkins endeavoured to set before the mind's eye of his congregation events in concrete form, to keep attention and to realise more fully his meaning. The technique was not always as effective as it might have been, since it could lead to over elaboration (as the retreat supper had found [p. 32]). The parable of the wedding feast and the guests is unduly detailed (S, 76–77), with the table and the like. If this is Ignatian concretisation, it here clouds rather than reveals the nature of the parable. Such a technique is clearly evident and more successful when, considering the raising of Jairus's daughter, Hopkins makes concrete Christ's going to the girl and the impediment of the healthy crowd to Jairus's daughter's safety:

> *a great crowd followed and thronged him.* Take notice of this.
> If there ever was a time when a man could have wished the
> road clear and no bar or hindrance in the way it was then. ...
> Fancy, my brethren, fancy that father: the crowd was
> between Christ and his daughter's life.
>
> (S, 31).

There are also hints, though no more than hints, of Hopkins's poetic language, in characteristic forms of vocabulary and syntax, the priest and the poet momentarily coming together, however different sermons and poems. On the Virgin as mediator, he uses 'heart' and 'tongue' (without definite article) to stand for activities of the whole person, and 'tell', derived from the loud peal of a bell, the tongue as clapper, has a poetic resonance: 'But when all is said heart cannot think her greatness, tongue cannot tell her praise' (S, 30). Hopkins's constant fascination with the natural world of beauty appears, above all, in Christ's beauty, for 'he is the hero' (S, 34). Beauty and strength go together, and although in Christ's passion 'this beauty [was] wrecked, this majesty beaten down. ... I look forward with eager desire to seeing the matchless beauty of Christ's body in the heavenly light' (S, 36).

Hopkins the priest, though, did not try to be Hopkins the poet when he was in the pulpit and the sermons present the public man, who spoke to a congregation, most confident in comparatively small churches, like Bedford Leigh, rather than the theatrical barn of St Francis Xavier's, Liverpool.

DEVOTIONAL WRITINGS 1880–89

The Devotional Writings are private notes Hopkins wrote for himself while on retreats, as commentary on the *Spiritual Exercises* [p. 22] or as preparation for confession. They are personal in a way that the sermons were not, himself in relationship to God. The arguments are more intricate, and the tone often darker than the sermons, since he is exploring his own failures and inadequacies before the love of God, love both given and demanded of him. As an individual, Hopkins recognises his distinct personality. Yet this individuality carries responsibility and at times a sense of shame. This 'taste of myself' is made up of 'my shame, my guilt, my fate ... [,] that selftaste which nothing in the world can match' (S, 125).

These retreat meditations, explorations of himself (that could lead to fits of horror [p. 19]), are largely commentaries on the *Exercises*, which at heart offer material, spaced over four weeks, for contemplation and exploration, intended to heighten self-awareness, yet also to urge us 'to rejoice in the great gladness of Christ Our Lord' (Loyola 1996: 328). Hopkins, like any individual, has many facets, and the darkness expressed, faced with his own sinfulness and God's grandeur, must be seen as an aspect of his contemplation, not his final state, just as he sees, besides the actual world, 'an infinity of possible worlds', like 'cleaves' or exposed faces of the pomegranate (S, 151). The poet is here as well as the priest in both meditation and language, convinced that words both literally and figuratively are part of our experience, since this world 'then is word, expression, news of God. Therefore its end ... is God and its life or work to name and praise him' (S, 129).

The very language he uses in his poetry, Hopkins here turns to naturally, since it is part of his normal language. As, in 'God's Grandeur' [p. 83], the 'world is charged with the grandeur of God', so in meditating upon the *Exercises* he declares: 'All things therefore are charged with love, are charged with God and if we know how to touch them give off sparks and take fire, yield drops and flow, ring and tell of him' (S, 195). Even at their darkest, the Devotional Writings show this belief in the continuing presence and power of God, just as the 'Terrible' Sonnets [pp. 107–14], while they may suggest despair, are indeed cries from the heart, yet affirm God's presence, however hidden, and above all the person of Christ.

Hopkins in his sermons and Devotional Writings, as in his poems and letters, insists upon the heroism of Christ, who comes as man and God, not simply because man has fallen and must be redeemed (see Devlin, S, 109). It is Christ that Hopkins constantly celebrates, God Incarnate, both human and divine, preferring the name 'Christ' to 'Jesus', the triumphant hero to the effete 'Gentle Jesus, meek and mild' favoured by Victorian piety. Christ suffered as a man, his beauty, reflective of his heroism, all marred, but even while suffering he was still that paradoxical God who offers his death for mankind's salvation and is yet the Pantocrator, ruler of the world.

Major production 1878-86: God, Nature and Mankind

Between leaving St Beuno's in 1877 and his appointment in Dublin in 1884, Hopkins wrote some twenty complete major poems, while another fifteen or so unfinished or minor poems survive. If often pressed for time, hence the incompleteness of some poems and fragments, it is still a respectable output, given the demands of parish, teaching, and spiritual duties, while this output also reminds us that to read only the accomplished poetry is to lose a sense of Hopkins's range and concerns. If he delights in nature and praises God through its exuberance and beauty, he also faces up variously to social disorder and his own necessary death. In the unfinished 'The Times are Nightfall' (undated; perhaps 1885–86), the darkening of society with the spread of industrialisation offers a bleak external world of winter and waste. This both picks up earlier gloomy apprehensions of the world where the blight of man's fall is only too evident in the industrialised world (at a political level, a feeling shared with Ruskin) and looks forward to the intensely dark inner landscapes of the 'Terrible' Sonnets. Again, an undated poem, 'To His Watch', is both exemplary as a Jesuit poem, following the *Spiritual Exercises* in making concrete the subject of meditation (death) in the time-pulse of both his watch and his heart, questioning which will die first, yet also looks to dissolution in death rather than the glory of nature or the hope of the resurrection.

'THE LOSS OF THE *EURYDICE*' (1878)

Hopkins's first major poem after leaving St Beuno's, 'The Loss of the *Eurydice*', offers an obvious connection in its subject matter with 'The Wreck', that first great poetic production, while the treatment shows quite other concerns. The *Eurydice* was a navy training vessel, returning from the West Indies with over three hundred and sixty on board, mostly trainee seamen. If the *Deutschland* struck and was broken over an extended period, the *Eurydice*, caught by a sudden squall, near the English coast, went down suddenly ('foundered') (White 1992: 296 & 495, n.12). Hopkins was more concerned here than in 'The Wreck' to 'tell the story' and employed a seemingly much simpler, four-line stanza, though he noted (*P*, 355) that the scanning runs on 'so that each stanza is rather one long line rhymed'. This stanza, in its (apparent) simplicity, might recall another startling loss, that of the *Royal George*, which foundered in fair weather and was commemorated by the eighteenth-century poet, William Cowper.

Hopkins though is particularly concerned with the crew, so many of them young 'boldboys soon to be men' (14), whose lives were suddenly ended. His phrase, 'hearts of oak', may invoke the very wooden ships, as in the eighteenth-century patriotic song ('Hearts of oak are our ships, gallant tars are our men'), but he means the men themselves, sailors who were the *Eurydice*'s freight – 'Lads and men her lade and treasure' (12). The treachery of sea and weather was the worse because of their very familiarity with England and the coast they were approaching, so the bells of the sheep on the Downs prove to be their funeral bells as the north wind, 'black Boreas', blows not out in the Atlantic nor in the notorious Bay of Biscay, but from England, the land that bred them. Hopkins was particularly drawn to the disaster not only by the scale and horror of suddenness (those who saw the ship disappear in the squall didn't realise she had gone down), but also by the freshness and the potential of the majority of the crew. He describes one dead cadet, washed ashore:

> He was all of lovely manly mould,
>   Every inch a tar,
> Of the best we boast our sailors are.
>   (74–76)

There is the immediate homoerotic charge of the youth's beauty, yet this leads on to other thoughts, of Englishness ('our sailors'), of potential, and of God's responsibility – the poem opens 'it concerned thee, O Lord'. The dead were on the threshold of their lives, in them the potential of 'leagues, leagues of seamanship' (82), something like the wound-up watch with its potential for running (*S*, 44), whether for evil or good, 'leagues' that

>   Slumber in these forsaken
> Bones, this sinew, and will not waken.
>   (83–84)

Hopkins then intertwines two of his concerns, his nation and its salvation, the need for England, by analogy, because not Catholic, to be kept from 'foundering'. The loss of these youths –

>   Those daredeaths, ay this crew, in
> Unchrist, all rolled in ruin –
>   (95–96)

– makes him, a Catholic priest, ask why God allowed them to perish, not only young, their potential lost, but also potentially without salvation. The link is then through the prayers of the women (mothers, wives) left behind, by extension becoming all women, and so linked to Mary as mediator with Christ, invoked particularly through her English shrine at Walsingham. The damned cannot escape hell, but since the fate of these souls is unknown to us until the Day of Judgement, those dead who are not yet in heaven can receive heavenly pity through prayer – ours and the Holy Mother's. Such priestly concerns were, necessarily, to be Hopkins's for the rest of his life.

OXFORD 1878–79: MEMORY AND EXPERIENCE

Hopkins had delighted in Oxford when first an undergraduate there: in a sense of adult freedom; in the ancient buildings, their Gothic style admired by Ruskin as truly reflecting the individual (and idealised) craftsman of the Middle Ages; and in the easy access to open space and countryside. In an abandoned fragment, 'What Being in Rank-Old Nature', Oxford's integration of natural and man-made finds expression in the elemental power of an ocean-wave that echoes in physical shape the reverberating power of a sound-wave, the impulse of the sea, imagined in motion, breaking, observed simultaneously from above and underneath:

> crumbling, fore-foundering, thundering all-surfy seas
> in; seen
> Underneath, their glassy barrel ...

(5–6)

Yet Hopkins had noted at Spinkhill and nearby Sheffield, the 'hollowness of this century's civilisation' (*L*, 2.97; [p. 31]), the encroaching darkness of the industrial age, the poisoning not only of nature but of our own environment, just as Ruskin recorded in 1859 in Rochdale, observing a ruined house, 'the garden, blighted utterly into a field of ashes, not even a weed taking root there', while a stream soaked by, 'black as ebony and thick with curdling scum' (Ruskin 1905: 120–21).

Without making Hopkins, or even Ruskin, into an eco-warrior, both valued natural beauty and an integrated society that recognised its responsibility towards (and indeed its gain from) a world of beauty, light, and justice. Hopkins had already reacted (some might say overreacted) to the felling of an ashtree in 1873 [p. 23] and the cutting down of poplar trees at Binsey, near Oxford, prompted 'Binsey Poplars' (1879), a lament for the loss of his 'aspens dear'. The poplars, providers of shade from the sun, are invoked in a composition of place, the sun an active force, 'leaping', that needed to be quelled by the straps of the branches, branches that are now themselves quelled,

> Not spared, not one
> That dandled a sandalled
> Shadow that swam or sank
> On meadow and river and wind-wandering weed-winding bank.
>
> (5–8)

Once gone, the beauty is gone for ever after 'only ten or twelve' axe strokes.

Such loss threatens Oxford itself in 'Duns Scotus's Oxford' (1879), though here Hopkins takes up another of his concerns, and celebrates the philosopher whom he so much admired, even at the expense of the goodwill of his fellow Jesuits [p. 26]. The octave's two quatrains contrast a harmonious Oxford with a darkening city. An expansive line embodying various experiences of delight, of noise that is musical, of nature, enfolding the man-made bells –

> Cuckoo-echoing, bell-swarmèd, lark-charmèd, rook-racked,
>   river-rounded
>
> (2)

– is set against a modern urban sprawl, 'a base and brickish skirt' of new and ugly housing and workshops, the sour Oxford (5–8) with which Hopkins's work as parish priest now makes him acquainted. From this modern Oxford, the sestet turns to Duns Scotus, the Franciscan teacher, who lived on the very air that Hopkins breathes, and to Hopkins's tribute to him, 'who of all men most sways my spirits to peace' (11). If the eye distresses, the mind has power to override it. Yet the Oxford Hopkins returned to was very different from that he remembered as a student; the University had changed little, but as priest he was drawn into town, not gown, while experience brought a sharp sense of civilisation's 'hollowness' and new faith and new ideas a devotion to the Virgin Mary, perhaps one of the most alienating marks of Catholicism for Protestants.

MARIAN DEVOTION

The Virgin Mary as the Immaculate Conception [p. 78] and the mother of God, already a vital presence in 'The Wreck' and 'The Loss of the *Eurydice*', is a devotion strong in Hopkins that many of his contemporaries would see as peculiarly 'unEnglish', identified with the popular superstition that Catholics practised 'Mariolatry', the worship of Mary, and so threatening a proper recognition of God's supremacy. The Catholic doctrine of Mary as mediator, which stresses her humanity, her love of mankind, and the power that as mother she has over Christ, is strikingly represented visually in Michelangelo's *Last Judgement* in the Vatican's Sistine Chapel, where Christ in majesty judges and Mary by his side is a pleader, not for the wicked but for us, frail and fallible humanity, devoted to her and through her to God. This devotion is seen in Hopkins in two poems that mark the beginning and the end of this period between ordination and the move to Dublin as Professor.

'THE MAY MAGNIFICAT' (1878) – 'THE BLESSED VIRGIN COMPARED TO THE AIR WE BREATHE' (1883)

'The May Magnificat', written during a return in Spring 1878 to Stonyhurst, was designed for a statue of the Virgin. Its title recalled the exultant words of Mary when, already pregnant, she visited her cousin Elizabeth. In the Magnificat (Luke 1: 46–55), named from its opening words, 'My soul doth magnify the Lord', Mary rejoices in the power of God. Hopkins muses on why May should be the month dedicated to Mary: her other feasts 'follow reason' – that is, Lady Day (25 March) is the feast of the Annunciation by the angel Gabriel that she will bear the Son of God (nine months later, at the Nativity – Christmas Day), while Candlemas (2 February), the Feast of the Purification, comes as required by the Law of the Old Testament forty days after Christ's birth. Is May then dedicated to Mary simply because things then are brighter than in any other month? Rather, Mary herself replies that it is a time of growth in everything, so that nature shares with Mary

> that world of good,
> Nature's motherhood.
>
> (27–28)

There is a delighted comedy, a universal laughter in nature's burgeoning and Mary's mirth in her own fecundity, which led to salvation, both hers and the world's. As Mary was joyful as she uttered the Magnificat, so also the fertility of creation, the natural world and the child in the womb, gives delight and salvation is linked to laughter – not always a quality identified with Hopkins or religion, but essential both to him and for him.

Once again at Stonyhurst in May 1883, Hopkins was asked to contribute to poems for Mary's statue. 'The Blessed Virgin Compared to the Air We Breathe' wittily traces an extended comparison between our envelopment in the air, essential to breath and life, and the all-enveloping love of Mary. Hopkins is not content simply with the air as breath, with Mary as the air which 'Let all God's glory through' (30), but explores the nature of the earth's atmosphere more scientifically and still finds, ingeniously, analogies with Mary's nature and power. She is the giver and the gift, wrapping us around (the blue of heaven understood as Mary's blue mantle), and while the air lets through the sunbeam directly, yet if there were no blue, the sun (understanding in the analogy, God) would be a 'blear and blinding ball' (97). The God of the Old Testament was the 'blinding ball', but with the Incarnation, God becoming human through the earthly mother, God is mediated through his mother, who at the poem's end is identified with the air we breathe, enfolding us as her body once protectingly enfolded God in her womb and as his mother:

> World-mothering air, air wild,
> Wound with thee, in thee isled,
> Fold home, fast fold thy child.
>
> (124–26)

GOD'S CREATION 1879–82

These Marian poems were occasional, to celebrate May as Mary's month. Other poems of this period – 'The Candle Indoors', 'Peace', 'Andromeda', 'As Kingfishers Catch Fire', 'Inversnaid', 'Ribblesdale' – indicate Hopkins's range and warn against too easily compartmentalising his output, since they both delight in God's creation and also sound darker notes, an awareness of mankind's and his own weaknesses. 'The Candle Indoors' (1879), a companion to 'The Lantern Out of Doors' [pp. 83–4], again draws on the Ignatian technique of composition of place to prompt meditation, though the initial situation, concrete as it is, seems also as casual as any observation from life. The candle burning in a window as he passes is no particular candle or window – it is 'some' candle, 'somewhere I come by' (1), striking for the way its light becomes liquid: 'puts blissful back | With yellowy moisture mild night's blear-all black', 2–3). The octave continues with speculation upon what he can't know: who is there at the window, man or woman ('Jessy or Jack'), doing what task. The very lack of an answer makes him the more eager ('the eagerer a-wanting') that someone is there to glorify God. But the sestet moves to himself and a kind of rebuke – he takes himself to task (there may be a hidden pun with the imagined 'task' which the unknown 'fingers ply'): before requiring others to glorify God by

their work, itself a way of praise (*S*, 240), he should do it himself.
And the beam of light becomes a rebuke, drawing on that of
Christ's – 'And why beholdest thou the mote that is in thy brother's
eye, but considerest not the beam that is in thine own eye?' (Mat-
thew 7: 3). Christ's beam is of course a block of wood, not a ray of
light, but the two words, rather than jostling, illuminate each other.
Hopkins was well aware of the semantic shift from the Bible's
beam to the candle's, yet things are transmuted in this poem, as the
candle's light had become moisture. So the candle passes over to a
rebuke uniting both light and heat, for such idle speculation:

> Come you indoors, come home; your fading fire
> Mend first and vital candle in close heart's vault ...
>
> (9–10)

The poem ends not with definite closure but a question, and becomes
a challenge, because while 'you' ('Are you that liar') is obviously the
traveller of the poem's opening, addressing himself, the shift to
second person allows the reader to be interrogated as well as the
poet's self. This reflects a meditative technique directed dramatically
to the reader as well as to the poet-priest and points forward
to likenesses as well as differences in the 'Terrible' Sonnets of
1885–86.

'ANDROMEDA' (1879)

Hopkins had already used allegory in the figures of Death and of
Hope in 'The Wreck' and drawn on Orion the mythical hunter as a
figure of God [p. 75]. Now, urged on by his increasing awareness,
after duties in Spinkhill and London and Oxford, of social issues, he
turned to contemplate the situation of the Church in the modern
world and in eternity. In classical mythology, Andromeda was a
princess whose father's kingdom was threatened by a sea monster,
placated only by the regular offering of a young woman. Chained to
a rock in the sea, Andromeda, left as sacrifice, was rescued by the
hero Perseus, who came on winged sandals, armed not only with
sword but also the snake-haired head of the Gorgon Medusa, whose
gaze, even after death, turned everything to stone. Rescued, Andro-
meda became Perseus's bride. The myth was popular for its romantic
rescue drama and while the application of a pagan myth to Chris-
tianity might seem strange, the Catholic tradition of reading the
Old Testament simultaneously as history and as foreshadowings of
Christ's coming (as Noah's ark is also the Church, in which salva-
tion is found; the brazen serpent raised by Moses, Christ on the

cross, against the venom of the Devil), allows also the extension of symbolic reading to secular texts.

That something more than simply the myth is meant here is made clear by the opening words: 'Now Time's Andromeda' – the poem is of its moment in 1879 and this Andromeda is the daughter of Time – is the Church as it exists temporally, the Church on earth. She is on 'this rock rude', both because Andromeda was chained, 'doomed dragon food' (4), yet also the Church was founded on St Peter, Christ punning on his name ('Thou art Peter and upon this rock I will build my church'), though 'rude' (in the sense of exposed, rough, primitive) suggests also the hurly-burly of the modern world. The Church is particularly threatened *now*: more than the 'many blows and banes' (6) of the past, she hears 'roar | A wilder beast from the West' (6–7). Here particularly commentators point rather wildly to the nature of this beast. Certainly, both the Church itself and external observers believed the nineteenth century was an age of indifference, of liberalism, of philosophical and scientific challenge – culminating, as explored wonderfully well by Owen Chadwick (1990), in secularisation. Perseus is Christ, coming, yet when? To the waiting victim, he seems to delay, Andromeda's patience, as though itself savaged by the dragon, 'morselled into pangs' (12), torn into small pieces, each of which is itself a shock of pain. Perseus treads air, supported by his winged sandals, and hangs – not 'in the air' as we might expect, but – with that imaginative surprise of poetry, 'His thoughts on her' (11), moving from physical to imaginative, as Christ, however apparently absent, never deserts his Church, his spiritual bride.

GREEN HOPKINS?

In 'Binsey Poplars' Hopkins lamented the destructive encroachment upon nature and he is often heralded as an ecologist before his time, though this is to misunderstand both his concern for nature and the increasing movement, prompted by Ruskin, against the fouling of the environment by industrial process and developments that produced the great nineteenth-century conurbations. Hopkins's concern was for the nature he loved and the encroachment upon God's creation by man, God's own favoured creation, who only too often seemed intent to give free rein to 'A wilder beast' ('Andromeda', 7). In three poems of this period (1881–82), Hopkins variously interacts with man's place in the natural world and with man's relationship to his and nature's creator.

'Inversnaid' (1881) is a virtuoso representation of a Scottish scene – the opening gives the rush of the stream, 'His rollrock highroad roaring down' (2), figured as human, a living entity in the 'groins of the brae' (10), 'groins' both a technical geological term and a reminder that Hopkins's study of the natural world goes beyond a general romantic glow. The stream, wild and untamed nature, is the very reason why it should be preserved from encroaching industrialisation:

> Let them be left,
> O let them be left, wildness and wet ...
> (14–15)

In 'As Kingfishers Catch Fire' (undated; it may belong to 1881 or be as early as 1877), Hopkins goes beyond the plea of 'Inversnaid' for the preservation of wildness. He develops the idea, of each thing having its own individuality and actively proclaiming it. Dynamism is suggested by observing a nature not static but characteristically in action: the kingfishers 'catch fire' in their sudden dart of colour, 'dragonflies draw flame' – even stones and bells, inanimate objects, do things and in doing so proclaim their inner beings, their *haecceitas*:

> As tumbled over rim in roundy wells
> Stones ring ... each hung bell's
> Bow swung finds tongue to fling out broad its name ...
> (2–4)

This point the traditional Romantic poet might reach, but Hopkins presses on and makes not only things actors, but Christ himself, playing on 'ten thousand' stages. For when 'the just man justices' he is part of this active universe and indeed in his justness 'Acts in God's eye what in God's eye he is – | Christ' (11–12). The beauty of nature extends into mankind and into moral qualities: if the kingfishers are beautiful in their nature, so too is man in being just and giving justice, when he is godlike in nature and function, sharing human and divine as Christ did by the Incarnation.

'Ribblesdale' (1883) takes up the idea of justice, not now though coming from man, whose fallen nature blights and destroys earth's beauty, but as a plea from nature itself, which has neither tongue nor heart to plead its cause, can only 'be', yet that being 'Thou canst but be, but that thou well dost' (5). Mankind, unlike the just man of 'As Kingfishers', is not here perceived in terms of heroic virtue, but as fallible, destructive, sinful, loved by God yet obstinate in opposition to his own good, 'dear and dogged man' (10). Earth, subjected to sin through man's fall, waits to be delivered, into what St Paul, quoted by Hopkins at the poem's head, calls 'the glorious liberty of the children of God' (Romans 8:21; *P*, 369). Man, who cares neither for his environment nor his salvation (a dark reminder of the dual nature of humanity, created yet sharing the divine, as Christ's incarnation reiterated), thriftlessly reaves ('plunders', 'pillages') 'our rich round world bare | And none reck of world after' (12–13). Earth is stained, wears 'brows of such care' through man's sinfulness (not just carelessness about his environment). Yet hope lies in this very care (playing between being worn out (care-worn) and cared for), since God has not abandoned the world, an object of 'care and dear concern' (14), where 'dear' doubles to convey lovingness and the great price paid by Christ as sacrifice to redeem mankind and with it, in justice, the physical world, restoring the 'lovely dale' from 'rack or wrong' (7–8).

PRIESTLY RESPONSIBILITIES

Between his appointment at Oxford (1878) and the Tertianship (1881), Hopkins wrote several poems that can be grouped together because of their concern with people, not the anonymous Jessy or Jack of 'The Candle Indoors', but individuals. Parish duties broadened Hopkins's experience and while not all these poems derive directly from these duties, he noted to Bridges that 'I find within my professional experience now a good deal of matter to write on' (*L*, 1.86).

'Brothers' (1880) draws on observation at Mount St Mary's, Spinkhill, describing with psychological acuity the body language of Henry, watching his younger brother's stage performance – Jack has no apprehensions about his success, but Henry, watching,

> drove, with a diver's dip,
> Clutched hands through claspèd knees ...
> (20–21)

While the opposition of the actor Jack's serene certainty and the auditor Henry's fears is comic, the love expressed in the body's agitation comes from feelings based in the heart, and in the paradox Hopkins has explored before –

> There's comfort then, there's salt!
> Nature bad, base, and blind,
> Dearly thou canst be kind ...
> (39–41)

And it is the heart's impulse, for good as well as evil, that impelled Hopkins to write 'The Handsome Heart' (1879). Wanting to give a present to a boy who had helped with duties in the church, Hopkins asked what he would like. The boy's simple, even naive reply, 'Father, what you buy me I shall like the best' (2), emphasises the rightness of the boy's heart – instincts, which are 'carrier-witted' as Hopkins's own heart had been in 'The Wreck', and the beauty lies not in anything physical, since

> Heart mannerly is more than handsome face
>
> (9)

– and the only gift Hopkins desires to give is the wish, the prayer, that the boy's life ('all your road your race', 13) will match his readiness now to deny the self.

From Wordsworth, Hopkins may well have learnt the strategy of encounter, that leaves the poet to question or meditate on what has unexpectedly been learnt. Hopkins said 'Brothers' was 'something in Wordsworth's manner' (L, 1.86) and in 'Cheery Beggar' (1879), an unfinished poem set near Magdalen Bridge in Oxford, priest and beggar, both materially poor (Hopkins was vowed to poverty), meet and as Wordsworth with the young, the old, the outcast, Hopkins admires a man whom want 'could not make pine' (7). Hopkins's own limited resources allow what he can give ('pence') to be significant rather than the condescension of the rich to the poor, so we focus on the beggar and that

> a gift should cheer him
> Like that poor pocket of pence, poor pence of mine.
>
> (8–9)

'The Handsome Heart' stresses that the 'Heart mannerly is more than handsome face' (9), yet questions arise again about Hopkins's response to beauty. He writes of women, of the Virgin Mary [pp. 50; 92–4], of Margaret in 'Spring and Fall' [pp. 103–4], yet there is no doubt that Hopkins is primarily interested in boys and men and that this interest can be, often disturbingly for the poetic effect, charged erotically as well as spiritually, not least because he insists on the material world – as it is God's creation, rather than anything evil, he of course must do so – and its beauty.

MORTAL BEAUTY

Hopkins was drawn to beauty long before reading Duns Scotus. Scotus, as Devlin points out (S, 120), says that 'the love of beauty is ... the initial impulse to the love of God', yet before and after reading Scotus, Hopkins was both drawn to beauty and repulsed by

it as a distraction from God. The danger is clear in the over-
whelming beauty of Digby Dolben [**pp. 13–4**], that helped draw him
to Church and God, yet also threatened him with a forbidden love.
This opposition, poetically fruitful, is explored in 'To What Serves
Mortal Beauty' (1885), where the question is answered first as 'dan-
gerous; does set danc-| Ing blood' (1–2), though beauty can lead to
higher feelings and even a glance (like a blow or a beam of light)
rightly taken can do more than gazing. Of course, all nature is
mortal, but the phrase 'mortal beauty' refers more particularly to
human beauty. There is the beauty of music, but also the beauty of
men like Dolben. Sometimes the reader feels an impulse to read
elements of certain poems as impulses of erotic desire (whether
recognised or suppressed by Hopkins) and these can distract from
the poem's clear intention. In 'The Furl of Fresh-Leaved Dogrose'
(1879), a young man's physicality is given peculiar emphasis, the
softness of face and cheek like the dog-rose sun-burnt, his hair
'like all a ravel-rope's-end' (5), bleached and wild. The poem leads
nowhere, but offers a picture for gazing on a young man as an object
of affectionate, even erotic contemplation. The lengthier yet aban-
doned 'Epithalamion' (1888), a wedding celebration, suggests also an
erotic pull upon the reader's attention which is not only overt but, in
its homocentricity, incompatible with heterosexual love. A prurient
sense of voyeurism is generated in the reader as the young man
comes upon a party of boys bathing and

> unseen
> Sees the bevy of them, how the boys
> With dare and with downdolfinry and bellbright bodies
>   huddling out,
> Are earthworld, airworld, waterworld thorough hurled ...
>   (15–18)

Prompted by the bathers, the man laboriously undresses to swim
too, the poem's very insistence that the man goes aside to bathe
separately only drawing attention to or creating a desire to have him
join the boys: the turning aside accentuates the obscene alternative.
Quite apart from the mildly ludicrous account of undressing, such a
homoerotic under-text may be one reason why 'Epithalamion' was
abandoned: it cannot with straight face be paralleled to heterosexual
marriage, even as a sacramental ceremony, as the increasingly frag-
mentary poem set out (but never arrived) to do.

Yet, in coming back to 'To What Serves Mortal Beauty', another
poetic course becomes apparent. The danger of mortal beauty is
freely admitted, but so is danger's counterpart, as beauty 'keeps

warm | Men's wits to the things that are; to what good means' (3–4), recognising that without love, the charity of St Paul that is greater than faith or hope, the impulse to others and to God, is missing. The last part of the octave exemplifies this by the famous episode from Bede's *A History of the English Church and People* (Bede 1968: 99–100), of St Gregory the Great, the Pope who sent Augustine of Canterbury to convert England, coming upon some boys in Rome for sale as slaves, 'wet-fresh windfalls of war's storm' (6). Struck by their appearance, Gregory, 'a father', both as priest and with tender feelings, asked who they were and determined their nation be given the faith. God-given beauty fulfilled God's purpose. Beauty is not to be feared, but met, and then beyond it, grace, 'God's better beauty' (14), be sought.

'Mortal Beauty' sets physical beauty against artistic beauty, wondering whether physical form may engross us more than the higher aesthetic forms of art (which as higher, are closer to God's beauty), may be 'prouder form | Than Purcell tune lets tread to' (2–3). It was Henry Purcell (1658/9–1695) that Hopkins had turned to (1879) as an individual whose music he hugely admired and where he could explore the complex relationship of art and the artist. One of Hopkins's tutors at Oxford, Walter Pater, had declared in his influential study, *The Renaissance* (1873) that 'All art constantly aspires towards the condition of music' (Pater 1928: 132). Pater, in opposition to Ruskin, divorced aesthetic and moral judgements: art was an end in itself, startling the human spirit 'to a life of eager and constant observation' (Pater 1928: 220). Hopkins had long engaged in 'eager and constant observation', but he would not agree that this was the end in itself. And yet if the work of art is neither good nor bad, so that the very angels cannot tell a man's nature by it, what is the relationship between art and artist? This complex of creativity and goodness is explored, if sometimes obscurely, in 'Henry Purcell'.

The sonnet (in Alexandrines – six-stress lines) opens obscurely (Hopkins was forced at least twice to explain it to Bridges). Hopkins as a Catholic hopes that Purcell may have experienced a 'fair' fate (may have a fair fate fallen to him) after death, even though a heretic – an insistence by Hopkins the convert on his desire for the conversion of England, which here sits rather uneasily. The opening does though suggest an intimacy of connection with Purcell, prompted necessarily by knowledge of his music, and that the artist and art cannot entirely be divorced nor the work and the 'listener's' feelings. Purcell is a great artist because of his penetration into the inner life, rather than the surface passions, allowing the 'rehearsal' (literally, here, the 'hearing again') 'Of own, of abrupt self there so thrusts on, so throngs the ear' (8), the sense of the 'very essence' of man being revealed (McChesney 1968: 89). Yet Purcell in the sestet is given his individual glory, his own self ('quaint moonmarks', 10), like a great seabird, the beat of whose wings 'fans fresh our wits with wonder' (14), rising from the 'thunder-purple seabeach', as 'his palmy snowy-pinions scatter a colossal smile' (13). Flight, which so fascinated Hopkins in birds, images too the flight of Purcell's imagination out of the 'seabeach' of the mundane world as the artist exerts his power.

PARISHIONERS AND OTHER PEOPLE

'The Bugler's First Communion' (1879) and 'Felix Randal' (1880) spring out of parish experience, in Oxford and Liverpool. In Oxford, Hopkins's duties extended to the army barracks at Cowley. Hopkins's patriotism, a very Victorian quality that he never lost, finds expression also in poems like 'The Soldier' [pp. 115–6]. No ideas of pacifism or conscientious objection enter (issues rather of the twentieth century): instead, the focus of 'The Bugler's First Communion' is on the boy's innocence and his desire to receive communion. Problems may arise over sentimentalism, surrounding the boy with an inhuman virtue, or the seeping in of erotic suggestion. On the first, Hopkins is not naive about the spiritual and moral dangers of army life, of the 'hell-rook ranks' (18). The second is less easy to cope with: the boy's innocence is imagined in tactile terms, as though inviting touch, whether 'Breathing bloom of a chastity in mansex fine' (16) or even more strongly in the boy's response to the priest's instruction, when he 'Yields tender as a pushed peach' (23). How far, the reader may wonder, legitimately if mistaken (or more properly, misdirected), has mortal beauty 'set dancing blood'?

Communion is the central rite celebrated by the Church and its doctrine was crucial to Hopkins – not just a commemoration as Protestants take it, but a renewal of Christ's giving of his body and blood at the Last Supper [p. 15]. The boy kneels while Hopkins as priest brings from the tabernacle of the altar (the 'cupboard') the already consecrated host, the body of Christ enclosed insignificantly ('low-latched') within a housing ('housel'), the appearance of bread that is now Christ's body. The poem becomes a prayer for the boy's safety in life as Hopkins, leaving his fate to Christ, declares though if his prayers are disregarded, they will 'brandle' ('shake') 'adamantine heaven with ride and jar' (46).

'Felix Randal' (1880) is less disturbing in its force. Felix the farrier or blacksmith is (or rather was) a handsome man ('big-boned and handsome-hardy'), but the process of his breaking down and remaking is Hopkins's concern, the realities of parish life, emphasised elsewhere [p. 33], evident in 'he cursed at first' (5). A colloquial language lies along with Hopkins's poetic language as though echoing the speech of Liverpool, familiar to Felix himself and so linking voice to sympathy – most obvious in 'all road ever he offended' (8) ('in any way in which he offended'), but 'all' (used five times in the poem), colloquialises 'anointed and all' (6), as it also emphasises the four diseases that contended to kill Felix. The Bugler received Holy Communion; Hopkins administered the last rites to Felix, both extreme unction, anointing with oil and prayers for someone close to death, as well as confession and communion ('and all'). The sestet, the meditation upon Felix's last days, considers how the strong man becomes a child to the priest (father) – the man was Felix Spencer, who died 21 April 1880, aged thirty-one (White 1992: 320); Hopkins was not yet thirty-six – loved with the tenderness of father to sick child, 'child, Felix, poor Felix Randal' (11). Felix's 'mould of man' ties in with a Victorian tradition in writing and visual arts of valuing physical labour and likening the working man to classical heroic images, found in Carlyle on history and in the central labourer of Ford Madox Brown's *Work* (Manchester Art Gallery). Felix's weakness works towards his likely salvation, yet the poem is oddly and effectively open-ended, defying the sonnet form's pull towards firm closure, so that Felix concludes not as a corpse, but as in life, using his physical strength to serve the strength of the work-horses, action harmonious and necessary:

> When thou at the random grim forge, powerful amidst peers,
> Didst fettle for the great grey drayhorse his bright and bat-
>   tering sandal!

>   (13–14)

'SPRING AND FALL' (1880)

'Spring and Fall', 'not founded on any real incident' (*L*, 1.109), has a girl as its primary figure – or rather, has a delicate interchange between an adult and a child, Margaret, where the undisturbed innocence of the child is reinforced by the ambiguity of whether the adult even speaks aloud or only meditates in this Wordsworthian encounter of innocence and experience. The old English form, 'fall', for autumn is tied in with the oppositions of the poem – child and adult, opposing seasons, purity and the primal stain of man's fall from grace. Margaret has instinctive perceptions, not knowledge, yet she responds to the autumnal fall of leaf:

> Margaret, are you grieving
> Over Goldengrove unleaving?

Leaves, like the things of man, you
With your fresh thoughts care for, can you?

(1–4)

The adult is mildly amused, yet also aware that while he can explain seasons, decay, the fall as doctrine, he also lacks Margaret's immediacy. The non-phatic voiced 'Ah!' is expressive of various feelings, as suggested here, none necessarily predominating:

Ah! as the heart grows older
It will come to such sights colder ...

(5–6)

Such experience clearly involves both coping with the world in which we must live and a loss of freshness, of the responsiveness of the spring in us. The adult does not intrude upon the child – there is no insistency as in Wordsworth's 'We Are Seven', where the adult comically retreats baffled. Rather, we move from the simple decay of autumn to the blight on man's physical and spiritual world:

Now no matter, child, the name:
Sorrow's springs are the same. ...
It is the blight man was born for,
It is Margaret you mourn for.

(10–11; 14–15)

The adult explains, to himself, to the reader, what the child now neither does nor could understand and the reader rests upon a sense of contained sadness without rough intrusion upon the girl, who must duly grow to the adult world. Here is the stillness of a moment caught in contemplation, of distance between child and adult, and yet of their necessary identity in being human.

WINEFRED, ECHO, SIBYL

While in Wales at St Beuno's, Hopkins had been drawn to Holywell, some nine or ten miles away, near the River Dee, a place of pilgrimage continuously from at least the twelfth century. Winefred was murdered by Caradoc after rejecting his advances: her uncle, St Beuno, restored her to life and she became a nun. From where her head lay, cut off by Caradoc, a spring flowed with healing powers (Milward & Schoder 1975: photos between 80 & 81). The attraction of St Winefred is clear in Hopkins's continuing determination to write a drama about her: three significant dramatic fragments seem to date from between 1884 and 1885, in which Hopkins's early interest in dramatic form, shown in the vivid 'Floris in Italy' [pp. 53–4], appears again and again in the range and tone of the spoken voice, of shifts of mood or sudden images, though his talent was not for playwriting. Caradoc's soliloquy after he has murdered Winefred is an effective exploration of the shifting moods of guilt – self-justification, denial, forced recognition by the blood on his sword (the 'workman' which still 'sweats' from its labour), a gradual realisation of self-destruction:

> I all my being have hacked in half with her neck ...
>
> (60)

The remarkable song, 'The Leaden Echo and the Golden Echo' (1882), was meant for the St Winefred drama. No indication is given where it would come in the action, though clearly its debate about mortal beauty links it to Winefred, whose looks were the cause of Caradoc's desire and her death. Reminiscent of the choruses in Greek tragedy, the song's long lines (the Golden Echo's eighth line has 41 syllables, surely the longest line in English poetry) demand vocalisation. Hopkins elaborates not the story of the drama, but a theme, as Greek dramatic choruses found analogies to the action, here the contrast between mortal and divine beauty. The song is a reinflection of 'Spring and Fall', aware of the Fall and consequent decay in time of everything mortal. The Leaden Echo descends, through fading of beauty, the onset of wrinkles and grey hairs, into despair, the lines narrowing down as though turning the screw upon the listener, passing from lament at loss to despair, then from despair's beginning to the fullest emphasis upon hopelessness in the face of the human condition with the fivefold repetition of 'despair'. The long lists serve both to emphasise the inadequacy of all means to preserve beauty – no 'bow or brooch or braid or brace, lace, latch or catch or key to keep | Back beauty' (1–2) – and the seemingly inevitable destruction from aging to decomposition:

> Ruck and wrinkle, drooping, dying, death's worst, winding
> sheets, tombs and worms and
> tumbling to decay ...
>
> (12)

In all this, the momentum of the lines is kept up by aural linkings, the initial 'b's and the dissolving from 'braid' to 'brace', from 'brace' to 'lace'. Then by an echo that is rhyme and something more, since the opposed meanings of the words introduce the opposition of Leaden and Golden, the poem's hinge takes us from 'despair' to 'spare', a device Hopkins might (though need not necessarily) know from Jacobean drama, where an echo off-stage repeats yet changes the meaning of the onstage character's words (see Webster's *The Duchess of Malfi*, V, iii). Out of despair may come salvation ('spare' doubles both 'forbear' / 'hold back', as in 'Spare your breath to cool your porridge', and 'save from death' / 'offer salvation'), for there is a way to climb, as the lengthening lines suggest the opening out, the climbing upwards towards the light or heaven. Here is the way to an eternal beauty, that of God, 'beauty's self and beauty's giver' (19).

Never part of the drama of St Winefred, but linked to 'The Leaden Echo' by its technical boldness and by its early drafts dating from the first drafts of Caradoc's soliloquy, is 'Spelt from Sibyl's Leaves' (1886), Hopkins noting rather wryly that it was 'the longest sonnet ever made and no doubt the longest making' (*L*, 1.245). But Hopkins's extreme line length and accentual handling makes it necessary (if these lines work at all) to take them slowly, at a speaking pace, almost unaware of the rhythm of a *line*, but rather aware of rhythm section by section.

The title refers to the Sibyl of Cumae, one of the prophetesses of the ancient world, described in *The Aeneid* (Virgil 1990: 70–71), divinely inspired, who foretold the future 'by signs and names [written] on leaves'. The leaves stay ordered in her cave, but are so light that the slightest breeze disturbs and whirls them in confusion. The Sibyls were also traditionally believed to have had premonitions of Christianity, hence the link in the poem with the Day of Judgement, supposedly foretold by the Cumaean Sibyl. The prophecy is 'spelt', that is, spelt out, deciphered with difficulty, both because of those 'signs and names', further darkened by the leaves being scattered, and because prophecies of the ancient world are famously ambiguous. The opening suspends us, with no verb, no activity, no subject referred to – 'Earnest, earthless, equal, attuneable': we must try as each word is made out to find its meaning, though the prophecy will not easily yield up itself. Discovering that the immediate subject is 'evening' as it strains to become night, so we turn back to that list of qualities: solemnity, detachment, overarching, vast are all suggested in the opening list, yet to give those meanings nowhere exhausts them. From qualities we move to a remarkably lovely picture of the oncoming night, the moonlight, the white light ('hoarlight') of twilight, the stars, even as the dappledness of nature, so loved by Hopkins, is hidden under darkness. This is a literal invocation of night, transferred at the end of the octave to symbolic meaning: 'our night whelms, whelms, and will end us' (8). Death and judgement, heaven and hell, are the 'four last things'. The physical world is dappled in its beauty, 'spare and strange', but as life winds down, as evening at the poem's opening passes into night, so the thread, 'once skeined stained veined variety' of life (11), will separate into the opposed absolutes of 'black, white; right, wrong', the starkness of statement, suddenly spelt out by the 'prophecy', emphasising the starkness of judgement. The prophecy becomes a warning that Hopkins, the believer, means all too seriously: 'reckon but, reck but, mind | But these two' (12–13). The Sibyl traditionally prophesied the Last Judgement: Hopkins urges the necessity of thinking beyond the forms of mortal beauty, beyond even the moonlight and stars of evening, to the darkness that comes in the end and the judgement that lies beyond it. His aesthetic concerns are crucially bound up with his continuing belief in God's existence and that belief's consequences when nature will be rolled away and God in glory revealed.

The 'Terrible' Sonnets: 1885–86

THE 'TERRIBLE' SONNETS

The 'Terrible' Sonnets or the Sonnets of Desolation are a group of poems from 1885–86, none precisely datable and their sequence not certain, linked by their dramatic representation of a religious experience, in itself common enough amongst the devout and often called, in the words of the great Spanish mystic, St John of the Cross (1542–91; Attwater 1965), the Dark Night of the Soul (John 1960: 26–29). Hopkins gives immediacy and intensity to his spiritual misery and desperation. There is some disagreement about which poems exactly should belong to this group. Generally the sequence (their order of composition not known) is of six: 'To Seem the Stranger'; 'I Wake and Feel'; 'No Worst There is None'; 'Carrion Comfort'; 'Patience, Hard Thing'; and 'My Own Heart'. 'Carrion Comfort' stands out because of its expansive use of unstressed syllables (apparent on the printed page); and because, some argue, its final mood is positive. But its optimism is qualified and hence aligns itself with the 'negative assertion' of the other sonnets. The coherence of this group is enforced by two pieces of evidence. First, they do not come in a period of poetic barrenness; other poems, finished and unfinished, can be assigned to 1885–86. So while the 'Terrible' Sonnets are not isolated productions, yet they are clearly related by shared experiences of suffering and inward struggle not apparent in other poems of the time. Second, Hopkins's own comments confirm that the experiences described were personal and bitter: sending Bridges two sonnets, he noted that 'if ever anything was written in blood one of these was' (*L*, 1.219) and later, of some sonnets, 'Four of these came like inspirations unbidden and against my will' (*L*, 1.221). Elsewhere he chose composition; here, not.

The experiences (since we have a biographical key) are seated in his appointment as professor in Dublin. Here, exhausted and depressed by the work of examining, affected perhaps by the poverty of the Dublin slums behind the city's Georgian grandeur, separated from England, from his family, isolated culturally and politically by the Irishness of those about him, in a narrower, less stimulating world than that of Stonyhurst or even parish work, and alienated by the struggle for Home Rule, which he believed should come but only because the alternatives were worse [**pp. 36–7**], Hopkins undoubtedly sank into depression in 1885 and 1886. This is evident in the most personal of these poems, 'To Seem the Stranger', and perhaps the one most determined by specific time, place and person:

> To seem the stranger lies my lot, my life
> Among strangers. Father and mother dear,
> Brothers and sisters are in Christ not near
> And he my peace / my parting, sword and strife.
>   (1–4)

Hopkins's sense of identity is strong enough to confirm that he is not a stranger to himself, yet he has the characteristics of the stranger, exclusion through difference and loneliness, the strangers amongst whom he lives enforcing the condition of strangeness. Yet that he lives amongst strangers throws us back to the opening verb, the ambiguity of 'seem': querying whether he really is a stranger or only seems so, confirms the central core of personality, even while it cannot relieve his loneliness or his bafflement. Separation from his family, by distance and by faith, is emphasised by the visual cleaving of the quatrain's final line, the forward-slash substituted for 'is', visual rather than verbal cementing closely the necessity of peace and parting (more usually opposites than companions), recalling that 'hard saying' of Christ, which Hopkins had experienced so painfully when confronting his family with his conversion: 'For I am come to set a man at variance against his father' (Matthew 10: 35). From family, Hopkins passes to his country (5–8), the convoluted syntax to (partly) express the intricacies of his situation. Acknowledging that 'Kind love' is still his, he turns to the highest cause of his sense of seclusion: that his prayers ('what word | Wisest my heart breeds', 11–12), are unanswered, excluded by the inscrutable ('dark') will of heaven or else which ' hell's spell thwarts' (13) – 'spell' as singular and the heavy stress on each word slowing utterance, avoids a mere rhyming jingle. Above all, perhaps, as man, as priest, as Jesuit, committed to serving God, he seems unable to offer anything. Without visible achievement, whatever later might be the consolation offered through St Alphonsus Rodriguez [**pp. 119–20**], advancing God's kingdom, delighting in God's love, seemed scarcely to be found in the interminable piles of examination scripts, so he is 'Time's eunuch' ('Justus Quidem Tu Es, Domine', 13 [**p. 120**]). Without God's response (not in material goods, but in spiritual consolation), he is but 'a lonely began' (14), the stranger who has made a beginning (convert, priest), but made no progress.

The 'Terrible' Sonnets are meditative poems, in that they observe and explore situations, but how different from the stimulus observed in 'Pied Beauty' or 'The Lantern Out of Doors' or even 'The Candle Indoors' [**pp. 94–5**], moving as that last does to rebuke and self-correction. Here the drama is at the moment of enactment, even when, as in 'I Wake and Feel', tenses shift disturbingly in suffering's progress. Meditation drove Hopkins within himself, to a personality and inner prospect that horrified him as he had found in 1883 [**p. 19**]. In 'The Wreck', though we are given the process of his own conversion, Hopkins primarily contemplates suffering through the agony and determination of the nun, while he, 'Away in the loveable west', his struggle over, is 'at rest' (185, 187). Now, mediator and participant, he experiences the storm, yet while the nun saw Christ loom up, a saving power, Hopkins sees no such comfort. All he can strive for is resistance to despair, the final sin that would damn him. Christ is absent: not because non-existent or because Hopkins doubts or disbelieves, but hidden, unanswering, while Hopkins's prayers are cries, 'like dead letters sent | To dearest him that lives alas! away' ('I Wake and Feel', 7–8).

THE 'TERRIBLE' SONNETS: THE DARK NIGHT OF THE SOUL

If 'To Seem the Stranger' is the most time-and-place specific of these sonnets, the others, amidst bafflement and pain, though not despair or disbelief, show Hopkins's experience of the Dark Night of the Soul, a period of desolation and aridity, a failure of prayer and devotion to produce a sense of God's response. Such experiences of spiritual 'dryness' are common enough and were recognised by St Ignatius and more importantly still by St Teresa of Avila (1515–82; Attwater 1965), whose mystical communion with God, above all in her famous ecstasies, was embodied by the Bernini statue in St Mary of Victory, Rome. In her Autobiography (written 1562), Teresa advises those who fall into the 'banishment' of the Dark Night not to be 'distressed or afflicted', however unfortunate it is for a soul 'that loves God to find itself in this state of misery' (Teresa 1987: 82–83). St Teresa, despite her associations with ecstacy and the high tide of the Counter-Reformation, both suspect to Protestant sensibilities, was an admired figure for some in Victorian England for her power and authority, a woman who reformed the Carmelite order in Spain and commanded others to the glory of God. George Eliot uses her in the 'Prelude' to *Middlemarch* (1871–72), an ironic parallel to the limitations of nineteenth-century provincial life. Hopkins, if he ever read *Middlemarch*, might well have identified himself with the novel's Dorothea and Lydgate, who aim so high, yet apparently achieve so little. Certainly, Hopkins read St Teresa's Autobiography, twice referring to a visionary passage that may have influenced the concretisation of feeling in 'I Wake and Feel the Fell of Dark'. Teresa describes a sense, during prayer, of being plunged into hell and closely confined in 'a cavity scooped out of the wall, like a cupboard' (Teresa 1987: 233). Hopkins recalled that cupboard, a 'little press in the wall', in 1873 and 1881, describing a nightmare (*J*, 238) and commenting on Teresa's experience (*S*, 138). The 'Terrible' Sonnets, then, explore the distress of the 'dark night', yet as Teresa urged, resist affliction and banishment from God.

THE 'TERRIBLE' SONNETS: DISTRESS AND DISGUST

Silence, emptiness, bodily weariness and sensory disgust combine in 'I Wake and Feel the Fell of Dark, not Day'. The link by stress between 'feel' and 'fell' emphasises the tactile oppressiveness of a skin or hide ('fell'), while that primary meaning of 'fell' is underpinned by the secondary meaning of 'terrible', 'implacable', as in Shakespeare's 'This fell sergeant, Death'. Instead of waking bringing daylight out of sleep's darkness, it brings only 'yet longer light's delay' (4), the horror of lying sleepless, echoing also, whether deliberately or unconsciously a passage in *Paradise Lost*, symbolic of the devil's snares, when the sailor, deceived, anchors himself to a marine monster (the devil symbolically), 'while night | Invests the sea, and wished morn delays' (Bk. I, ll.207–8). That Hopkins's night-horror can also be taken symbolically is enforced by the temporal shift from literal to figurative in the second quatrain, as hours of waiting for daylight become 'years', life itself, and he takes us now not into Teresa's little cupboard, but the very Victorian institution of the 'dead letter' section of the Post Office, where misaddressed letters are gone over to be sent back or else are, eventually, destroyed. Hopkins, turning back upon himself, to blame not the 'dearest him' but himself, finds himself 'heartburn', a term for 'indigestion' that suggests the condition's discomfort while drawing in the whole range of feelings associated with the heart: the distaste recalls the 'old and terrible afflicting thought and disgust' of the 1883 Retreat notes (*S*, 253), while bitterness, gall, sent by God, like the pangs of indigestion, rise in him – God's decrees 'Bitter would have me taste: my taste was me' (10).

The rhetorical play of 'have me taste: my taste was me', with verb-pronoun-noun becoming noun-verb-pronoun, 'me taste' becoming 'my taste', passive to active, is entirely serious, in forcing Hopkins to recognise his very body is his own bitterness. He aligns himself with the damned ('the lost'), yet also recognises, just in the nick, the 'saving grace', as in all this group of poems, that neither life nor spiritual progress is yet complete. He and the damned exist in their full physicality, 'their sweating selves' ('selves', stressing individual identity, a significant key term for Hopkins), but the damned are of course worse. Their spiritual journey is complete, and plunged in despair by eternal separation from God they suffer in body and spirit. Hopkins ends on the words 'but worse', applied not to himself in a common way of images: 'brighter than … ', 'braver than … ', but to the ones in hell. The eye of hope is not yet shut.

It is a slight hope, but in the Dark Night Hopkins clings to it, as St Ignatius advised anyone struggling in this desolation: 'and let him think that he will shortly be consoled, making diligent efforts against the desolation' (quoted *S*, 204). In his Dark Night, writing a sonnet 'in blood', others coming 'like inspirations unbidden', Hopkins was still a poet, alert to the discipline of the sonnet. The 'Terrible' Sonnets do not flail wildly or become incoherent, however painful Hopkins's situation: on the page the sonnets, except 'Carrion Comfort', are notable for a brevity (compare the appearance of any one with 'Spelt from Sibyl's Leave' or even 'Henry Purcell'), their conformity to iambic pentameter, the omission of unstressed syllables, hinting at the poems' compression, a denseness that is sometimes obscure, but always opens to the glimpse of hope, however limited.

'No Worst, There Is None' conveys the horror of desolation, yet leads surely to that glimpse of hope, however limited. 'No Worst' opens with the vertiginous realisation that the agony of the Dark Night is infinite, need never be plumbed, as yet more pangs will yet 'wilder wring'. The sufferer is hurled ('pitched') beyond the extent (the 'pitch') of grief. 'Pitch' also suggests (Hopkins knew the musical term well) tension beyond the normal tuning level of grief (all order is broken here), as there may further be a suggestion of tar, the pitch-blackness of St Teresa's vision of hell. The sestet makes concrete that sickening giddiness of the opening's realisation, as the mind, that grasps that the worst has not, never will come, induces the terrible vertigo of mountains, 'cliffs of fall | Frightful, sheer, no-man-fathomed' (9–10). However much these are terrors created by the mind in meditation, they are real enough to the sufferer. Then, shifting from self to regarding self as a third person, Hopkins exclaims in a moment of (dramatic) realisation: 'Here! creep, | Wretch, under a comfort serves in a whirlwind' (12–13), sharing with others at the end of their tether (King Lear in the storm might also come to mind, with his 'poor naked wretches') points of rest even if they are only death and sleep. But with them some point of rest, some relief from 'no worst' can be found.

The waiting which St Ignatius urged, that 'diligent effort against the desolation', is evident in 'Patience, Hard Thing'. Patience, as against the terror of being 'Pitched past pitch of grief', would seem desirable, but unlike other heroic virtues it is passive, enduring rather than acting: 'To do without ... and obey' (4). Yet Patience expands into images of growth (ivy) and the very quality becomes a comfort of Christ, a sweetness likened to the honeycomb, filled by the continued patient activity of bees. Consolation seems more assured here and it is glimpsed, quite literally as an image, at the end of 'My Own Heart Let Me More Have Pity On', where the bitterness of gall and heartburn, the terror of cliffs of fall, is exchanged for the tenderness of soul towards heart, so that wryly the soul is rebuked as 'poor Jackself' (9), Jack as common man (compare 'Jessy and Jack' in 'The Candle Indoors'), the wryly affectionate comic tone here reflecting Hopkins's self-deprecation [p. 5], even while reintegrating soul and heart into a single self, which must give over self-examination and turn to comfort rather than suffering, to accept God's will, however inscrutable. The colloquialisms of 'God knows when' and 'God knows what' ('size at' (11), essentially 'grow', is frankly obscure) emphasise the need for patience, the hope that Ignatius gave 'that he will shortly be consoled', and at the poem's end, Hopkins opens on a God-given moment, future yet certain. The smile of God unlooked-for will break upon him, 'as skies | Betweenpie mountains', and light 'a lovely mile' (13–14). However dark the night that Hopkins suffered, and his sufferings need not be doubted, the poems constantly end in assertion, however negative in tone, and in the consolation of faith.

THE 'TERRIBLE' SONNETS: 'CARRION COMFORT'

'Carrion Comfort' is distinctively more expansive than the other 'Terrible' Sonnets, as a glance at the printed page shows, and it has been claimed it should not properly be included with them because of its confident account in the first part of the sestet (9–11) of Hopkins's joyous progress, through trial, to conversion. Yet the poem's ending is as dramatically startling and dark in effect as any of the other 'Terrible' Sonnets, even while, like them, 'Carrion Comfort' shares, besides the discipline of the sonnet form, an underlying template of spiritual meaning, religious imagery, and the Bible.

The negative assertion of the opening ('Not, I'll not, carrion comfort, Despair, not feast on thee') presents a struggle as dark as 'I Wake and Feel the Fell' or 'No Worst, There Is None'. The repeated 'not', six times in the opening four lines, conveys a sense of desperation. Despair is food, but food for a scavenger that gluts itself on chance-found dead flesh, disgusting food for a repulsive creature, jackal or vulture, into which Hopkins seems urged to transform himself. Despair might comfort those who abandon the struggle and find themselves, belly-full, at rest. Yet despair is the condition of the damned, eternally separated from God, whose sweating selves Hopkins identified with (in 'I Wake and Feel the Fell'), even while keeping himself apart. He holds to the Catholic grace of choice, oddly expressed as it might seem in the negatives of 'not choose not to be' (4), a real choice, as opposed to the Calvinistic horror of pre-destination, where our salvation or damnation is already settled, despite any effort of ours. Yet in this opening, dramatically, Hopkins is a man at the end of his tether, literally so in the images of untwisting strands, the rope or fabric of his being unravelling, slack yet still holding.

The second quatrain (5–8), with its gasps and cries of present suffering ('ah!' and 'O' were added during the writing process to enforce that sense), might be expected, as commonly in sonnet form, to develop the opening and we may understandably read 'O thou terrible' as referring to Despair. It becomes clear on closer reading that God is the terror, God in his majesty rather than the obvious manifestation of love. Despair is dead (not therefore powerless), is carrion; God is a living lion, the lion of Judah, King, arbiter of justice. Hopkins felt impulsions towards being the questing scavenger: now God becomes the hunter-lion, Hopkins the living 'prey' – lions traditionally do not eat carrion. Underlying this figure of rough power ('rude' is adverbial = 'rudely') is a God who once thought the pursuit worthwhile, who once valued Hopkins the living prey. The image of flight ('me frantic to avoid thee', 8), expresses the terrifying yet essential process of conversion that Hopkins when a student finally acknowledged that he must undergo and which he had described in 'The Wreck' – 'I did say yes | O at lightning and lashed rod' (9–10). Simultaneously, this flight is given a wider application by being modelled on a series of quotations from the Book of Job (*P*, 375) – 'Thou huntest me as a fierce lion' (10: 16); 'thine eyes are upon me, and I am not' (7: 8); 'For he breaketh me with a tempest, and multiplieth my wounds without cause' (9: 17). The references are subdued poetically, but for the reader aware of them Hopkins appears not alone in being cast down – many, Job amongst them, have suffered the Dark Night – and the same hope might come for Hopkins that ultimately came to Job, whose trials vindicated him and God blessed him more than before.

Why, though, God's trouble to seize Hopkins? and why (though the question is temporarily deferred), after producing fruit and harvest, cast him down into darkness again? This rough handling by God of the unwilling soul leads to other biblical imagery, already drawn on by Hopkins in 'Barnfloor and Winepress' [**pp. 50–1**], where the harvest is 'Scourged upon the threshing-floor' (6), a flail used to separate the grain from the heads of wheat. And now the threshed corn is fanned, tossed up into the breeze, to separate wheat from chaff ('and fan, | O in turns of tempest, me heaped there', 7–8). After the series of questions in the second quatrain – why 'on me | Thy wring-earth right foot rock?', why 'lay a lionlimb against me?', and so on – the opening of the sestet provides a series of answers: out of that 'rude' handling came harvest and came too for Hopkins the unusual effects, in this sonnet series, of joy and laughter. Even in the Dark Night he can recall such delight in submitting, kissing the rod or 'Hand rather' (11).

But a further ambiguity, after rod or hand, opens at a further question about whom did his heart 'cheer' – God or himself in that context. Who is the hero? God for seizing him or himself for submitting to God (the paradox of winning salvation by submission). Hopkins ends with the triumphant struggle with God (12–14), in which both won, a moment intensely personal, yet sustained also by a Biblical parallel, where Jacob wrestles all night with an angel, who proves (Hopkins accepted the interpretation of a puzzling text) to be God himself: Jacob declares, 'I have seen God face to face, and my life is preserved' (Genesis 32: 30). Despair, that carrion, seems answered, even as Hopkins reverts to the desperate darkness of the poem's opening in another seemingly undesired struggle. Who was the hero on 'That night, that year | Of now done darkness I wretch lay wrestling with (my God!) my God' (13–14)? The past tense is emphatic enough ('now done darkness'), yet the agonised cry 'my God!', doubled with the recognition of whom he was resisting ('my God'), dramatically impels Hopkins and us into what is still a present tussle in the dark.

Soldier, ploughman, navvy

Hopkins had drawn on his experiences as parish priest, which provided him with 'a good deal of matter to write on' (*L*, 1.86), for 'The Bugler's First Communion' and 'Felix Randal' [**pp. 102–3**]. Three poems written in Ireland, 'The Soldier' (1885), 'Harry Ploughman' (1887), and 'Tom's Garland: Upon the Unemployed' (1887) deal, apparently, with similar experiences, though it is soon clear that Harry and Tom are types rather than the particular Felix, while The Soldier is a generic figure, any and all soldiers, rather than a specific youth like the Bugler Boy. These later poems and figures are intricately woven with Hopkins's political and social awareness, marking him as attached to his own time, someone essentially conservative, gloomy about Ireland's political prospects (though Irish matters enter none of these poems directly), and reflecting upon the labouring man's innate nobility, even while driven to consider casual labour and the consequent unemployment that produced 'Loafers, Tramps, Cornerboys, Roughs, Socialists and other pests of society' (*L*, 1.274; even amidst the gloom, he could not resist a good list). Hopkins's gloom was fed no doubt by his personal unhappiness and the Irish crisis that threatened violent means to desperate political ends. He might well look back to the political chaos of Paris in 1871 when the Communards burnt the Tuileries Palace and Town Hall, threatened the Louvre museum with the same fate, shot hostages, including the Archbishop of Paris, and were in turn slaughtered. Such a mood is expressed in the unfinished 'The Times Are Nightfall'.

'The Soldier' opens dramatically with a vocal response ('Yes'), as though to some remark or sudden thought. Why seeing a soldier, do we bless him? Hopkins has uttered the blessing, in the street, as a habit almost automatic and reflects upon it – the phrase 'bless him' suggests the colloquial, the unthinking. Such an impulse is now less common, partly at least because most soldiers are no longer notable by scarlet uniforms ('Our redcoats'), as British soldiers were until the Boer War, nor are they usually seen in the streets in uniform. While the British Army has hardly been inactive during most of the past century, nor has ceased to be, the 'enterprise of Empire', expansion in Africa and political conflicts on India's North West frontier (Afghanistan was a name as familiar to Hopkins as it has been only too familiar in Britain over the past forty years), involved policies very much in the late nineteenth-century consciousness. So soldiers, voluntarily risking their lives, a bulwark of civilisation, might well be blessed, in the casual way of blessing.

Yet Hopkins, while ready to bless, was not naive about the character and behaviour of soldiers: his parish experiences had taken him to Cowley barracks, amongst the poor, and even lower to 'filthy places' and 'dens of shame' [**p. 33**]. To him, soldiers might be heroes, they were hardly saints – being, 'the greater part, | But frail clay, nay but foul clay' (2–3). They could be seen and identified on the streets and if better disciplined than the 'brutal and licentious soldiery' of the eighteenth century, they were no moral exempla. So why do we bless a soldier? Because the heart, again, in its pride, leads us astray as it declares the soldier's calling 'manly' and identifies the frail clay with the noble action and ideal. The sestet then explores the paradox of Christ's approval of the soldiers' actions in war. Hopkins draws on the long tradition of Christ as captain of an army, the Church on earth or Church Militant, developed further by St Ignatius, a former soldier, who organised the Jesuits along military lines. So Christ, who fought and suffered heroically on earth, applauds when he sees some great deed: 'For love he leans forth, needs his neck must fall on, kiss' (12), an action shaped by the language of the Gospels. But if we set this concept of God's military power against the deed of soldiers, however heroic, and however their frail nature is acknowledged, we may well be squeamish about the analogy. Warfare, killing, and the ambitions of Empire are not so easily justified by God's approval of slaughter. The First World War, if nothing else, stands between us and Hopkins. As a Christian he draws in Christ as a Victorian could, but not as a poet, even a Christian poet, can now. 'The Soldier' functions, and to the modern reader is limited, by being a poem fixed in its time.

'Harry Ploughman' was conceived by Hopkins 'altogether for recital, not for perusal' (*L*, 1.263), by speaker and chorus – speaker to have the sonnet's fourteen lines and chorus the five 'burden-lines' ('Head and foot, shoulder and shank', 4), which do not rhyme but end with exactly the same word as the previous line. Felix Randal, admired for his physical beauty, was broken by illness and had to be 'reconstructed' as 'a heavenlier heart' (6). Harry the Ploughman, though, is beautiful, active, the labouring man as hero, as that central figure in Ford Madox Brown's *Work* [**p. 103**]. Harry has bodily strength and beauty, his arms hard as the farm's hurdles or movable fencing, in contrast to the soft down ('flue') on his arms. The tactile being of the man shows form related to function: firm as a tree trunk ('beechbole'), but not therefore passive: he is called, like a soldier to duty: 'as at a rollcall' (9). The plough seems to control him ('all quail to the wallowing o' the plough', 13), yet here is 'Churlsgrace', a compounding (literally in word form) of the rough person, the labourer, with beauty in action and (implied at least) the grace of God. The portrait does not lead into a specific Christian interpretation, but ends rather with his boots: Hopkins himself admitted the ending to be unsatisfactory in construction, as though boots were bound (as in 'Tom's Garland') to give him trouble, Harry's feet hidden in bluff hide (rough leather).

'Tom's Garland', yet another sonnet despite appearances, fourteen lines with two codas (tail-pieces) of three lines each, may mislead us initially by its subtitle, since only in the second coda (18–20) do the unemployed appear. Tom himself, a navvy, one of vast numbers of labourers engaged throughout the nineteenth century in cutting canals, railways, roads, helping to change the face and life of Britain, exemplifies the dignity of labour, that wants not rank or wealth, that wants no higher honour than being part of his country. England is imagined as a human figure: 'lordly head, | With heaven's lights high hung round, or, mother-ground | That mammocks, mighty foot' (10–12), an image drawn from the fable of the body, government as head, labourer as foot, invoked in Shakespeare's *Coriolanus*. That Hopkins had the play specifically in mind is clear from 'mammocks' ('rips up', 'tears'), a rare word used to describe Coriolanus's son tearing a butterfly, though here the navvy tears up the earth to the greater good of his country. The image of the state as a human body was a long established one in political and social thought, emphasising an organic and necessary relationship of part to part, each in its own station, if the commonwealth were to flourish for the good of all. Hence, Tom's garland of honour, which oddly at first is identified under his feet, in the hobnails of his boots, that rip out 'rockfire' (3) – his is an iron garland of the circling nails, opposed to the head's golden garland (the 'heaven's light', 11), the foot in the fable, and therefore its garland, necessarily being opposite to the head. This is not immediately clear and Hopkins found it necessary to explain the poem's underlying structure in detail (*L*, 1.272–74). 'O, once explained, how clear it all is', he wryly exclaims. Tom has work, wages and therefore food, hearth and contentment ('Heart-at-ease' against 'heartsore', 7) and if he occasionally thinks of his situation (interposed in a three-line parenthesis), 'he his low lot ... swings though' (5, 8), that is, he tosses such concern away 'as a light matter' (*L*, 1.273). But Tom is part of the Commonwealth: it is a darker vision on which the poem closes, in men turned beasts, the unemployed whose 'packs infest the age' (20).

Final poems: 'Fresh Woods'

Although the remaining poems that Hopkins wrote, in 1887 to 1889, were indeed his final poems, he himself had no apprehension of their finality. Creatively he had largely escaped from the Dark Night of the

'Terrible' Sonnets, though both 'St Alphonsus Rodriguez' (1888) and 'Justus Quidem Tu Es, Domine' (1889) reinflect his acute sense of pointlessness, near hopelessness, expressed in the earlier poems. Hopkins, though, having no necessary apprehension of death, was not shaping his poetic production as a final statement nor distilling the wisdom or imaginative power of his art. Few of us shape our lives, least of all the end of it, in that way and with Hopkins, rather, there are new directions, abandoned projects, possibilities in a life that might have stretched well into the twentieth century. Five poems show old interests freshly explored, new perspectives.

Hopkins called 'That Nature is a Heraclitean Fire' (1888) a sonnet, though if finished it is probably his most irregular effort, running to twenty-four lines, with no clear marker at the end of fourteen lines before the codas begin. Heraclitus, a Greek philosopher who flourished about 500 BC, believed 'everything flows' and that 'the world is an eternal and ever-changing modification of fire' (Barnes 1987: 39; and see 100–126). Hopkins may also have been struck by Heraclitus's insistence on the unity of opposites (Barnes 1987: 39), since such paradoxes lie close to the heart of religious doctrine, while in the poem's larger structure the flux of Heraclitus's world is set against yet reconciled to the permanence of God. Hopkins here returns to the great flow or flux of nature in its variety, its piedness – the clouds constantly moving and changing shapes in a play of the material world –

> Cloud-puffballs, torn tufts, tossed pillows flaunt forth, then
>   chevy on an air-
> Built thoroughfare: heaven-roysterers, in gay gangs they
>   throng ...
>
>   (1–2)

Another world is opened out by this inverted perspective from the solid world of earth to the roads and inhabitants of the sky, as earlier in Wales he had called forth the stars as 'fire-folk' in 'The bright boroughs, the circle-citadels there!' ('The Starlight Night', 2–3) [pp. 81–2]. Now, Hopkins has moved on, for though nature's bonfire (drawing on Heraclitus's claim that fire was the universal element) burns on, yet 'quench' nature's 'bonniest, dearest to her, her clearest-selv'd spark, | Man', and once dead, like the bonfire's spark, how quickly Man's 'firedint, his mark on mind, is gone' (11–12). 'Ashes to ashes', yet this is not a pessimistic poem. Rather, its optimism, though only achieved through images of bonfire and spark derived from an ancient Greek, finds out of shipwreck ('Across my foundering deck', 18) a dramatic impulse that clears the way to a Christian truth: 'Enough! the Resurrection, | A heart's-clarion!' (16–17). God paradoxically became man and Hopkins, in a unity of opposites of immortal and mortal, can become immortal and permanent (unlike the transient sparks that fly upwards: Job 5:7). Hopkins is only a contemptible fragment, 'Jack, joke, poor potsherd' (23), yet since Christ too became 'Jack, joke', they both are immortal diamond and this Jack (Hopkins) indeed, in the apparently redundant repetition that emphasises the paradox and closes up the poem in a final short line, 'Is immortal diamond' (24). The opposites of bonfire spark and eternal diamond fire, of pagan philosophy and Christian theology, of Christ's dual nature, sharing godhead with mortality, of mankind finding a god-like nature in the soul, are reconciled in the overarching form of the sonnet, its contrary impulses brought into harmonious vision.

Two sonnets, 'In Honour of St Alphonsus Rodriguez' (1888) and 'Justus Quidem Tu Es, Domine' (1889), might seem to stem from Hopkins's concern about his lack of achievement [p. 37] and the desolation of the 'Terrible' Sonnets. Yet both indicate how far Hopkins was exploring very different ways, personally or at least poetically, since that Dark Night of 1885–86. 'St Alphonsus Rodriguez' is far from the subjective horrors of the 'Terrible' Sonnets, an objective celebration of another person, yet the obscurity of Alphonsus's life, taken as a reflection of Hopkins's feelings about his own situation, can be consolatory as well as celebratory. It is a public poem, unlike the intimacy of the 'Terrible' Sonnets, asked for by the Jesuits of Majorca (L, 1.292–93), and the sonnet, Hopkins noted, knowing only too well Bridges's difficulties of understanding, '(I say it snorting) aims at being intelligible' (L, 1.293). Alphonsus Rodriguez (1531–1617; Attwatter 1965), after the death of his wife and children, became a lay member of the Jesuits and served as doorkeeper or porter at the House in Majorca for over forty years. He had been canonised in 1888 and his first feast day was to be celebrated on 30 October that year. While he made a deep impression by his wisdom and spirituality, his achievements were not obvious and the poem explores the nature of heroic virtue, requirement for a saint. Anyone may be a saint in God's eyes, but what caused Alphonsus to be recognised by the Church? He was not a founder or organiser like Ignatius Loyola, not a mystic and administrator like Teresa of Avila, not a theologian like Thomas Aquinas. While Hopkins never thought of himself as a saint nor likely to be one, Alphonsus's obscurity, working at a menial task, vibrates with Hopkins's own obscurity and educational drudgery. What serves God? The glory of sainthood 'is a flame off exploit' (1), but while this is most obvious in action that the world sees and admires, in the imitation of Christ as heroic warrior, explored in 'The Soldier' [pp. 115–6] or symbolised in the Perseus of 'Andromeda' [pp. 95–6], such holy war is not necessarily external and dramatic. Where 'war is within' (6), there is no obvious struggle, 'Earth hears no hurtle then from fiercest fray' (8) – and it was that conflict 'within' we are allowed to say, if he could not, that Hopkins endured in the Dark Night and in the drudgery that he endured in Dublin. Yet such struggle is as heroic as any, for God works in all things and in all actions,

> who, with fine increment
> Trickling, veins violets and tall trees makes more[,]
> Could crowd career with conquest ...
>
> (10–12)

And the poem ends with Alphonsus's achievement in a manner that almost seems commonplace, dreary, yet the verb 'watched' alerts us to the constantly living spirit of the saint, faithful to his task,

> while there went
> Those years and years by of world without event
> That in Majorca Alfonso watched the door.
>
> (12–14)

If 'St Alphonsus Rodriguez' allows us (as it could not its original or intended readers) to see how in some measure it reflects Hopkins's own concerns, so too does 'Justus Quidem Tu Es, Domine'. Here also though, while the sense of unfulfillment – he strains, 'Time's eunuch' (13) – echoes the 'Terrible' Sonnets, God is not absent and Hopkins objectifies the drama by starting from a puzzle that has long vexed religious thinking (if God is just, why do we see the good suffer, sinners prosper?) and he quotes directly from Jeremiah, one of the Old Testament's great prophets, who preached for years and yet failed to persuade the Jewish kingdom to change its ways. Tensions therefore are set up between the prophet and Hopkins's own meditation upon this problem of God's justice, between also Jeremiah's despair and his hope. What might seem, without knowledge of the title's Latin quotation, simply Hopkins addressing God, becomes an exploration and a dialogue. 'Righteous art thou, O Lord, when I plead with thee; yet let me talk with thee of thy judgments: Wherefore doth the way of the wicked prosper?' (Jeremiah 12: 1). The pleading before a just judge becomes at the end a prayer for help – for release from time's sterility through the desire for rain. The appeal of this cry to twentieth-century poets is obvious in the whole structure of T.S. Eliot's *The Waste Land*, a poem that might seem to spring from the sonnet's final words: 'send my roots rain'.

'The Shepherd's Brow' (1889), a strange poem moving between the epic grandeur of the fall of the angels from heaven (echoing Milton's *Paradise Lost*) and the insignificance of man, a 'scaffold of score brittle bones', allows also the grotesque but comic glimpse of Hopkins's own face in the distorting reflection of a spoon's bowl. The shepherd, out in the fields, faces the lightning and acknowledges 'The horror and the havoc and the glory | Of it' (2–3). Thunder accompanied the rebel angels' fall and so it is an appropriate musical underpinning or bass (the metaphor draws on Hopkins's renewed interest in musical composition), asserting God's glory as well as the epic horror of the rebels' overthrow. But as for man, the second quatrain demands, those brittle bones, gasping for breath, the very breath a reminder that death inevitably comes ('our *momento mori*', 7), what instrument plays the sustaining undertone to our condition? – 'What bass is *our* viol' (8) (a viol is an early string instrument). Man is ridiculous, scarcely can lay claim to 'tragic tones' as Satan's fallen crew might, for Jack (again, generic for all men) is a man, but only just. Man scrapes an existence and his body is shameful, with its excrement ('voids with shame', 9). Transferring from the general to the particular self, Hopkins pauses on his self-pitying representation, as though, caught in the midst of the every-day act of eating, he sees his distorted image in the spoon. We may leap forward to T.S. Eliot's image of futility in 'The Love Song of J. Alfred Prufrock' – 'I have measured out my life with coffee spoons', but more crucially should look back to a Victorian delight in grotesque forms, particularly in the way a spoon, like a funfair's distorting mirrors, can, upright, show us thin and sourfaced or, sideways, fat and jolly. The distorted image is both the 'bass' to the human condition, restoring a sense of proportion to humanity's 'tragic woe', and a reminder of how Hopkins delighted in the comic verse of Edward Lear. Made ludicrous, all our endeavours perhaps, momentarily, rendered futile, yet the perspective tames our tempests, grants a sense of proportion.

What seems undoubtedly Hopkins's last poem, 'To R.B.' (Robert Bridges), dated 22 April 1889, is not, as might be expected, a tribute or dedication to Bridges, but rather an explanation or 'apologia' for Hopkins's own 'lagging lines' (11), poetry that had no longer 'The roll, the rise, the carol, the creation' (12). It is a poem about poetry from one poet to another. The octave represents the process of artistic creation, that process of inspiration and the poem 'left behind' by it – very much a Romantic conception of poetic process – in the 'fine delight that fathers thought' (1), like a spur or the blowpipe's flame: Hopkins writing on the *Spiritual Exercises* had drawn on the blown flame, though to very different purpose (*S*, 242).

Inspiration, the fine delight, is the father, but the mother must endure the gestation of the child/poem for nine months, even nine years. To Dixon, apropos of music, Hopkins wrote, 'The disproportion is wonderful between the momentary conception of an air and the long long gestation of its setting' (L, 2.135; P, 388). After this impersonal (not therefore lifeless) account, Hopkins considers his own poetic case: 'I want the one rapture of an inspiration' (10), where 'want' does double duty both as 'lack' and 'desire', feeling himself in a 'winter world' (13). And yet the whole poem demonstrates the paradox of a poem about not being able to write poetry. Just as Yeats in 'The Circus Animals' Desertion' despairs of creation unless he lies down in the 'foul rag-and-bone shop of the heart' and in despairing has made a poem, so Hopkins shapes into a gracefully colloquial line the 'winter world' that 'yields you, with some sighs, our explanation' to conclude a fine sonnet that shows Hopkins engaged with the mysteries of his poetic craft even as the end of his life, all unsuspected, approached.

The Letters

The letters of Hopkins reveal him as man, priest and poet. They give biographical information about his early religious life; his decision to give up poetry on entering the Jesuits; his training and priesthood; his thinking about other poets: the rejection of Tennyson, the constant return to Milton, praise however qualified for Wordsworth and Walt Whitman, delight in Edward Lear; and his study of poetry, its rhythms and structures, that led to Sprung Rhythm. If not as entertaining or penetrating as the correspondence of the greatest letter-writers of the nineteenth century – Elizabeth Gaskell or Charles Dickens or Edward Fitzgerald, for example – Hopkins's letters trace his friendships, help us understand his poetry, with their detailed explanations of poems, and place him firmly in nineteenth-century life, an important corrective to the view of Hopkins as a twentieth-century poet

There are important series of letters to his family and to friends, three in particular, Coventry Patmore, R.W. Dixon and Robert Bridges. This range allows us to see that Bridges was not the only person Hopkins remained in touch with and shows how, as any letter-writer will, he wrote differently to different people. With Bridges he is on equal terms poetically, despite Bridges's persistent obtuseness about Hopkins's poetic aims and achievement and the constant tension over Hopkins as Catholic and Jesuit. With Dixon, a poet he immensely admired, Hopkins was often severely critical, yet since Dixon was an Anglican clergyman, they had in common the fact of belief and an understanding of the priestly office and duties. With Coventry Patmore, like Hopkins a Catholic convert, a poet who had given over poetry by the time he and Hopkins began to correspond in 1883, Hopkins was so intensely attentive to his poetry that Patmore declared he was stimulated to write again.

Hopkins's early letters relate mainly to his undergraduate days and immediately afterwards. His first experiences at Oxford are detailed with delight to his mother – rooms, friends, activities – in marked contrast to the painfulness and stiffness in writing to his father regarding his conversion (*L*, 3.91–5). Yet the continuing series to his mother shows Hopkins still in touch with his family, even if necessarily seeing far less of them, and his reconciliation with them. He sent his poems to his mother, one of that hidden audience that knew Hopkins's work in his lifetime. The life-long series of letters to Alexander Baillie, a Presbyterian and effectively a non-believer, shows how Hopkins could maintain friendship with those of very different religious opinions, as well as offering an often fascinating critical discussion of poets, sometimes expressed humorously – 'I have begun to *doubt* Tennyson' (*L*, 3.215) – and the nature of poetic language.

With Coventry Patmore, Hopkins began to correspond only in 1883 [**p. 38**]. Patmore, twenty years Hopkins's senior, was like him a Catholic convert and a poet, though by 1883 he thought his poetic life finished. Hopkins's criticism of Patmore's poetry, his 'careful and subtle fault-finding' (*L*, 3.324), based on a high estimate of a subtle and ironic writer, Patmore declared 'the greatest praise my poetry has ever received' (*L*, 3.324). More surely than Bridges, though often baffled by Hopkins's difficulties, he recognised the genius, the 'pure gold imbedded in masses of impracticable quartz' (*L*, 3.353 note).

Hopkins first wrote to R.W. Dixon in 1878 and the survival of both sides of the correspondence allows us to see directly Dixon's admiration of Hopkins's poetry, even if sometimes mixed with bewilderment. Dixon was ten years older than Hopkins and while a tenuous master–pupil relationship from Hampstead existed [**p. 7**], it was rather as a poet, long known and admired, that Hopkins contacted him. There was a sympathy between them, one priest to another, a sympathy conspicuously lacking in Hopkins's friendship with Bridges. To Dixon, Hopkins could write and expect to be understood, that the 'only just judge, the only just literary critic' is Christ (*L*, 2.8). It was to Dixon also that Hopkins could reveal the strange paradox of a classical scholar who was often at odds with the religious culture of his studies, finding in Greek mythology false history and false religion: if we face heathenism, 'literally words would fail me to express the loathing and horror with which I think of it' (*L*, 2.146). A depth of feeling about the truth of Christianity is revealed not to be found when writing to Bridges. While Hopkins's detailed consideration of Dixon's own poetry has only a specialised interest, since despite Sambrook's sympathetic study (1962), his poetic reputation has not flourished, the two men's letters show bonds of sympathy that helped sustain Hopkins.

While the correspondence with Bridges begins early and, with breaks, was sustained to the end of Hopkins's life, it is here considered last because it links naturally into Part III of this study. Bridges as friend, poet and editor, established a critical tradition that shaped early perceptions of Hopkins's poetry and can still skew our reading of it. It is a one-sided correspondence. While preserving all of Hopkins's letters to him (except two, which he deliberately destroyed), Bridges destroyed all his own letters when they came back to him after Hopkins's death. We can nonetheless form a good idea, from Hopkins's reactions, of their relationship, as well as a sense of Hopkins's diplomacy and self-assertion. He neither broke with Bridges nor simply accepted his comments on poetry or religion. Hopkins admired Bridges's poetry, but was at pains to point out that Bridges often, quite wilfully, misunderstood his, whether in detail or over the principle of Sprung Rhythm. Yet despite differences, in Hopkins's teasing defiance of Bridges by declaring himself 'in a manner ... a Communist' (L, 1.27) or in objecting, as 'strange and unpleasant', to Bridges's assumption that Hopkins's own beliefs had no reality for him (L, 1.148), the two remained friends. Hopkins felt he could unburden himself to Bridges, acknowledging in 1883 that 'there is no likelihood of my ever doing anything to last' (L, 1.183), or offering a glimpse in 1885 of 'that coffin of weakness and dejection in which I live, without even the hope of change' (L, 1.214–15). Hopkins offered much detailed criticism of Bridges's poetry and Bridges responded to Hopkins's, even if declaring he would not read 'The Wreck' again 'for any money' (L, 1.46). Hopkins asked him to do so, none the less, since 'Besides money, you know, there is love' (L, 1.46). Friendships can survive diverse personalities, may be built upon them, and at least Bridges, however misguidedly, felt that Hopkins was a poet and that his poetry must, eventually, be published. It took the best part of thirty years, though.

FURTHER READING

Criticism of Hopkins's poetry is dealt with in Part III. McChesney (1968), though, offers a careful commentary on the poems from 'The Wreck', onwards. Useful, though needing some caution when they expand into interpretation, are Mariani (1970) and, on 'The Wreck' and the sonnets, Milward (1968) and Milward (1969).

3

Criticism

Introduction

Hopkins felt the lack of readers and it was only in 1918, nearly thirty years after his death, that an edition of his poetry appeared and widespread reading, response and criticism were possible. Although Robert Bridges was scarcely the most sympathetic of critics, yet he held that he had a responsibility to Hopkins, to publish him and to prepare the ways to publication. And despite Bridges's reservations throughout those thirty years, expressed again at the first edition's publication, he unwittingly held back Hopkins to a time when everything Victorian in society and art was being challenged or rejected and Modernism was the dominant movement in literature and the arts, whether the poetry of T.S. Eliot and Ezra Pound, the fiction of Virginia Woolf and James Joyce, or the music of Stravinsky and Schoenberg. Modernism in literature stressed linguistic texture and detail, stressed discontinuity and intensity, so that Hopkins, though all his work was completed more than a decade before the Victorian age came to an end, was hailed both as a new writer and as a Modernist.

It was as a Modernist or at least a Modern – effectively a twentieth-century writer, not a Victorian – that Hopkins was treated through the 1920s and 1930s and on to the mid-century. Yet others perceived, very early, that historically and therefore aesthetically Hopkins was a Victorian, a current of thought culminating most obviously in Alison Sulloway's *Gerard Manley Hopkins and the Victorian Temper* (1972), but fed by the publication in the 1930s onwards of Hopkins's letters, journals and devotional writings.

Such assessment and reassessment complicated further the reading and understanding of Hopkins, since the terms 'Victorian' and 'Modernist' are not equivalents, the first being primarily chronological, the second aesthetic, assessment complicated too by the personality and career of Hopkins, who as a committed Catholic and priest, did not fit easily with the Victorian polarisation of Protestant Christianity and doubting secularism nor with the agnostics of the twentieth century who treated religious experience as neurotic or comic. Hopkins's delight in language and verbal virtuosity, despite links to the exuberance of Dickens or the dialect of William Barnes, might make him a Modern, but the intensity and sincerity of his Catholic belief and experiences ultimately set him off from the aesthetic and atheistic attitudes (often collapsed into a single expressive entity) of Modernist writers and critics. For Hopkins a poem must mean as well as be.

After a brief consideration of who were Hopkins's earliest readers, this section looks at the critical explorations, often a grappling with meaning and technique, charted by Hopkins himself and responses during his lifetime. Attention is given to how Bridges prepared an audience for the 1918 publication and critical responses to that event. The embracing of Hopkins as a Modern is traced and the counter-current of Hopkins as Victorian. But Hopkins has claims to be a poet beyond or apart from both those terms, as a poet of nature, as a religious poet, and as an exploiter of techniques and theories. Attention will be given to traditions of reading of particular poems and a conclusion, 'Shaping the Reputation', will attempt to 'place' Hopkins critically at the mid-twentieth century and into the twenty-first century.

Earliest readers

Hopkins admitted wryly that his oddity, deprecated by Robert Bridges, might arise through lack of audience. Yet we should not think of him as entirely without readers until Bridges commented upon his work. He must surely have been encouraged, however fleetingly, by the schoolboy success of 'The Escorial' [**pp. 44–5**] and of 'Winter with the Gulf Stream' [**pp. 46–7**]. At Oxford, Hopkins published 'Barnfloor and Winepress' [**pp. 50–1**] in the *Union Review*. Within the Jesuits, he was known as a poet and was encouraged to write the May verses [**pp. 93–4**] and the Silver Jubilee poem [**p. 79**]. But these poems, even the Marian poems and the Silver Jubilee verses, were in Hopkins's early style, conventional in technique at least, and therefore unlikely to startle or give offence. The problem of criticism arose with 'The Wreck'. Accepted for publication, it did not appear and finally was returned, without comment. Rejection, especially after acceptance, was bitter to Hopkins, for this was the poem where, on his superior's hint, and with a new rhythm in his ear, he felt he might write poetry again. Once or twice it again seemed a poem might be published, but none were. While size of audience may not count for much, silence and incomprehension are not encouraging.

HOPKINS AS CRITIC

Hopkins was a critic, not systematically, often casually, of the poetry and poetic diction important to him and which helped shape his perception of what poetry ought to be and what his own poetry strove to be. C.C. Abbott observes that Hopkins's criticism probably 'dates him with more certainty than any other part of his writing' (*L*, 1. xvi note), yet Hopkins's criticism is significantly different from the expectations raised by his time and his contemporaries. While a young man he was necessarily influenced by the Romantic and earlier Victorian poets. If Keats's sensory delight infuses 'A Vision of the Mermaids' [**pp. 45–6**], yet it was Wordsworth rather than Keats that remained important to him. Wordsworth's sonnets might have an 'odious goodiness and neckcloth about them which half throttles their beauty' (*L*, 1.38), yet beauty was there still in the precision of syntax and perception, while Wordsworth, however unlike his beliefs, in youth or age, were to Hopkins's own, was a man who had seen '*something*' beyond the ordinary (*L*, 2.147) as few others had, and that '*something*' was deeply serious and deeply worth trying to understand and to emulate, however differently inflected by Hopkins's own beliefs.

It was the lack of seriousness, of precision in thought, a lifelessness of language matched to mechanical exactness, a failure to find the essence of poetry (however impossible that might be to define or illustrate) that Hopkins increasingly found fault with in his Victorian predecessors. Tennyson, Browning, perhaps Matthew Arnold, were the established living poets of Hopkins's youth and he rightly admired Tennyson for his lyrical beauty and Browning for a willingness to experiment with language ('Gr-r-r – there go, my heart's abhorrence! Water your damned flower-pots, do!'), but Tennyson's exactness of syllables and metres in 'Locksley Hall', high technical achievements, eventually wearied him (*L*, 2.19), while Browning had energy but no subtlety, 'a way of talking ... of a man ... saying that he meant to stand no blasted nonsense' (*L*, 2.74).

All this was untrue to nature: a statement that opens the whole question of what is nature. To define what he means by truth to nature, Hopkins invokes that most Victorian of critical adages: the touchstone of 'the highest or most living art is seriousness; not gravity but the being in earnest with your subject – reality' (*L*, 1.225). By this criticism, Hopkins rejects the Catholic poet, Dante, but embraces Milton in *Paradise Lost*: the theology of the poet is *here* less important than the conviction of the poet. Dante, knowing it is all invention, delights in putting his enemies into Hell regardless of merit, while Milton believes as Puritan *and* poet that something is at stake. The intricate verbal texture of Milton, his controlled yet variable rhythms, are all directed to a purpose and so Milton is a poet admired and used as a model by Hopkins [**pp. 132; 178; 184–5**].

Hopkins stressed both Milton's meaning and his technique. His academic training in Classics led Hopkins to listen to rhythm and to think about rhythm, stress, and language. He developed theories about the 'counterpointing' of ideas and rhythm in the choruses of Greek tragedy and, criticising Robert Bridges's rhythms, observed 'I have paid much attention to Milton's rhythm' (*L*, 1.37). He might seem to contradict himself when he claims strict metrical regularity in 'The Wreck', even while declaring that his rhythms 'go further than [Bridges's] do in the way of irregularity' (*L*, 1.45, 38), yet the very nature of Sprung Rhythm is to allow rhythmic variation within a stress pattern that is meticulously established and followed [**pp. 68–9**], since what Hopkins sought, unlike his Victorian predecessors and incomprehensibly to Bridges, was nearest to the rhythm of prose while never becoming prose, that is, 'the native and natural rhythm of speech, the least forced, the most rhetorical and emphatic of all possible rhythms' (*L*, 1.46). The voice is key to understanding Hopkins – listen, speak him aloud, but Bridges could not hear: fortunately, other readers even in Hopkins's lifetime could, as could the new readers of the twentieth century.

None the less, Hopkins hoped to convert Bridges, first and fore-most, to an understanding of 'The Wreck' and sympathy with it, as he sought by explication to persuade Dixon and Patmore. He acknowledged faults, oddity, obscurity, noting, almost wistfully, in the year before he died, 'what I want ... to be more intelligible, smoother, and less singular, is an audience' (*L*, 1.291).

HOPKINS: POET IN WAITING

In October 1918, Hopkins's poems were finally published in reason-ably complete form. Bridges had had copies of them for many years and was effectively regarded (mistakenly, but understandably) as the copyright holder. He clearly recognised Hopkins as a major poet, yet essentially lacked either sympathy or understanding of Hopkins as Catholic, priest, and poet. Even his praise was usually qualified: in

1878 he acknowledged the 'poetry is magnificent but "caviare to the general"' (Phillips 1992: 91) and in 1914, when urged to prepare an edition, refused on the grounds that the poetry was of a 'very difficult & unpopular nature'; its publication could lead only to 'adverse criticism & ridicule' (Phillips 1992: 242).

And yet the existence of a poet unknown though potentially exciting was emerging, if often obscured by Bridges's own efforts to prepare for the 1918 edition. In 1893, Bridges arranged for eleven poems of Hopkins, seven of them complete, to be included in Alfred Miles's *The Poets and the Poetry of the Nineteenth Century* (Miles 1906: 179–88). Bridges's introduction declares that if all Hopkins's poems were gathered, they are 'so full of experiments in rhythm and diction', they would appear 'a unique effort in English literature' (Miles 1906: 179–80), praise qualified not only by there being no collection, but more devastatingly by the critical qualification: 'Most of his poems are religious, and marked with Catholic theology, and almost all are injured by a natural eccentricity, a love of subtlety and uncommonness' (Miles 1906: 180). Further, Bridges stresses Hopkins's distance from 'the ordinary simplicity of grammar and metre' (Miles 1906: 182), impudence coming from the Bridges of syllabic metres and grotesque insensibility to language. Bridges released a few more poems in his vastly popular anthology, *The Spirit of Man* (1916), though less than one stanza of 'The Wreck'.

Still, Hopkins was becoming known, perhaps only to a small number, but those with some influence. And if there was a growing impression, promoted by Bridges, of Hopkins's unconventionality, there was too a growing impression of someone who should be read and should be made available. Roger Fry, a pioneer of the Modern, organiser of the 1910 Post-Impressionist exhibition in London that Virginia Woolf saw as the moment when sensibility shifted from Victorian to Modern, was enthusiastic in 1896 after seeing poems in manuscript, including 'The Windhover' (Fry 1972: I, 165). Hopkins was duly to be caught up in the mood that rejected Tennyson, rejected the Victorians, notoriously in Lytton Strachey's lively if mendacious *Eminent Victorians* (1918), and that embraced the very qualities in poetry that Bridges saw and denigrated in Hopkins. Hopkins was being removed, by Bridges and by Fry, though in very different ways, from the Victorian era to the Modern.

Robert Bridges's edition of Hopkins in 1918 is curious in one respect: there is no introduction, but, printed after the poetry, a long Preface to the Notes, an account first of editorial procedures and then a critical summary. At least Bridges's eccentricities did not intrude immediately on the reader, though there clearly enough.

Questions of taste come first: affectation in metaphor; the 'perversion of human feeling' in religious reference; the forcing of emotion into theological or sectarian channels; and, for good measure, the 'exaggerated Marianism' of some pieces (Jenkins 2006: 50). These faults are few, Bridges admits, yet affect his liking 'and more repel my sympathy than do all the rude shocks of his purely artistic wantonness' (Jenkins 2006: 50). Content and technique he condemns both. Even when Bridges allows, later, that 'this poet has always something to say', the observation comes among faults gathered under the twin extravagances of Oddity and Obscurity (Jenkins 2006: 50). Hopkins's use of language is often ambiguous, rhymes often peculiar and therefore repellent, indeed when Hopkins 'indulges in freaks, his childishness is incredible' (Jenkins 2006: 52). Special notice was reserved for 'The Wreck', acknowledged as a 'great metrical experiment', standing, in notorious phrase, 'like a great dragon folded in the gate to forbid all entrance' (Jenkins 2006: 117). The more sympathetic reader might well feel the forbidding dragon to be not 'The Wreck' but Bridges.

When the poems appeared in a second edition (1930), the reputation of Hopkins had shifted. In only twelve years he had become known as a major poet for the twentieth century. Now Charles Williams, a devout Anglican, introduced the volume. He stressed what he felt to be a neglected feature of Hopkins's technique, his alliteration, contrasting it with Swinburne's, a close contemporary of Hopkins's, concluding that 'the astonishing thing about Swinburne is not [alliteration's] presence, but its uselessness, as the admirable thing about Hopkins is not its presence but its use' (Hopkins 1930: x). Hopkins is a poet fully in control, technically, a poet not of word-play but of passion, a point illustrated from the opening stanza of 'The Wreck', that dragon in the gate, 'in which the intense apprehension of the subject provides two or more necessary words almost at the same time' (Hopkins 1930: xi). Hopkins's language vitalises the reader and makes it necessary to read, to react with, the whole poem. The linguistic devices

> persuade us of the existence of a vital and surprising poetic energy; ... they suspend our attention from any rest until the whole thing, whatever it may be, is said.
>
> (Hopkins 1930: xii)

The poems have not changed between 1918 and 1930, but the reader has and Williams goes on to see Milton as the great forebear of Hopkins. Neither was a mystic, though both on the verge of mystical vision. Their vision is complex, yet controlled:

The simultaneous consciousness of a controlled universe, and yet of division, conflict, and crises within that universe, is hardly so poignantly expressed in any other English poets …

(Hopkins 1930: xiv)

Coming to know Hopkins: 1935-60

Increasing interest in Hopkins's poetry duly led to editions of his Letters (Vols 1 & 2, 1935; Vol. 3, 1938), Journals (1959), and the Sermons and Devotional Writings (1959). How important these are in understanding the man, priest and poet is shown by this study's reliance on them. The introduction to the first two volumes of the letters (those to Bridges and the correspondence with Dixon) includes an important critical assessment by the editor, C.C. Abbott, an essay 'towards the understanding of a poet for whose work I have a particular reverence and affection' (L, 1.x). He stresses that since the 1930s, Hopkins has been accepted by the young as a con-temporary, though emphasising that Hopkins was an Englishman and a Victorian: 'He may be a strange Victorian, but he belongs to that company' (L, 1.xxi). What Abbott identifies as the essential qualities of Hopkins as a poet include the very features that Bridges too identified, only to condemn. Abbott, aware of weaknesses in what is often *experimental* work (L, 1, xxiii), yet sees in Hopkins's poetry 'a magnificent concentration by the elimination of weak words and the determination to say nothing at second hand' (L, 1.xxii). And for Abbott, with whatever other qualifications, 'The Wreck' is not a dragon denying entrance, but the triumphant gateway, since 'it made his style, and his confidence in himself as poet, secure' (L, 1.xxvii). Abbott also distinguishes between the phases of Hopkins's poetic production, finding the exuberant nature poetry of 1877–80 the most immediately attractive, while in the mature middle period (1880–83), he finds a 'clouding over of that fresh vision' and, drawing on Hopkins's own words, 'a mood more charged with meditation that fathers a weightier utterance and demands for its expression a more intricate music' (L, 1.xxxvii). The last phase, for Abbott, the 'Terrible' Sonnets, is 'a chart of despair, agony, and frustration' (L, 1.xxxviii), with no relief or serenity in Hopkins's last years, and Abbott declares the 'pity of these poems is hardly to be borne' (L, 1.xxxix), reminding us that Hopkins's poems appeared in 1918, at the end of the First World War. The poet Wilfred Owen, killed in that war, had stated that 'My subject is War, and the pity of War. The Poetry is in the pity' (Owen 1963: 31), and while Hopkins was, for many of his early readers, a Modernist, he could also be seen as a poet struggling with his own experience of war against a deadly enemy. That perception shapes many readings of the poetry, since it brings life and poetic career to a desperate climax, rather than to the comparative relief and new experiments earlier suggested here [pp. 117–8]. Abbott, though he has none of Bridges's distaste for Catholicism, is cautious about Hopkins as a religious poet: while not a mystic, Hopkins reveals 'the loveliness of God's kingdom on earth, the beauty of those made in His image, and the pains of mortality' (L, 1.xliii).

No such assessment of the poetry is made by Graham Storey in his introduction (1959) to the Journals, though the journals themselves feed into our understanding of Hopkins's eye and exultation. Devlin's edition of the *Sermons and Devotional Writings* (1959) is more revelatory, since while it says nothing directly about the poetry, it rightly emphasises Hopkins as priest and the excitement that could be stirred in him by religious feelings and ideas, things that some critics shy away from, as though it were possible to make Hopkins into *merely* a nature poet. Devlin notes how striking is 'the objective enthusiasm which wells up in him unfailingly when some lofty theme or subtle overtone attracts him' (S, xiv), and points to the centrality for Hopkins, as in Christianity itself, of the Incarnation, Christ coming as man, and the Great Sacrifice of Christ on the cross, as well as Hopkins's insistence that these events were not dependent on the Fall of Man. They would have taken place even if there had been no Fall and so all creation is dependent upon the decree of the Incarnation (S, 109), hence Hopkins's constant linking of nature, God's creation, with God's purpose and meaning. Devlin sees stages in Hopkins's work, essentially those of Abbott, that take their inflections from the central truth, a shifting from the presence of God's design or inscape in inanimate nature (Abbott's 'nature' poetry of 1877–80), to the working out of that design, by stress and instress, in the minds and wills of men (S, 109).

Hopkins as Modern: 1918–30

In 1950, surveying, as his title stated, *Crisis in English Poetry 1880–1940*, Vivian de Sola Pinto placed that crisis as beginning about thirty years before the outbreak of the First World War, and as part of a larger moral, intellectual, social and economic crisis, the effects of which were felt throughout the first half of the twentieth century (Pinto 1958: 9). Whatever the rights or wrongs of Bridges's delay in publishing, many felt that Hopkins benefited from being published as a 'Modern' in 1918 rather than a Victorian in 1890. If a new kind of poetry, indeed of literature, was needed to express a 'schism in the soul' (Pinto 1958: 12) and if poetry, indeed all writing, must be 'difficult' to express that crisis and that schism, demanding the reader should work in the enterprise of exploration and expression, then Hopkins in his language, in his rhythms, in the 'Terrible' Sonnets, could be hailed as a Modern. Pinto stressed, rather distorting the biographical evidence, that the 'Terrible' Sonnets, showing 'a new starkness and clarity', were among 'the great tragic utterances of the modern crisis, representing not only the agony of the dying priest to whom his religion brought no comfort, but the complaint of modern humanity', isolated, 'faced with the horror of spiritual disharmony' (Pinto 1958: 79).

Modernism in literature was characterised by a breakdown or abandoning of plot in fiction; of a freeing of poetry from strict metres or logical sequence, with a structure compressed and fragmented, built up through images and symbols; the representation of a world both mundanely ordinary and yet sensational for the (ideally) vivid consciousness of the individual experiencing it; an ironic note, too (very remote from Hopkins, even at his most playful), that allowed perspectives on experience and individuals as the artist stood aloof from the 'young man carbuncular' of *The Waste Land*. Yet the very 'difficulties' that Bridges had so insistently stressed in his 1918 Preface – ambiguity of language, rhymes repellent, freakish and childish – were things that Modernism embraced.

The early critics were well aware from Bridges's Preface and notes of when Hopkins died, his subsequent obscurity, his Catholicism and priesthood. But the focus was on the Modern rather than the Religious, still less (by most) on the Catholic. The 1920s and 1930s saw a reaction against the formalised religion of the Victorians, though artists embraced their own creeds of Socialism, Marxism, Freudianism, or Fascism. Even before the 1918 publication, J.M. Hone noted (1917) that Hopkins was 'in reaction against most of the literary influences of the nineteenth century' (Roberts 1987: 11), and by the 1930s it was (virtually) a dogma that Hopkins belonged, as in some sense he did, 'temperamentally and technically to the 20th century' (Roberts 1987: 20). Along with an appeal to Modernism, the early twentieth century saw a reaction against Romanticism and a discovery of the Metaphysical poets, principally John Donne, who were praised by twentieth-century critics for their direct use of the speaking voice ('Busy old fool, unruly Sun' or 'For God's sake, hold your tongue, and let me love'), a characteristic that many critics picked up from Hopkins's own Preface and his declaration that but 'take breath and read ... with the ears ... and my verse becomes all right' (*L*, 1.79).

The early critics of Hopkins's poetry were remarkably welcoming, especially given Bridges's caveats, and while many naturally hedged their bets, they found much of interest and value. Technique necessarily figured largely. E. Brett Young in 1918, pre-publication, while seeing aspects of the 'elaborately wrought verse' as no more deserving of attention than the 'curious decoration of a missal', goes on to praise adventures in technique, 'a subtlety of workmanship', as Hopkins strove to translate 'the delight of a quick eye into terms that would please a subtle ear' (Roberts 1987: 74–75). Others, while admitting that difficulty of technique, insisted it lay in the very nature of Hopkins's enterprise and need. If for Hopkins poetry meant difficulty, 'he wrote it to say more than could be said otherwise; it was ... a packing of words with sense, both emotional and intellectual' (Roberts 1987: 84), while Theodore Maynard, recognising the priest, hailed him as a Modern, his poetry showing the heroism of a saint, 'as if every word had been born in anguish and had awoken with a cry' (Roberts 1987: 88). While comparatively little emphasis, beyond the biographical fact, was placed upon Hopkins as Catholic and priest, some reviewers noted it, and if the *Dial* (1919) thought him 'too prevailingly theological to gain a wide reading' (Roberts 1987: 116), others variously stressed Hopkins's power as a Catholic poet or a Modernist in crisis trying to reconcile faith with experience. The *Saturday Westminster Gazette* (1919), the anonymous reviewer very likely a Catholic, thought Hopkins's 'mystical passion ... coloured by a deep consciousness of the greatness and terror of that Power which he feels in closest contact with his soul' (Roberts 1987: 99), but the secular I.A. Richards (1926), acclaiming Hopkins's demands on the reader, found a modern (or Modernist) 'appalling tension' between belief and experience (Roberts 1987: 145). This difference between the *Gazette* and Richards highlights a debate that continues, about the nature of Hopkins the Catholic [**pp. 162–4**]. Whether to reject or accept Hopkins, though, virtually ceases to be an issue, because the critics who took over from the early reviewers were not ones to waste time on a poet they felt to be of no value or incomprehensible.

That Hopkins was guilty of no 'innocuous Victorian smoothness' (Roberts 1987: 135) and had an 'acutely conscious modern mind' (Roberts 1987: 96) became the accepted critical viewpoints, rather than that he was 'immediately incomprehensible', with 'a discordant defiance of verbal beauty actively unpleasant' (Roberts 1987: 112), though as late as 1936, G.M. Young, reviewing the *Oxford Book of Modern Verse* in the *London Mercury* rejected modern (not just Modernist) poetry in general and Hopkins in particular. Young declared that there had been an abandonment of a poetic tradition, 'not a development but a catastrophe, a gash at the root of our poetry' (Young 1937: 202). Hopkins, indeed, is the chief legislator of the new mode, and Young enters into a perilous contradiction when he declares 'the greatest admiration' for him as a poet, yet Hopkins's theories on metre seem 'as demonstrably wrong as those of any speculator who has ever led a multitude into the wilderness to perish' (Young 1937: 202).

Part of Young's concern clearly is about Hopkins's influence on other poets, and this is a question often raised in early reviews: how would Hopkins be absorbed and what would his effect be? The most sensible thought his techniques were so distinctly his own, that no true poet would imitate Hopkins and after all, Hopkins himself said that studying masterpieces made him 'admire and do otherwise' (*L*, 1.291). It was variously claimed that the younger generation, of W.H. Auden, Stephen Spender and C. Day Lewis, were trying to imitate his 'tremor of expectancy' (Roberts 1987: 36), though perhaps the only wholly successful 'imitator' has been Dylan Thomas, in the exuberance of poems like 'Fern Hill' and the word-compounding and dark symbolism of the 'Altar-wise by Owl-light' sequence.

HOPKINS AS MODERN: 1930–60

The new phase from about 1930 of Hopkins criticism, that sees him as a Modern, though increasingly conditioned by the publication of the Letters, Journals, and Devotional Writings, was conditioned too by a shift into academic discussion. This phase is highlighted by William Empson's *Seven Types of Ambiguity* (1930). As critical close reading developed in university studies, so the linguistic texture of poetry was emphasised, as well as the poem as a free-standing object, not to be contaminated by historical or biographical infor-mation, Cleanth Brooks's *The Well Wrought Urn* (1947) being the most influential study. Empson's book struck at the very objections Bridges had raised to Hopkins's poetry and struck too at the Victorians: difficulty was a mark of modern poetry and ambiguity of language was inherent in all poetry. For Empson, much Victorian poetry was bad because it took from the Romantics the idea of poetry as per-sonal expression, but without doing the necessary work (Empson 1965: 17), so that poetry became an emotional bath in which to wallow without thought or effort. Empson rightly asserted (and felt the need to assert) that poetry was not simply a matter of 'Pure Sound' and 'Atmosphere': meaning mattered, while by its nature, language is constantly open to alternative meanings, which the reader needs to take on board.

With Hopkins, Empson first chooses 'Spring and Fall' [pp. 103–4] and focuses on 'will' in l.9: 'And yet you *will* weep and know why'. Is 'will' the future – 'you will weep in the future and *then* know why' – or is it an emphatic auxiliary – 'you insist *now* upon knowing why you weep': the child's perception and the poem's meaning would be very different according to which is chosen, though Hopkins makes clear that if it represents the child's demand for present enlightenment, it is refused: 'Now no matter, child, the name'. Empson's close focus upon a single word, not the poem as a whole, insists that *both* meanings are possible, because the ambiguity allows it and the complexity represents the poet's state of mind. Later, Empson chooses one of Hopkins's greatest and most discussed poems, 'The Windhover' [pp. 84–6], to show 'the use of poetry to convey an indecision, and its reverberations in the mind' (Empson 1965: 224). Empson sees an opposition in the poem, the 'active physical beauty of the bird' being 'the opposite of [Hopkins's] patient spiritual renunciation' (Empson 1965: 225). These 'Freudian' opposites intrigue Empson and he seizes on the word 'buckle' (to be followed by most readers since, however mistaken some of their interpretations), which in its ambiguity can connect or disrupt: connect if taken as in fastening a belt, or disrupt if taken as a bicycle wheel crumpling up. Empson's delighted pursuit of the ambiguous leads him away from the simpler to the more complex reading, since Hopkins's 'buckle' is the integration of forces into a greater singleness, not a disastrous smash. The religious element of the poem is not seriously investigated, Modernism commonly disregarding the spiritual experience in favour of the mundane or naturalistic, though Empson's own hostility to God, stimulatingly if perversely manifest in *Milton's God* (1961), is here absent.

Empson, at Cambridge, was a student of I.A. Richards, a pioneer of close reading, as was Elsie Elizabeth Phare, who wrote the first single author study, *The Poetry of Gerard Manley Hopkins* (1933). Phare found it useful to look back from the twentieth century to the Romantics and to Wordsworth in particular, to 'place' Hopkins, eliding the Victorian age. Yet she does not see Hopkins inheriting Wordsworth's power of representing the primitive or tracing the 'primary laws of our nature' in incidents of his own everyday experience (Phare 1933: 47). She finds herself uncomfortable, in a way not provoked by Wordsworth (nor, by implication, by the Victorians), in the representation of the Bugler's first communion (Phare 1933: 48), clearly as a result of the conflict in the poem between declared spiritual delight and undeclared sensual desire [p. 102]. Yet if Hopkins fails for her in simplicity and directness, he succeeds in 'The Bugler' in the exploration of 'his own complicated reactions to the incident' (Phare 1933: 50), and it is this psychological quest, written with the whole man, in which 'he never separates soul and body', never attempts 'to emerge all spirit', that demonstrates his 'peculiar adequacy to experience' (Phare 1933: 75). While Phare recognises Hopkins's belief and priesthood, she values more highly what may be thought a twentieth-century concern with inner struggle. Phare does not make Hopkins a Modernist, but she does make him a Modern, troubled as twentieth-century artists were (or were supposed to be), yet bold enough never to take refuge in an imaginary world, 'nor even in a world purely of the spirit' (Phare 1933: 76).

If Phare, relating Hopkins to a tradition stemming back to Wordsworth, used that tradition to question part of his achievement, she none the less praises the inward struggle and its representation. Not all critics were so discriminating nor indeed so understanding of the nature of poetic structures. Yvor Winters in two essays, published in 1932 and 1949, the second reprinted in *The Function of Criticism* 1966 [1957], while acknowledging Hopkins as 'a truly great poet' (Roberts 1987: 225), doubted whether being 'a radical technical innovator' was sufficient to make him a greater poet than those less radical. Hopkins, he declared, 'can express with his violent rhythms an extremely special kind of excitement arising from religious experience, but he can express little else' (Roberts 1987: 225), a judgement amplified in 1949, by devising a tradition and theory of poetry that by-passed the Victorians, according to 'a particular theory of poetry' (Winters 1966 [1957]: 37), in which Hopkins comes off decidedly worst. Winters's 'particular theory' seems so general as to be unhelpful to any kind of conclusive comparison: 'A poem is a statement in words, and about a human experience, and it will be successful so far as it realizes the possibilities of that kind of statement' (Winters 1966 [1957]: 37). Winters's bewilderment in the face of 'No worst, there is none' [pp. 111–2] and 'The Windhover' [pp. 84–6] suggests an inability to understand the working of image or metaphor. That he dismisses the opening of 'The Windhover', with its 'dapple-dawn-drawn falcon' as 'merely description' (Winters 1966 [1957]: 49), suggests the critic's inadequacy rather than the poet's. A more successful attempt to understand Hopkins's use of language and his aesthetic approach is Geoffrey Hartman's in *The Unmediated Vision* (1966). While he can be obscure at times, Hartman is alert to how language works in poetry and like Phare, though expressing it differently, he explores (and elevates) Hopkins's fascination with physical beauty and the beauty of the Incarnation: 'Christ, as he appears in Hopkins, is dangerously near to physical man, while man is still dangerously near to physical beauty' and it is 'The Windhover', rejected by

Winters, that Hartman sees as the finest outpouring by Hopkins of that praise of 'the eternal nativity of Christ in the physical and sensuous world' (Hartman 1966: 60).

Another version of Hopkins as a Modernist, is John Wain's 'An Idiom of Desperation' (1959). Wain first acknowledges that Hopkins was of course a Victorian, who necessarily drew materials from his literary environment, though his structures were entirely different. Indeed, any affinities with poets of his age are with the Nonsense poets, Lewis Carroll and Edward Lear [p. 58], where what is in their minds turns out to be 'nightmare, guilt, privation, and dread' (Wain 1966 [1959]: 60). Wain offers as example of difference a comparison of Bridges's 'London Snow' and Hopkins's 'Felix Randal', concluding, against Winters's judgement, that Hopkins 'has life, waywardness, density, action, where Bridges gives us nothing but a picturesque scene' (Wain 1966 [1959]: 59). Identifying in Hopkins two qualities, irreducibility and simultaneity, as Modernism's hallmarks of poetry, Wain traces these characteristics through the Romantics and French nineteenth-century poets, to place Hopkins in a tradition, yet also isolating Hopkins bleakly as desperate, since only 'someone who was completely alone could have produced an art that takes so little and gives so much' (Wain 1966 [1959]: 69). This may be a gnomic conclusion, yet Wain both 'places' Hopkins as modern, while stressing his individuality and power.

Accepted first as modern or even a Modern, Hopkins gradually came to be seen as a Victorian, in his origins and in his concerns. The shift can be traced during the 1930s in the writings of F.R. Leavis. Leavis proclaimed that aesthetic judgement is the business of the mind, not merely of the feelings. In *New Bearings in English Poetry* (1932), exploring the poetry of Modernism, he identified Victorian poetry as the end product of a tradition, stemming from the Romantics, which rejected 'Wit, play of intellect, stress of cerebral muscle', which 'could only hinder the reader's being "moved"' (Leavis 1963: 16). The Victorian poets, recognising an alien world, took refuge in dreams; the Modern poets face the alien, recalcitrant, and unpoetical (Leavis 1963: 21). Hopkins is a great poet because he had mind, sensibility, and spirit, and he has the technique too, bringing poetry closer to living speech, a poet who must be read with the body as well as the eye (Leavis 1963: 140). Leavis, indeed, sheers away from Hopkins as Catholic and Jesuit, the technique being that of a great poet (a great 'modern' poet) 'when it is at the service of a more immediately personal urgency, when it expresses not religious exaltation, but inner debate' (Leavis 1963: 147). Hopkins stands here with Ezra Pound and T.S. Eliot.

Hopkins as Victorian

Yet even as Leavis declares Hopkins is 'now felt to be a contemporary', he acknowledges him historically as a Victorian who, recognisably a Modern, is likely 'to prove ... the only influential poet of the Victorian age, and ... the greatest' (Leavis 1963: 156). Leavis took this further in an 'Evaluation' (1944), prompted by the centenary of Hopkins's birth and reprinted in *The Common Pursuit* (1952). While Hopkins is superior as poet, he is placed alongside Tennyson and Matthew Arnold as a 'nature poet', a term 'applicable enough for one to accept it as a way of bringing out how much Hopkins belongs to the Victorian tradition' (Leavis 1962: 45). And now Leavis too admits that it is impossible to discuss Hopkins for long without coming to his religion. Hopkins, put down by others as 'the devotional poet of a dogmatic Christianity', is 'rescued' by his religious interests being bound up with 'a vigour of mind that puts him in another poetic world from the other Victorians' (Leavis 1962: 48). So Leavis separates Hopkins from the other Victorians and yet plays down his religious experience, finding that the 'Terrible' Sonnets were produced by a personal rather than a religious pressure (Leavis 1962: 57).

HOPKINS THE VICTORIAN: RESPONSES 1917–40

To the earliest readers it was clear that chronologically Hopkins was a Victorian, for while Robert Bridges did not provide a biographical outline to the 1918 *Poems*, his notes give dates. Yet, even allowing for Bridges's cautious preparations for the poems' publication, for most readers Hopkins came suddenly upon them, fully formed, in a world very different from that of Tennyson, Browning or Matthew Arnold, a world very different too in its political and social landscapes. Accordingly, Hopkins was treated by many as a contemporary and a Modern rather than as a Victorian and a Victorian poet. Already in 1917, J.M. Hone had claimed, in clear terms of praise, that Hopkins was 'in reaction against most of the literary influences of the nineteenth century' (Roberts 1987: 11), and even those earlier readers who condemned Hopkins still condemned him as a Modern rather than as a Victorian. In 1934 Edith Sitwell, a poet sensitive to the movement and sound of language, named names when she found Hopkins's rhythmical principles arose from feeling and instinct, principles the same as those of Ezra Pound, Wilfred Owen and T.S. Eliot (Roberts 1987: 271). Yet by the 1930s a different kind of perception was gathering. Humphry House, in reviewing Phare's book [**pp. 138–9**], declared that Hopkins's very appearance thirty years after his death had helped wrench him out of context, indeed that 'in the whole structure of his thought and imagery Hopkins does not belong to our generation at all' – House was born in 1908 – 'and that his adoption into it is excessively misleading' (Roberts 1987: 263). Yet how distinctive Hopkins is, however part and parcel of his own age, is apparent when a year later (1935) House placed him not as a Victorian, nor even particularly as a Catholic or Mystic, since the 'Terrible' Sonnets did not represent the Dark Night of the Soul [pp. 107; 109–10], but something 'more elementary and universal' (Roberts 1987: 308). Hopkins might be Modern or Victorian, yet he was also himself alone and not easily to be bent to the agenda of another, of T.S. Eliot, for example, that 'high-priest' of Modernism, who by the mid-1930s increasingly conservative in politics, religion, and poetry, rather startlingly declared Hopkins, however metrically innovative, unable to help in 'the struggle ... against Liberalism' (Roberts 1987: 286).

HOPKINS THE VICTORIAN: THE BIOGRAPHICAL SHAPING 1930–92

Necessarily, readers of the poetry did not find it easy to see Hopkins as a Victorian when they had little beyond a general biographical sense. But in the 1930s, as the Letters and Journals appeared, and then in the 1950s the revised Journals and Papers and the Devotional Writings, not only was a large body of original writing available, interesting in itself, but also material towards a biography. Stimulated by Hopkins's burgeoning poetic reputation and by such publications, investigation of Hopkins's life, material and spiritual, gathered momentum, through to the 1990s.

The first biography in any formal sense, G.F. Lahey's *Gerard Manley Hopkins* (1930), predated the publication of Hopkins's letters and journals, but drew on documentary evidence to show the 'evolution' of Hopkins's character (Lahey 1930: vii). In a short book, Lahey, himself a Jesuit, seeks to individualise Hopkins, while also providing context and interpretation of the man and his poetry. The family background, especially its artistic interests, is touched on, and Hopkins's over-sensitive nature in the face of moral disorder and physical ugliness (Lahey 1930: 3). Early poetry (including 'A Vision of the Mermaids' and 'Spring and Death' [pp. 45–6; 58]) is quoted to suggest links with the Romantic tradition. Moving to Oxford, Lahey lightly sketches in the importance of Oxford, as an intellectual 'theatre of great activity' (Lahey 1930: 15), with key figures amidst the 'intellectual undercurrent' being Jowett, Liddon, and Walter Pater [pp. 11–2; 101]. Friendship is also emphasised, in Bridges, who might,

Lahey recognises, have reservations about Hopkins's religious ideals and 'Marianism', but should be defended (Bridges only died in 1930). Digby Dolben he deals with boldly, though in a way that might make later biographers pause, if the dangers of 'mortal beauty' come to mind rather than Lahey's eulogistic insistence upon 'a mind no less penetrating than his friend's, and a soul sensitive to the seductive glow of nature and of art' (Lahey 1930: 27).

Lahey then moves to the shape of the priest's career, quoting from the journals, and bringing out Hopkins's interest in Duns Scotus – a very un-Victorian characteristic, but fundamental to understanding Hopkins and his modes of perception. Perhaps most surprising to the modern reader is Lahey's final section, dealing with the Dublin years. While acknowledging Hopkins's sorrow at separation from friends and family and at the political situation [pp. 36–7], he finds Hopkins came as a 'worthy complement' to an 'assemblage of choice spirits' (Lahey 1930: 139). While startling, it is at least worth pausing upon, since Lahey had contacts with people who had known Hopkins in Dublin or were still at the National University. Already there was a biographical tradition, which Lahey wanted to counter, 'tragic portraits of an exiled Englishman slowly dying to loneliness, drudgery, and despair' (Lahey 1930: 140). Yet there was an internal, spiritual sorrow, springing from true mysticism: 'Hopkins, smiling and joyful with his friends, was at the same time on the bleak heights of spiritual night with his God' (Lahey 1930: 143). And yet the 'Terrible' Sonnets are not tragic, for they are only terrible in the way that the beauty of Christ is terrible – here 'Golgotha and Thabor meet' (Lahey 1930: 143), the places of the crucifixion and of the transfiguration, where the incarnate God respectively suffered and showed his transcendent power. Fahey's insistence points to the debate on the nature of Hopkins's religious experience and its re-enactment in the poetry: his Hopkins is Victorian, but also a Catholic and, distinctively, a Jesuit.

The first full biography, by Eleanor Ruggles (USA, 1944; Britain, 1947), could draw, as Ruggles recognised, on a full body of biographical materials in the letters and the first edition of the Journals and Papers (1937). Out of this mass of prose there emerges 'the elemental figure of a man in a predicament whose appeal ... [lies] not only in his writings, but also in his situation, in the austerity of his choice, the persistent humanity of his weakness' (Ruggles 1947: 9). The conflict, pursued by others, between vocation as priest and vocation as poet, is established at this opening and highlighted later again (Ruggles 1947: 156), though Ruggles is not really prepared to go into the issue of whether his priesthood damaged Hopkins as poet. Ruggles does not regard Hopkins primarily as a Victorian and has little sympathy with his choice of Catholicism and the Jesuits, praising Pusey at Oxford over Newman, since Newman 'renounced freedom of inquiry and bound his eyes ... with the bandage of a final creed' (Ruggles 1947: 41). Yet despite the assertion that Hopkins appeared in 1918 as a poet of 'absolute sincerity' who 'transcended his native era' (Ruggles 1947: 8), Ruggles does pay attention to the Victorian world in which Hopkins lived and by which he was formed. The Victorian world she represents is that imagined in the early-twentieth century, rather than the more complex and sensitively interpreted one of recent historical and literary investigation, so that she often delights in stark contrasts, of a 'penny plain, twopenny coloured' kind. When Hopkins, a boy in Hampstead in 1852, looks over London from the vantage of a tree top, Ruggles extends the view into a heady world of Dickensian oppressiveness, where in 'the cholera-ridden slums of all the great industrial cities thousands of other children were living like animals, and dying like them' (Ruggles 1947: 11). The same love of contrast is seen in later juxtapositions, of the rebellious schoolboy Hopkins linked to the 'socialists and nationalists' of France and Italy (Ruggles 1947: 18), or Newman, concealing from himself the 'disintegrating patchwork of his Anglican faith' (Ruggles 1947: 53). Yet it is misleading and unfair to characterise this pioneering work, as John Pick does, pejoratively, as popular and readable, compounding this with the observation that 'it would be too harsh to say that the work is a frustrated historical novel' (Pick 1968: 322).

Though Ruggles begins by placing Hopkins as someone who 'transcended his native era', she does give an account of Oxford and the conflicting claims of Jowett and Pusey in religious thought and enquiry. She traces back the Oxford Movement [p. 10] as an awakening, touches only slightly on Hopkins's own process of conversion to Catholicism, then does give detailed attention to his noviciate. Clearly, though, Ruggles is embarrassed by the Jesuits, since for her – and, as a biographer primarily of the poet, one partly sees why – the 'important feature of the next five years is the fact that at the end of them Hopkins began again to write poetry' (Ruggles 1947: 95). Psychologically, Ruggles sees Hopkins as one of the 'twice-born', those 'complex, sombre, and ardent personalities', who 'must be first broken on the wheel of spiritual crisis, then reassembled and reanimated by the working on them of divine grace' (Ruggles 1947: 119). While the Jesuits 'broke' Hopkins, Ruggles still uses the term 'divine grace', the poet as gifted from God, and she sees poetry, certainly Hopkins's poetry, as closely linked to a divine power, since for such a personality, the incentive to write again 'must come with the force of a revelation' (Ruggles 1947: 113), and the nuns of the

Deutschland, part of that revelation, 'became to Gerard Hopkins what Beatrice was to Dante, the boy "Lycidas" to Milton, Lincoln to Whitman' (Ruggles 1947: 114).

Ruggles passes fairly rapidly over Hopkins's priestly career. Liverpool was where Hopkins 'first shows traces of that irredeemable despondency by which the last years of his life were to be warped' (Ruggles 1947: 151) and her Dublin is very different from Lahey's 'assemblage of choice spirits'. Shortly after his arrival, Ruggles claims, Hopkins 'underwent a nervous collapse' and she sees Hopkins's life shaped by a (possible) instinct that he had not long to live (Ruggles 1947: 191, 199–200). Yet the poetry written in Ireland was the most individual and masterly, even while Ruggles havers over Hopkins's inner state: depression, despair, 'if indeed it may be called despair' (Ruggles 1947: 211); and offers a modern (1930s/ 1940s) Freudian alternative to the 'dark night'. Was he a mystic unanswered? a neurotic unrelieved? (Ruggles 1947: 211) – Ruggles is not going to answer those questions.

If Ruggles draws back from the Jesuits, seeing the system as breaking Hopkins, Alfred Thomas's focus in *Hopkins the Jesuit: The Years of Training* (1969) is a detailed account of Hopkins's Jesuit training, both what it was and how, though in many ways entirely ordinary in its routines, it yet set Hopkins apart as a particular kind of Victorian, who not only embraced Catholicism, but also the Society of Jesus, a body regarded with suspicion by many Catholics as well as by Protestants. Thomas, himself a Jesuit, writes in detail, as Fahey did not, and with sympathy, as Ruggles could not. He tracks the years between conversion (1867) and the Tertianship (1881–82), setting down 'exactly and in detail' what happened to Hopkins in those years, while making no claim to be able to 'pluck the heart' from Hopkins's mystery: 'for me the enigma remains' (Thomas 1969: ix).

Thomas explores Hopkins's training in detail, concerned, as one who was trained nearly a century later, to bring out both the ordinary round of the Society and what might strike the modern Jesuit as strange (Thomas 1969: 28). In considering Hopkins's conversion and his religious life, Thomas gives no sense amongst the Jesuits of cynicism or hypocrisy or envy such as Bridges hinted at [**pp. 13; 21–2; 124**], though evoking the sometimes alien image of the Jesuits in the 1850s and 1860s (Thomas 1969: 15–19). Amidst the routine, Hopkins was also aware of contemporary events – the Society necessarily carried his interests well beyond England – including the occupation of Rome in 1870 and the expulsion by the new Kingdom of Italy of the Jesuits from their properties in Rome (Thomas 1969: 100–101). Thomas underlines Hopkins's personal development, for in closely observing the particularities of nature, Hopkins 'perceived an unmistakable regularity, and this notion combined with his religious outlook to produce in him a sacramental view of nature' (Thomas 1969: 85). Thomas resists the idea, at least in terms of Hopkins's training and his situation at the end of the Theologate at St Beuno's (1877), when he was not allowed to enter the fourth year of theology, that this was a major disappointment. Indeed, Thomas disputes Devlin's claim (S, xiii-xiv) that Hopkins was three times disappointed in expectation of a full and useful life, respectively as scholar, preacher, and academic writer (Thomas 1969: 182). So Thomas, while not concerning himself with the Dublin years nor primarily offering an interpretation or critique of Hopkins or the poetry, does stand against the 'dark' Hopkins, that desolate and tragic figure.

Writing sympathetically as an agnostic about her favourite poet, Paddy Kitchen in 1978 could draw on extensively published sources and had examined the originals of the Journals, so she knew the omitted Confession notes (J, xx; Saville 2000: 35). Kitchen's references to these notes prove something of a tease, since, when drawn on, they are less exciting than Kitchen initially suggests (Kitchen 1978: 70) – evidence of masturbation and looking up bad words in the dictionary. It was a pity House and Storey so emphasised them by omission: Norman White's later discussion (White 1992: 113–15) is useful and sensible. They do play though into Kitchen's stress on Hopkins's nature and the poetry as personal expression.

In charting Hopkins's life, the biography begins with a prologue summarising the Oxford Movement, since it so much provides the context of Hopkins's early life and his eventual conversion, Kitchen providing a reasonable if somewhat picturesque account, stressing the serious and absurd sides of the Oxford Movement and its members. She also stresses the early influence of Ruskin and sees his 'association ... between acute physical perception of nature and high moral perception' (Kitchen 1978: 23), as the foundation of Hopkins's speculations about art and of his thought. Yet if as early as 'The Escorial' [pp. 44–5] Kitchen identifies 'Storm, shipwreck, physical and moral endurence' as 'popular Victorian themes' (Kitchen 1978: 26), she also offers a Hopkins made alien to his own age and ours by being a Jesuit. For while becoming a Catholic was commonplace among his associates, being a Jesuit surrounds him with 'an aura alien to most readers today' (Kitchen 1978: 112). She sensibly stresses at the end, though, that to speculate whether Hopkins would have been a different poet is useless, since 'he *was* a Jesuit, and his decision to become one was no more arbitrary than most people's choice of career' (Kitchen 1978: 231). While acknowledging Hopkins was a

Victorian, Kitchen none the less approaches him from a psychological perspective and finds him finally to be a poet of the inner, personal life. Through poetry 'he was expressing his intellectual and emotional needs' (Kitchen 1978: 40). She claims that Hopkins's 'sexual orientation was never conclusively evolved' (Kitchen 1978: 62) and on Digby Dolben, follows House in accepting that 'Where Art Thou Friend' [pp. 54–5] is addressed to Dolben. Like Phare [pp. 138–9], Kitchen looks at 'The Bugler's First Communion' as a poem deeply embarrassing, but turns the embarrassment the other way, so it is not a bad poem, but utterly central to Hopkins, demonstrating that his feelings 'were in no way silenced nor his expression of them anything other than explicit' (Kitchen 1978: 192–93). For Kitchen, Hopkins's emotions 'ranged freely' within the limits set by the Jesuit regime (Kitchen 1978: 167), while the 'Terrible' Sonnets are 'painfully clear' as a narrative of the state of Hopkins's mind and feelings (Kitchen 1978: 218). At the heart of the mystery for Kitchen is a Victorian, made stranger still to us by being a Jesuit, who yet could 'recreate the moment of arousing wonder at physical attraction and ... describe the experience of barren despair' (Kitchen 1978: 232).

If Kitchen has a very proper enthusiasm for her subject, Norman White's 'literary biography' of 1992 is the fullest and the best to date. He places Hopkins in his times, while properly insisting that being a Victorian was not something antiquated and quaint at the time, so that Hopkins's university and personal education took him into 'a subtle and confused modern English world more suited to experiment and individual response than to the judgements of an imposed doctrinal framework' (White 1992: viii). This Hopkins is modern not by being of the twentieth century, like Eliot or Woolf, Pound or Joyce, but by being of his own time, his nature and work shaped by circumstances and personality. That conflict between individual response and doctrinal framework is a key to White's interpretation of Hopkins, so that while he rightly finds 'an overall and coherent pattern cannot be imposed on the works' nor the life (White 1992: vii), he none the less pursues the conflict he finds in Hopkins's nature, in a powerful and original temperament, 'a strange mixture of innocence and expertise, of old prejudices and clear-sighted observations', that worked against his achieving happiness and success (White 1992: vii). By entering the Catholic Church and then choosing the Jesuits rather than Oratorians or Benedictines (both possibilities), Hopkins, White suggests, attempted 'to simplify his problems and evade his demons by complete submission to ancient comprehensive ideological systems' (White 1992: vii). So Hopkins's beliefs impose 'a moral grid' on his richly vigorous personal responses to experience in the Welsh poems following 'The

Wreck', yet in Ireland, new power and originality were 'forced into his poems of self-examination' (the 'Terrible' Sonnets) by 'his diminished loyalties and ... isolation' (White 1992: viii). Hence, while an 'overall coherent pattern' cannot be imposed, White does suggest a tragic dimension to Hopkins's life and a direct interaction between his life, belief, vocation, and his poetry.

The narrative and detail of the biography are wonderfully sustained, without the more garish colouring of Ruggles – indeed, White is at pains to stress long periods in Hopkins's life where, at least externally, nothing happened. Detailed attention is rightly given to Oxford and White draws the reader in to the controversy between High Church and the liberal camps, with the opposed figures of Pusey and Jowett (White 1992: 98–103), Hopkins, though tutored by Jowett, choosing the High Church, since 'Jowett's moral short-comings were of a piece with his aesthetic philistinism' (White 1992: 99). Ruskin too is a dominant figure, first discovered at Oxford, all Hopkins's debts to Ruskin stemming from 'Ruskin's great principle, that art should be made, not by learning from general ideas or words, but by looking at natural objects' (White 1992: 75). From Ruskin too came the 'elegiac inference', to predominate in Hopkins's poetry, 'that natural beauty was unique, momentary, and vulnerable to time and man's impiety' (White 1992: 75–76). With Dolben, again, White sees the opposition in Hopkins's nature, spiritual and carnal desire mixing, Hopkins finding in Dolben elements of himself, just as he recognised too in Whitman 'aspects of his own temperament which he dared not name' (White 1992: 110). White's argument that Hopkins combined oppositions, lassitude and activity, physical desire and religious 'sublimation' (White 1992: 110–16), seems only too natural in a young man of some sensitivity and cultivation. And if his suppressions might make it doubtful that Hopkins 'ever achieved complete coherence' – though who indeed ever does? – this leads, White suggests, to a Hopkins seemingly 'always afraid of his unconquered demons', so he 'took strong measures to keep them down' (White 1992: 129).

These 'strong measures' underpin White's careful account of Hopkins's conversion and becoming a Jesuit. If White suggests the Jesuit regime was harsher than Thomas does, this is in part emphasis, in part also an answer to the question Why the Jesuits? White argues that Hopkins was hoping to impose on a '"sordid" and unpredictable existence a sense of rightness and order' (White 1992: 186). Increasingly, Hopkins becomes isolated, a 'lonely spectator' (White 1992: 201), with a distinct, even peculiar, vision and expression. If 'The Wreck' is 'unmistakably a Victorian sea-disaster poem' (White 1992: 252), it looks forward less to the joyful Welsh poems than to the tragic Dublin ones (White 1992: 256). Perhaps White overemphasises the personal here, since while his claim that rejection of 'The Wreck' for publication meant Hopkins never attempted a poem even half so ambitious is true in terms of length, a poem such as 'The Windhover' is equally remarkable in technique and content. White's Hopkins does become increasingly isolated, given to misanthropy and loneliness (White 1992: 288), doomed to end his life in the place 'the least congenial' (White 1992: 367; [p. 36]). If this account brings out the contrasts White develops in his biography, this is partly because these contrasts lie at the root of his interpretation of Hopkins's poetry and in his placing of Hopkins as artist in the Victorian fragmented world, 'with no language but a cry' (White 1992; 401). It was not only biography, though, that was concerned increasingly to 'place' Hopkins as a Victorian.

HOPKINS THE VICTORIAN: CRITICAL APPROACHES 1944–72

Biography repositioned Hopkins as a Victorian, while Victorianism in the mid-twentieth century had itself been 'repositioned' from the oppressive restrictions of a dark and (at best) quaint age to one of dynamism and radical achievement, not least because the term itself was recognised as too limiting, given the span of the historical period from early Dickens in the 1830s to the poets of the First World War, from the reign of William IV to that of George V. Hopkins himself was increasingly and properly seen as a late Victorian, a period when the High Victorianism of Tennyson and Browning, Dickens, Thackeray and George Eliot, was being challenged. As early as 1944, an important article by Austen Warren, 'Instress of Inscape', suggestive rather than detailed, praising the 'Middle' Hopkins from 'The Wreck' to 'Tom's Garland' and 'Harry Ploughman' as a period of experiment that 'startles us by its dense rich world ... its plenitude and its tangibility' (Warren 1966 [1944]: 168), began to indicate the poet's roots not in Romanticism or High Victorian poetry, but in the Ritualist Movement, with Keble and Pusey; in Pre-Raphaelitism, both visual and the verse of the Rossettis; and in the Aestheticism of figures like Walter Pater, which valued the intense feeling of the moment over the meaning. Warren rightly pointed to Hopkins as English, a British not an Italian Catholic, and the four great shapers of his mind – Pater, Ruskin, Newman, Duns Scotus – as British, an inflection often earlier ignored. For Warren, exploration of Hopkins's poetry starts from the institutions and the movements in which the poet was involved, a poet who 'gloried in the range and repertory of mankind' (Warren 1966 [1944]: 171), drawn to his antitypes: soldiers, miners, manual labourers.

Two important studies, exploring at length Hopkins's likeness to his fellow Victorians and their ideas, apppeared in 1968 and 1972. Wendell Stacy Johnson's *Gerard Manley Hopkins: The Poet as Victorian* is concerned to explore Hopkins as a Christian poet, a poet of nature, and, with special emphasis, a Victorian poet (W.S. Johnson 1968: 2). For Johnson, Victorian literature is haunted by the question whether man, 'the creature who turns attention inward to himself', is in harmony with the external order or alienated from it (W.S. Johnson 1968: 2), and he sees Hopkins as a poet confronted by a post-Romantic problem in a self-conscious age. Two qualities of the Victorians are especially explored: self-consciousness, recognised in a simultaneous self-probing and self-masking; and, second, an ambivalent attitude to the natural, temporal world, embodied in imagery, both literal and metaphorical. The Victorian relationship between ego and image, or self and nature, is 'a tense, problematic one', not the harmonious interaction that Wordsworth, arch-Romantic, believed in (W.S. Johnson 1968: 9). Drawing out the contrast between two 'spiritual' autobiographies, Wordsworth's *The Prelude* (written 1805) and Thomas Carlyle's *Sartor Resartus* (1833–34), Johnson finds Carlyle's irony, ambiguity, fictionality exemplifying the divide between the Romantic assertion 'I am' and the Victorian question 'Who am I?' (W.S. Johnson 1968: 12). Hopkins's poetry may be more successful than that of other Victorians, 'in coming to terms with self-consciousness, in controlling doubleness, ambiguity' (W.S. Johnson 1968: 23), yet engage he must with those terms. Johnson contrasts usefully Victorian imagery of nature with Romantic, in Christina Rossetti's 'Goblin Market', where the earth's fruits are tempting yet dangerous; and in painting, where Holman Hunt's *The Scapegoat* (1854–55; Manchester Art Gallery) and Millais's *The Blind Girl* (1854–56; Birmingham Art Gallery) carry a moral significance (influenced by Ruskin). Hopkins, like other Victorians, had to realise, that 'this nature is sometimes stormy, that animal beauty is distracting and ephemeral, that every flower and fruit is merely mortal, and that the source of light is the source also of blinding, blasting energy' (W.S. Johnson 1968: 42). Underlying all this is Johnson's insistence on Hopkins as Catholic and priest, as well as Victorian, who resolves (or attempts to resolve) those ambiguities of 'Who am I?' in a Christian poetry structured in the three necessary stages: of nature; of grace from God the Father; and of grace from Christ (W.S. Johnson 1968: 146). Nor can Johnson quite forget the Modern world, for, taking the spoon image in 'The Shepherd's Brow' [p. 121], he finds, in its reduction of the heroic, that Hopkins 'predicts now the way in which Victorian self-consciousness can finally become, as in Eliot's "Prufrock," a kind of self-mockery', an inversion of grand Romantic expectations (W.S. Johnson 1968: 144).

Johnson stressed the Victorians' question 'What am I?' and traced the self-consciousness of the age and its doubleness of representation. That same self-consciousness and questioning lie at the heart of Alison G. Sulloway's outstanding study, *Gerard Manley Hopkins and the Victorian Temper*. Sulloway suggests that Hopkins is placed firmly in the centre of the Victorian tradition, his very nature showing 'the shifting spirit, now exuberant, now tentatively hopeful, or at least reconciliatory, now gloomy, if not actually apocalyptic' (Sulloway 1972: 1). While natural, given when his poetry was published, the 'unconscious supposition' that Hopkins 'was mostly excluded from the drama of the Victorian age' is not true; indeed, Hopkins's manner as well as his matter is more often than not a reflection of self-conscious Victorian England (Sulloway 1972: 5). Sulloway explores this interconnection through four principal topics: the Tractarian wars; Ruskinian aestheticism; the Victorian concept of a gentleman; and the nineteenth-century apocalyptic mood.

Oxford and Hopkins's undergraduate experience up to his conversion and entry into the Jesuits is the conflict zone of the Tractarian wars, not so much the earlier days of the Oxford Movement [**p. 10**], but rather the opposition of High Church and the 'liberals', of Pusey and Keble against Jowett and the *Essays and Reviews* (1860), a publication that questioned (in very mild, qualified ways) both the absolute truth of Scripture and High Church thinking. Sulloway's account of Oxford in the 1860s, its serious-minded Oxonians and the passion for Oxford herself, focuses on the crisis of faith in the individual, compounded by similar crises involving friends, university, country, and Church. Prepared forthrightly to expose the falsity of the position of Pusey and other Tractarians who clung to the Church of England, Sulloway finds they wanted to pick and choose amongst Catholic dogma, 'they wanted Catholicism without Papal infallibility' (Sulloway 1972: 57), a position Newman had rejected and one Hopkins too was to reject as logically impossible. Oxford's 'alarms and excursions' contributed to an atmosphere of imminent crisis that Hopkins endured during his undergraduate days, and which feed the moral crises in so much of Hopkins's poetry (Sulloway 1972: 26–27). But more importantly still, though aligning himself with the High Church rather than the 'liberalism' of Jowett, Hopkins heard the missionary note in Jowett, the 'disposition to sacrifice personal comfort, even personal health, for idealistic ends' (Sulloway 1972: 36), that brought him to Catholicism, priesthood – and the Jesuits.

An excellent chapter on Ruskin, exploratory and suggestive, beginning with the proposition that if Hopkins's poems would not be what they are without the *Spiritual Exercises*, 'to praise, reverence and serve the Lord', it is equally true of the poems without Ruskin's works (Sulloway 1972: 64–65). Hopkins, Sulloway argues, is doing what Ruskin outlined for the Christian artist, and 'inscape' and 'instress' are the artist's description of things and the perception (as artist) of what lies behind, while Ruskin's 'three steps' towards a completed art work are Hopkins's sketching or describing natural things; his awareness of his 'fury', 'passion', 'admiration', or 'enthusiasm' for Nature's self; and Hopkins's nature poems themselves (Sulloway 1972: 71). In perceiving 'what lies behind', Ruskin was insisting on a sacramental view, a 'grace' that increased our spiritual strength and was in some measure a help to salvation. For Hopkins, the 'sacramental energy' needed for the role of Jesuit missionary was inseparable from the sacramental energy required of a Ruskinian artist (Sulloway 1972: 81). Neither Ruskin nor Hopkins, though, found nature perfect, since wherever they looked in the phenomenal and spiritual world they saw 'paradoxes, dichotomies, antitheses, and contradictions': such contrasts they explained as the consequences of 'man's original fall from grace' (Sulloway 1972: 90).

The concept of the gentleman, however it may make us uneasy in phrases such as 'one of nature's gentlemen' or declarations that dead criminals were 'real gentlemen', was undoubtedly a key area of cultural conflict in the Victorian period. Sulloway, recognising the contradictions, paradoxes and problems, pursues the idea well, claiming that Hopkins, like Ruskin, tries to 'subdue the romance of chivalry for domestic consumption' (Sulloway 1972: 119). It is part of their Englishness and Ruskin saw the duties of the gentleman, as a Christian, included giving his 'full energies' to 'the soul's work ... the taking of the kingdom of heaven by force'. Whenever the Christian fails, he can no longer be an artist, for 'even the Orpheus song is forbidden him' (quoted Sulloway 1972: 122). So with certain poems of Hopkins, which only yield some of their ambiguities when, 'behind the gnarled syntax and the cascade of metaphors', is discovered 'the new Victorian gentleman, struggling to adapt himself to the diverse responsibilities he had assumed' (Sulloway 1972: 128). If in 'Brothers' [p. 98] Sulloway sees the danger of beauty, the actor John, the master rather than the servant, as the gentleman must be, 'the dazzling performer, who is heedlessly selving himself *above* his audience like some latter-day Lucifer', in 'St Alphonsus Rodriguez' [pp. 119–20] the 'breach between nature and grace is healed, for the Author of nature is also the Author of grace' (Sulloway 1972: 148, 156).

The Victorian Apocalyptic Vision leads to the 'Calamitarian Mode' and to 'The Wreck', a pivotal work because the only major

Victorian work in distinctively aesthetic form that treats Apocalypse as 'indisputable prophecy' (Sulloway 1972: 194). Hopkins, in 'The Wreck', adopted an archetypal model that permitted him to encompass much of the troubled times he lived in (Sulloway 1972: 158). In contemplating the godless present with its tide of secularism that Oxford had once seemed a bulwark against, but which a poem like 'Andromeda' [**pp. 95–6**] acknowledges is no longer so [**pp. 9–10; 160–1**], Hopkins draws on the Apocalypse of St John the Divine, with its 'apocalyptic rhythm from horror and carnage to joy in expectation of the second coming' (Sulloway 1972: 159). In 'The Wreck' and its storm, Nature is 'both sinner and sinned against, both the destructive agent and the symbolic victim of the doom she precipitated' (Sulloway 1972: 175). The Nun becomes the body of the Church to her saviour, Christ, and Hopkins has translated a contemporary 'ordeal of the waters' into 'a mystical event' (Sulloway 1972: 194).

Nature into religion

It is impossible to talk about nature in Hopkins, and his artistic training and artistic beliefs (his aesthetics), without being drawn on to religion and to technique. The following discussion necessarily touches on nature, aesthetics, briefly on science, then religion, as separate elements, before dealing more particularly with technique. Yet all the time, actual or implied cross-references are necessary, because in Hopkins all these aspects interact. The damage if Hopkins is not approached with this understanding is clear in Bridges's early treatment of Hopkins's texts. To publish a sonnet's octave but not the sestet, skews the relationship of nature to religion, skews exposition to resolution, and obscures the integral form of the sonnet's structure. Bridges sought to make Hopkins safe, as an English nature or pastoral poet, playing down the 'embarrassment' of religion, betraying Hopkins's technical skill. The categories in what follows should be seen, then, not as fixed, only as convenient.

NATURE

As just mentioned, Bridges would have preferred to place Hopkins in a pastoral tradition, away from the hazards of doctrine, away from a Catholicism which would be 'foreign' to English-language readers.

Hopkins's observation and responses to nature were related to his early experience and training, developed and modified by his persistent attempts to perceive, understand, and theorise. He was trained in drawing, looking, and reproducing, by his aunt, and Hopkins's family was artistic. Hopkins himself seems to have followed Ruskin's *Elements of Drawing* (1857), with its emphasis on the training of the eye (Phillips 2007: x), to see what is there in nature, 'rejecting nothing, selecting nothing', whether the glory of the stars or the filth of a polluted stream in Rochdale [**p. 91**].

A useful introductory study of Hopkins's experience of the natural world is Peter Milward and Raymond Schoder's *Landscape and Inscape: Vision and Inspiration in Hopkins's Poetry* (1975), providing visual images particularly of St Beuno's and the Welsh countryside, for Hopkins's creativity ingenuity is 'in going beyond the objective reality into a world of his own insight and making' and the photographs allow us to see him 'in action on the world around him' (Milward & Schoder 1975: 9). Milward offers a commentary on 'The Wreck' and some of the Nature sonnets that followed, including 'Hurrahing in Harvest', 'God's Grandeur', 'Pied Beauty' and 'The Windhover', the last illustrated by the stuffed bird in St Beuno's, labelled 'windhover'. The commentary goes beyond simple equation of picture and words. Milward rightly characterises the alternating structure of 'The Wreck', yet as Hopkins turns his eyes 'outwards to the sufferings' of the nuns and 'inwards to his responsive sympathy and consequent rebirth in spirit' (Milward & Schoder 1975: 18), the exploration goes on to Job, Isaiah, and other Biblical examples, and finds in God's finger, touching poet and nun, a likeness to Michelangelo's God in the Sistine Chapel, reaching out in an energy-charged gesture to Adam.

On the natural scene, Milward finds Hopkins a poet in the Romantic tradition, 'stirred from his inmost depths by a power of divine inspiration' (Milward & Schoder 1975: 29), yet he stresses also how nature and God are inseparable for Hopkins. The poet looks up at the clouds of 'Hurrahing in Harvest' and their 'lovely behaviour', but in his heart recognises within the clouds the presence of 'Christ, King, Head', and so receives 'the inspiration of the "arch and original Breath"' (Milward & Schoder 1975: 31). A sense is given of the religious templates or structures underlying natural representation, so that in the same sonnet, Milward points out, the idea of the Saviour gathering in harvest, links with Ruth and Boaz gleaning at harvest end (Ruth ch.2), and then through Ruth to the royal house of Israel and so to Christ's descent from King David (Milward & Schoder 1975: 31).

More particular studies of Hopkins's relation to sight and the natural scene are included in R.K.R. Thornton's *'All My Eyes See': The Visual Work of Gerard Manley Hopkins* (1975). Important here is Jerome Bump's survey of 'Hopkins' Drawings', which while aware of the 'necessarily amateur nature' of Hopkins's work, sees him as part of a nineteenth-century trend away from the picturesque tradition of the Romantics, of nature to be experienced as an end in itself, towards 'drawing as a means of acquiring useful knowledge' (Bump 1975: 70–71), a mix of the aesthetic and scientific in which Ruskin's was the greatest influence. Bump suggests Gerard's sketches with their 'distinctively *unifying* design' (Bump 1975: 74) give insight into what Hopkins means by 'inscape'. Norman White's 'Hopkins as Art Critic', in the same collection, asserts that morality was for Hopkins the basis of the aesthetic and ties this in with Victorian attitudes to visual representation, where an extraneous message was expected, and so people 'were unable to see a painting for what it actually was' (White 1975: 91). The Pre-Raphaelites painted just such pictures, as with Madox Brown's *Work* or Holman Hunt's *The Light of the World*, and White, claiming the influence of painters on Hopkins, suggests his mind 'worked in very much the same kind of way' (White 1975: 91).

NATURE AND AESTHETICS

Both Bump and White call in question the 'innocence of the eye' (Ruskin 1907: 3 note), since how we see and how we react will be conditioned by environment, nurture, and assumptions. Ruskin demanded observation and representation should take account of the particular – the form of a leaf, the structure of the rocks – and raised this to a theory of art. Yet Hopkins, deeply influenced by Ruskin, met other aesthetic theories at Oxford, was indeed tutored in 1866 by Walter Pater, one of the most influential art theorists of the late nineteenth century. Alison Sulloway identifies Pater's 'established order of things' with Hopkins's 'inscape' and Pater's 'the nobler elements in that order' as 'instress' (Sulloway 1972: 45). She goes on to suggest that Pater's writings express a weariness or desire to escape, seen too in Hopkins's undergraduate poems such as 'The Alchemist in the City' [pp. 56–6] and 'Heaven-Haven' [pp. 51–2]. Pater's aesthetic of 'art for art's sake', so opposed to Ruskin's concern with the moral basis of art, is viewed from a fresh perspective by Denis Donoghue in 'The Oxford of Pater, Hopkins, and Wilde' (1994). While serious on the influence of Pater, and well aware of religious difference and the stronger influence of Ruskin, Donoghue finds Pater and Hopkins linked by their interest 'in art, aesthetics, and homoerotic sentiment' (Donoghue 1994: 98), though their 'Oxfords' were very different. Pater had little time for Oxford as loving mother or intellectual powerhouse, and showed nothing of Hopkins's numinous style in describing Oxford (Donoghue 1994: 99). Slight yet lively, the piece throws useful light on art theories and on different attitudes to Oxford.

The presence of Pater in Hopkins's aesthetic development is also recognised by Hilary Fraser, for while Pater (like Wilde later) embraces the subjectivism that Ruskin and Matthew Arnold sought to avoid, he also, like Ruskin, attempted to develop 'a quickened, multiplied consciousness', aiming to distinguish and fix 'delicate and fugitive detail' in the struggle to discern truth (Fraser 1986: 73). If Hopkins did not content himself with Pater's seizing and experiencing the exquisite moment, was not satisfied egotistically to be the subjective and sole centre of his own world, burning with a 'hard, gemlike flame' (Pater 1928: 221), none the less Pater fed into Hopkins's developing exploration at Oxford of Nature and the idea of Beauty and the purpose of art.

And it is Hopkins's Oxford education more widely that is key to Hilary Fraser's scholarly, densely argued, yet readable *Beauty and Belief: Aesthetics and Religion in Victorian Literature* (1986), the most thorough and stimulating study of nature, religion and aesthetics in Hopkins. Fraser sees a hallmark of the Victorian age as its 'all-pervasive, deliberate, and rather self-conscious concern with the relationship between religious and aesthetic experience' (Fraser 1986: 2). Theories designed to reconcile the claims of Christianity and beauty, morality and art, proliferated amongst the Victorians, a proliferation quite natural since traditionally religion and art have sought to express and embody non-material ideal truths in a physical form (Fraser 1986: 1), necessarily drawn from the natural, phenomenal world. Fraser's beauty and belief reciprocally work upon each other: the Oxford Tractarian, John Keble, for instance, gives 'orthodox definition' to Wordsworthian nature by an 'innovatory aesthetic theory of sacramentalism' (Fraser 1986: 39). For since the sacraments, centrally holy communion, are means to receive God's grace, the sacramental principle may in turn 'be extended to nature', for when a mind is 'incited by God to see the supernatural in any good or beautiful action or object', it is an equivalent to 'the giving and receiving of Christian sacramental grace' (Fraser 1986: 40). Newman, too, assumed 'a direct parallel between religious and aesthetic experience' (Fraser 1986: 63), while Ruskin and Matthew Arnold, if more concerned with the moral implications of arts and aesthetics than the strictly theological (Fraser 1986: 107), yet assumed a relationship between religion and aesthetics and sought 'to impose order on the chaos and instability' of the temporal situation and 'to synthesise the fragmented details of the actual into a harmonious and unified ideal' (Fraser 1986: 111).

On Hopkins, Fraser argues that his theory of inscape is often regarded as 'the philosophy of a solitary mystical and poetical visionary', particular to him (Fraser 1986: 67), yet as an attempt to relate ideas about beauty, art and religion, 'inscape' places Hopkins 'very centrally in the post-Romantic religio-aesthetic tradition which defines Victorian aesthetic thought' (Fraser 1986: 67). Rather than a split between priest and poet, Hopkins's priestly vocation on one hand and on the other his practical genius and intense vulnerability to beauty, 'these two aspects of his life are subtly related rather than being ... radically divided' (Fraser 1986: 67–68).

Fraser's exploration begins from the question of perception and Hopkins's central concern: 'Why do some things in nature and in our experience suddenly strike us as special and in some way significant?' And, do these insights afford 'some intimation of the divine'? (Fraser 1986: 69). If so, what is the relationship between the natural object or experience and God? At Oxford Hopkins had studied philosophy and the question raised by the German philosopher, Immanuel Kant, would be particularly significant to someone attracted to physical beauty: how can the pleasure of aesthetic experience be justified in terms which would commend universal assent? (Fraser 1986: 80). Hopkins asks just such a question in 'To What Serves Mortal Beauty' [pp. 99–101] and his solution is the development of inscape and instress, so that in 'The Windhover', the 'bird is both a unique entity ... and the carrier of universal and essential truth' (Fraser 1986: 87). Man in Nature perceives Christ, 'the ultimate inscape', and gives glory because 'made, to give God glory and to mean to give it' (Fraser 1986: 94, 96; quoting S, 239). Hopkins's is a solution to the Romantic subjectivism that lies behind Kant's question: if I am the centre of perception, then how can my (aesthetic) pleasure be justified in terms which would command universal assent? Hopkins finds it in Christ, so that 'Mortal Beauty' 'does this: keeps warm | Men's wit to the things that are; to what good means'. Such a discovery, though, still does not necessarily command universal consent, grounded as it is in faith.

NATURE: GLORY AND DARKNESS

Milward and Schoder celebrate the exuberance of Nature and the glory of God as Hopkins depicts it in the Nature sonnets that followed 'The Wreck', indeed show how even in the storm and the destruction of the *Deutschland*, Hopkins is confident of God's presence and purpose [p. 75]. Yet however true of Hopkins's exultant Welsh poems, this vision of Nature was one variously challenged in the nineteenth century and in Hopkins's own experience. No longer was there confidence in God's design and a benevolent Nature. Observation of Nature's bounty also suggested Nature's casualness and cruelty. As Nature, 'red in tooth and claw', gripped by Necessity, had seen come and go a thousand types or species, so man, the highest form, had no guarantee of permanence. And Hopkins's own experience, of 'the weariness, the fever, and the fret' of teaching and parish duties, produced at times a sense of the slime from which we come and towards which, at times, we seem to retrogress, 'To man's last dust, drain fast towards man's first slime' ('The Sea and the Skylark' [p. 82]), a darkness compounded in the 'Terrible' Sonnets by the horror of God's absence, expressed in a mental landscape of 'cliffs of fall' or in a vision of the end in 'Sibyl's Leaves' [pp. 106–7], as 'earth her being has unbound ... | ... quite | Disremembering, disremembering'.

The Victorians inherited from the Romantics an idea of Nature as benevolent, yet counter to this benevolence in Nature, Wordsworth declared in *The Prelude* that he grew up 'Fostered alike by beauty and by fear', and Hopkins, for whom Wordsworth was a man who '*saw something*' (L, 2.147), may well have seized, in *The Prelude* (published 1850), on the disturbance and strangeness of the descent into Italy (Bk VI, ll.617–40), with its 'sick sight | And giddy prospect of the raving stream' opening on to 'Characters of the great Apocalypse'. E.E. Phare, while finding Hopkins's mind one that could not easily submit 'to the arbitrariness of actual experience' (Phare 1933: 55), argues it had that sense of strangeness 'characteristic of the religious mind', even if not completely at home in either the geometric world of religion or the unruly world of Nature (Phare 1933: 56). Sulloway more insistently presses the point that for Hopkins Nature is not so much 'unruly' as fallen, corrupted, however 'fortunate' the Fall was, leading on as it did, theologically, to the Incarnation and salvation. In this, Hopkins inherits also from Ruskin, since both saw everywhere in the physical and the spiritual worlds 'paradoxes, dichotomies, antitheses, and contradictions', explicable only through 'man's original fall from grace' (Sulloway 1972: 90). Nature was imperfect, though rather than Phare's geometrical/unruly opposition, Sulloway points to Hopkins's belief in explanation and purpose in God's creation and plan.

Science out of nature

It is useful here as context for three important studies by J. Hillis Miller, Tom Zaniello, and Patricia Ball, to sketch (and no more than sketch) the changing perceptions as science developed out of nature in the nineteenth century. The eighteenth century saw a sudden surge in scientific investigation, inextricably linked to developments in technology and in transport that brought the factory system, steam power, and gas lighting. Such progress could be viewed optimistically easily enough, as in Joseph Wright's great picture of *Experiment with an Air Pump* (1768; Tate Gallery), while Wright's later pictures of the industrialist Richard Arkwright's mill working at night is more Romantic than threatening, even if industry is identified with William Blake's 'Dark Satanic mills' and Ruskin's later observation of the trickle of filth at Rochdale (Ruskin 1905: 121). Science, which had been a field for amateurs, particularly for naturalists like Gilbert White, in his *Natural History of Selborne* (1788), became increasingly professional (Allen 1978). Botany and zoology took over from Natural History, and physics, mathematics and astronomy became more and more specialised, though the last at least was a field where the amateur still did and still does have contributions to make. Observation was crucial, but now it was linked to closer investigation and explanations and theories. Geology developed, and along with it an interest in fossils that extended far beyond digging them up for exhibition in cabinets of curiosities. When and how had the rocks been formed? What were fossils and what did they tell of? What was the testimony of the earth?

Time and space were expanding: millions, not hundreds of years, were needed to form sedimentary strata, while if the Solar System expanded outwards with the discovery of two new planets (Uranus, 1781; Neptune, 1846), beyond it and beyond our galaxy, were other galaxies still. Where did this place man in such vastness and did it correspond to the Biblical account? The creation of the world, if not Adam and Eve, could no longer be in 4004 BC. The opening of Genesis might be seen poetically, not as literal days, but as ages. Even so, what of fossils and their implications for evolution, a changing world rather than something stable, created once and to remain unchanged until the Apocalypse? Perhaps man, then, the highest work, God's chosen, would vanish in turn as fossil species had. Theories of evolution had been around long before Charles Darwin. Genesis itself is such a theory, stressing the breaks (days) rather than continuity between each stage. In the early nineteenth century two great French scientists, Frédéric Cuvier (1769–1832) and Jean Lamarck (1744–1829), took up opposing views. Cuvier proposed a series of catastrophes, between creation and the Flood, to account for geological change and the fossil evidence (echoed in Britain by Robert Chambers's anonymously published and immensely popular and crudely popularising work, *The Vestiges of Creation* (1844)). Lamarck favoured an idea of gradualism, a modification of forms, rather than Cuvier's more spectacular cataclysms.

In all this, God existing still, not yet dead as the German phil-ospher, Friedrich Nietzsche, was later to proclaim, becomes *absent*, because unnecessary, an idea explored by J. Hillis Miller in his study, *The Disappearance of God* (1963), who besides Hopkins, considers Browning, Emily Brontë, and Matthew Arnold. Miller sees this as a phenomenon peculiarly of urbanisation, an overwhelming development in the nineteenth century. 'Life in the city is the way in which many men have experienced most directly what it means to live without God in the world' (Miller 1975: 5), as the system of symbols 'binding man to God has finally evaporated' and modern times begin 'when man confronts his isolation, his separation from everything outside himself' (Miller 1975: 7): Hopkins was appalled by Liverpool's squalor [**p. 33**] and his own alientation was later expressed in 'dead letters sent | To dearest him that lives alas! away' [**p. 110**]. The development of engineering and science is crucial in the development of nineteenth century urbanisation: together they help change the very way society perceives itself.

It was perhaps the effect of Charles Darwin's *Origin of Species* (1859) and, to a lesser extent, Charles Lyell's *The Antiquity of Man* (1863) that was crucial to the late Victorians, Hopkins not least. Both careful works of science, though approachable in their style, neither offered anything new in their basic background, but were seized on, Darwin in particular, as new in implications, and chal-lenging to Christian belief when mapped onto theology. The chal-lenge was most strongly felt in Britain by Protestant fundamentalists, like the distinguished marine biologist, Philip Gosse, who found, as his son, Edmund Gosse, described in *Father and Son* (1907), an irre-concilable division between his scientific and theological beliefs. Many Catholics and Anglicans, though, used to thinking, at one level, of Genesis as a poetic account, had no difficulty in relating the Biblical creation symbolically to a new understanding. Certainly, to come closer to Hopkins, Catholics, many of them Jesuits, had long been working active scientists. Indeed, one of the most eminent astronomers of the Jesuit order, Stephen Joseph Perry, was based at Stonyhurst (Zaniello 1988: 60; *J*, 419).

Yet the nineteenth century, for all its advance in science, saw in some quarters an obscurantist reaction. While in Britain, attitudes seem largely responses to Darwin and his followers, in Europe such reaction was tied up with political concerns too, expressed as a fear of 'Modernism'. The election of Pope Pius IX in 1846 had been welcomed, but with the seizure of Rome by Mazzini and Garibaldi in 1848, proclamation of a republic, the Pope's flight and eventual restoration by French troops, Pius turned his face against liberalism in all areas: political; theological; scientific. In the Syllabus of Errors, a decree issued in 1864, it was stated that the Pope could not and ought not 'to reconcile himself with progress, with liberalism, and with modern civilization' (Chadwick 1990: 111), while the First Vatican Council (1869–70) published in 1870 not only the dogma of Papal Infallibility, but also a firm denunciation of Modernism in all its manifestations (see further Chadwick 1990: 111–13; Vidler 1974: 146–56). And though Hopkins's 'Andromeda' [**pp. 95–6**] gives a sense of the Church embattled against Modernism as the Church 'hears roar | A wilder beast from West than all were', he yet maintained his strong scientific interests (Ball 1971: 115).

Hopkins's scientific contributions are considered in chapter 5 of Tom Zaniello's *Hopkins in the Age of Darwin* (1988), a study which, if not directly about the poetry, is suggestive about the intellectual and specifically scientific context in which that poetry was written. How, asks Zaniello, did a Victorian poet, with a keen interest in science, confront the revolutionary problems generated by the discoveries known collectively as the Age of Darwin? (Zaniello 1988: xiii). Zaniello looks at Oxford, in Hopkins's time, and at Hopkins's interest in language and perception in relation to the major challenges to theology by supporters of Darwin, most notably T. H. Huxley. As another dimension to the Oxford of Tractarianism, Zaniello points to the wide interest in science at Oxford, marked by the opening of the Oxford University Museum, and notoriously by the 1860 meeting of the British Association for Science, when Huxley and Samuel Wilberforce, Bishop of Oxford, debated Darwinian evolution. Zaniello gives an account of the atomist theory, which argued, as Darwin's evolution could be seen to do, that all physical activity and development came from a random fall of atoms, rather than divine plan (Zaniello 1988: 35–36). Atomism was a form of materialism, and while Stonyhurst was scientifically active, with Stephen Perry heading its meteorological station, the Jesuits were also necessarily alert to the doctrinal implications of the First Vatican Council, which amongst its decrees expressed concern to rescue those sunk in the abyss 'of Pantheism, Materialism, and Atheism' (Zaniello 1988: 87). Hopkins was no progressive, but his critique of Darwinism reveals the 'flexibility' of someone who wished 'to accept Darwin's findings' without rejecting traditional religious beliefs (Zaniello 1988: 112–13).

Patricia Ball's *The Science of Aspects* (1971), a study of science and the treatment of fact in Coleridge, Ruskin and Hopkins, returns us more directly to critical consideration of the poetry, and offers a bridge across from nature and science into religion. This is clear, focused, and usefully exploratory, about nature and science, but also aesthetics and religion, in ways entirely helpful to the (slightly advanced) reader. The title, 'The science of aspects', is taken from Ruskin, who declares a study needs to be made not only of the *nature* of things, but also their effect from that 'aspect' upon 'the eyes or heart' and Ball focuses upon the strands of Romanticisms and Ruskinianism in Hopkins's work (see Ball 1968, below), linking the observation of the prose to the revelation of the poetry.

Romantic subjectivism, which draws all experience to the poet's self, Hopkins, as did Ruskin, denounced ('your d – d subjective rot'; L, 1.84; Ball 1971: 103), yet this was not to deny the 'central self', which delights, not in introspection, but the revelation of the distinctive self, a revelation loved by Hopkins 'as it emerges in the act rather than as it beholds itself in the egotistical consciousness' (Ball 1971: 105). Hopkins sought a term ('inscape') for his experience that 'in the behaviour of what is watched, there is identity to be appreciated, the marks of individuality to be divined, the expression of personal being to be discerned' (Ball 1971:108). The 'pure' facts are not passive, but charged and potent. Hopkins's descriptive prose, with its appetite for fact and strong intellectual drive to understand the universe, to uncover its laws (Ball 1971: 118), was a preparation for the poetry, as Hopkins's power lies in the ability 'to keep us in the presence of the thing itself while he demonstrates its properties and exposes the laws of its being' (Ball 1971: 123). Fact is placed in a dependent relationship, as in the structure of 'The Wreck', where Part Two reflects Part One's psychological evolution from crisis to insight, a context which defines the value of the facts of storm and death.

Religion

Hopkins was pained by Bridges's assumption that religion and his Catholic belief had no more meaning for him than they did for Bridges: as if 'you were only waiting with a certain disgust till I too should be disgusted with myself enough to throw off the mask' (L, 1.148). However Hopkins might, especially in his later years, feel desolation, the silence of God, he never ceased to believe in God's existence and the truth of the Catholic Church. Religious in himself, he was also a religious poet. But is he a *religious* poet, rather than someone simply 'bringing in' religion? And what kind of effect does his religion have on the way he writes and hence what kind of religious poet he is? These are questions raised, though hardly answered, by the early critics: they knew he was a Catholic and a Jesuit, but either skirted this, denigrated it, or touched on it only to pass on. Some of this at least was an unease by British readers at a systematic religion, as against a general sentiment of religious cosiness, or else outright hostility in the Modernist movement to absolutes, including religious belief. In a useful discussion, Gerald Roberts, in his Introduction to the *Critical Heritage*, agrees that while Hopkins's mind '*does* show through' in the poetry, it is 'a Catholic and a Jesuit one, and not to be appreciated without some effort and conscious rejection of bias by the reader' (Roberts 1987: 6). Roberts highlights the early critical theme of the dichotomy between poet and priest, found for example in *Time and Tide* (1935), which declared Hopkins a 'split man', poetry and religion 'pulling opposite ways' (Roberts 1987: 31), though in the same year Desmond MacCarthy, more sympathetic religiously, suggested the two vocations led rather to a 'peculiar concentration' in the poems (Roberts 1987: 31). As well as the 'split' between poet and priest, dichotomies found by earlier critics include oppositions both of sensuality and art to religion.

Some early critics had no difficulty with the religion: Clutton-Brock (1919) thought Hopkins had 'the audacity and the good faith' of the religious poet, so that in 'Heraclitean Fire' [pp. 118–9], his 'passion strikes sparks' in 'a fierce utterance of belief fiercely worn' (Roberts 1987: 86). Others were dismissive: 'too prevailingly theological' (Roberts 1987: 116); or, uncomfortable with the issue of religion, found, like I.A. Richards, Hopkins 'intellectually' (that so-English damnation) 'too stiff, too "cogged and cumbered" with beliefs, those bundles of invested emotional capital' (Roberts 1987: 145). Yet others called on Freud to picture Hopkins 'fumbling in the dark, his brain tortured by religious phantasies by which he sublimated his remarkable sensuality' (Roberts 1987: 149), or if accepting the genuine nature of Hopkins's belief, the 'violent rhythms' express little else than excitement, and 'even the religious experience is incomplete' (Roberts 1987: 225).

Even so responsive a critic as F.R. Leavis shies away from the religious dimension, though not denying it: he acknowledges 'inner, spiritual, emotional stress' in 'The Wreck', but finds 'terrible doubt' rather than faith in the later sonnets (Leavis 1963: 143, 151). Again, while finding Hopkins's religious interests combine with 'a vigour of mind that puts him in another poetic world from the other Victorians', Leavis declares the Christianity to be 'dogmatic' (strictly true, but the sense here is clearly pejorative), with 'consequent difficulties and delicacies' (Leavis 1962: 48), presumably for poet and readers alike, though the meaning is unclear. Amongst the earlier critics it is again Elsie Phare who is most alert to Hopkins's adequacy to experience, so that for 'all his unhappiness, spiritual and mortal', he never takes 'refuge in an imaginary world, nor even in a world purely of the spirit' (Phare 1933: 76), while her account of 'Harry Ploughman' [pp. 116–7] might serve as a paradigm for Hopkins as poet: Harry is 'a creature', who 'exercising all the powers with which he is endowed',

> merely as a by-product flashes off beauty, unknown to him-self, giving intense pleasure to the eye of the beholder, as well as giving satisfaction to the Creator who sees his creature using its faculties to their utmost.
>
> (Phare 1933: 73).

A modern critic, Helen Vendler, rightly insists that those who feel the Nature sonnets 'spoiled' by the 'tacking-on' of a moral 'after a brilliant sensuous rendition of the world' fail to recognise Hopkins's compulsion to render 'his secondary interior intellectual process, as well as his primary sensuous process' (Vendler 1995: 20). Yet when we ask what kind of religious poet Hopkins was, we may be baffled by what the terms mean: mystic; contemplative; meditative; devotional; sacramental; sentimental. Was Hopkins a mystic, someone who had direct experience of God, such as St Teresa of Avila describes, whether in the oppression of the damned or Christ's appearance in 'most sacred Humanity, in all the beauty and majesty of His resurrection body' (Teresa 1987: 233–34, 196)? Few people are mystics and few (except loosely) believe Hopkins to be a mystic: though Sulloway strongly suggests that Hopkins, writing to Bridges (L, 1.66), hints that Christ had appeared to him at one time or another and that in 'The Wreck' Hopkins translated a contemporary 'ordeal of the waters' into 'a mystical event' (Sulloway 1972: 184, 194). Geoffrey Hartman, sceptical about such claims ('in no way a mystic'), allows a possible exception in 'Carrion Comfort' (Hartman 1966: 54), though there the wrestling with '(My God!) My God!', since based on Genesis's Jacob and the angel [p. 114], is metaphor rather than a personal experience.

Of the other terms used to characterise the poet Hopkins, it is perhaps best to offer rough definitions before turning to the more detailed studies produced since 1940. 'Contemplative' implies ima-gining and emotionally responding to some image or event, such as Christ in Majesty or (in the rosary) the Virgin as Joyful or Sorrowful Mother. 'Meditative' is a more active application of thought to the unravelling of doctrine, seen at a simple level in 'The May Magnifi-cat' [p. 93], where the poem is an unpacking of the links between Virgin and month. 'Devotional' is directed to lead others to a better religious frame of mind; it may express the poet's devotion to God or the saints but seeks a more public audience; 'devotional' may shade or collapse into 'sentimental', with demands upon the readers' emotions falsely achieved. Yet this series indicates how shifting, opal-hued, the terms are, especially when used loosely.

ANGLICAN AND TRACTARIAN?

While Hopkins is best categorised as a Catholic poet, he came out of a High Anglican and, at Oxford, a Tractarian background, through the influence both of Liddon [p. 12] and of John Keble [p. 10]. Hopkins was responsive, certainly in his early poetry, to the Tractarian poetic tradition, which found its most popular expression in Keble's *The Christian Year* (1827), a series of devotional poems tied, as the title suggests, to the Christian (Anglican) calendar. It is this influence that Margaret Johnson traces in *Gerard Manley Hopkins and Tractarian Poetry* (1997), touching also on R.W. Dixon, Christina Rossetti, and Newman, to argue that the roots of Hopkins's technique lie not in the *Spiritual Exercises* [p. 22], but in a tradition stemming back through Keble to Wordsworth. Looking at the relationship between theology and poetics, Johnson links each chapter by the 'argument about the Incarnation' (Margaret Johnson 1997: 11), the divine act central to Hopkins's thought and poetry, a doctrine taking in also the Eucharist and issues of Transubstantiation and the Real presence. Johnson traces Tractarian poetry back to Coleridge and Wordsworth, later placing Hopkins's 'The Escorial' [pp. 44–5] in this tradition, where both choice of building and brilliancy of detail ('a Pre-Raphaelite painting in motion') show it to be 'a shell enclosing nothing' (Margaret Johnson 1997: 213–14, 205).

Wordsworth's sense of the numinous (the presence of the divine in natural objects or places) was a powerful influence on Keble and through him on Newman, though Tractarian poetry was modified by vital theological needs that Wordsworth's early work, close to pantheism, God being in and inseparable from physical nature, failed to supply (Margaret Johnson 1997: 19–20), The essence of Tractarian poetry, Johnson insists, is 'a revelation of the divine' (Margaret Johnson 1997: 29). Johnson labours rather at showing likeness in the use of analogy in Keble and in 'The Wreck' – analogy is a common enough poetic technique. More importantly, though, in a discussion of 'Barnfloor and Winepress' [pp. 50–1], Johnson points to specifically religious features – prefatory biblical quotation; natural images to convey specifically Christian message – that Hopkins adopted from Keble, even while he 'collapses' the distance between God and nature, God and humanity, humanity and nature (Margaret Johnson 1997: 41). Hopkins's attempts to show the interfusion of God and the world, though, were not Roman Catholic, but 'already present in Hopkins' Tractarian poetry' (Margaret Johnson 1997: 45). Where both Keble and Hopkins use the stars as analogies or metaphors, Keble seems 'pallid and trite', while Hopkins explores the mystery within the physical object, 'just as the barn exists to hold the harvest; so that all things are formed by the stress of God's presence' (Margaret Johnson 1997: 57).

TRACTARIAN INTO CATHOLIC

With conversion, however close his doctrinal beliefs had been to Catholic, Hopkins entered a new religious world, that had lasting consequences for his poetry, especially since long poetic silence allowed him to absorb the more fully Catholic practices, including forms of prayer and attitudes to the dead. Ian Ker so argues in *The Catholic Revival in English Literature, 1845–1961* (2003). To show the change in Hopkins's style as a result of his conversion, Ker points to 'the unliterary language of a now largely discarded Catholic piety', the rhythms and diction of which would appear to outsiders 'foreign and unEnglish' (Ker 2003: 47), and to show this shift compares 'Barnfloor and Winepress' from before Hopkins's conversion and 'The Bugler's First Communion' from after (Ker 2003: 43–44). Ker highlights new concerns and new rhythms, which emphasise Newman's own insistence on Catholicism being 'business-like', professional in its concept of priesthood, unlike the 'genteel family conversation of an Anglican vicarage' (Ker 2003: 42, 49), though being 'business-like' can embarrass, in a word like 'treat' ('To his youngster take his treat!'), a quality highlighted by Phare in our awareness of an uncomfortable 'lusciousness' in the boy with the image of a 'pushed peach' (Phare 1933: 48). Ker also moves with 'Felix Randal' [pp. 102–3] to the importance for Catholics of the dead, who are not excluded from the community of the living: we can pray for them and they can pray for us (Ker 2003: 55). This is a cultural loss to Protestants, of purgatory, of the invocation of the saints: so that Tennyson in *In Memoriam* cannot pray for the dead Arthur Hallam, but Hopkins can pray for Henry Purcell (Ker 2003: 53).

SACRAMENTALISM: THE INCARNATION

The seven sacraments – baptism, communion (the eucharist), confirmation, confession, marriage, ordination, extreme unction – are all regarded as channels by which God's grace is given to the faithful. Other experiences may be seen as giving access to grace, connecting us to some power beyond us, and so be deemed sacramental. Hilary Fraser distinguishes between Wordsworth's and Hopkins's understanding of the sacramental value of Nature. Wordsworth's 'natural sacramentalism' takes 'no account of circumstances which took place after the creation of heaven and earth – the coming of evil, sin, and suffering ... Christ's incarnation, miracles, the Redemption': Hopkins's Nature was sacramental in that it was symbolic of a divine creator (Fraser 1986: 70).

Christ's Incarnation, which is unnecessary for 'natural sacramentalism', is fundamental to Christianity and fundamental to Hopkins's theories of perception, beauty, and poetry. He saw the Incarnation as an act of love, rather than a ransom [p. 134]. Inscapes, 'versions of the whole nature of Christ', become a re-enactment, in God's creation, of the Incarnation, exemplified by Fraser in the nun's experience in 'The Wreck', in 'her recognition of Christ in the inscape of the storm, and the utterance of her cry, as conceiving him anew' (Fraser 1986: 94, 93). While Margaret Johnson reinforces this sacramental vision, identifying it in the Tractarian understanding of Nature as a sacrament (Margaret Johnson 1997: 221), the concept has been much argued over. Earlier, the American critic, Yvor Winters, decrying the kestrel in 'The Windhover' as symbolic of Christ, had denounced 'pretentious remarks' about the sacramental view of Nature as merely foolish (Winters 1966 [1957]: 55), while Marshall McLuhan in 1944, presumably the provocation to Winters's dismissal, claimed Hopkins 'habitually shifts his gaze from the order and perspectives of nature to the analogous but grander scenery of the moral and intellectual order', the 'book of nature' providing a parallel with the 'supernatural revelations' of scripture (McLuhan 1966: 83).

HUSK AND KERNEL

Critical and scholarly investigation of Hopkins's sacramental beliefs have proliferated. A tough study, not to be read through at one go, is Jeffrey B. Loomis's *Dayspring in Darkness: Sacrament in Hopkins* (1988). Bedevilled occasionally by its language ('another rapt theophanic experience of Ignatian meditative colloquy' – an extreme but not unfair example), it usefully takes a long view of the poetry, not just sacramental doctrine, and provides an overview, critical but not unsympathetic, of other studies. Loomis develops his view of sacramentalism from the accepted idea of the sacraments being outward and visible means by which invisible grace may be obtained, so developing the distinction of husk (the outer form) and kernel (the inner significance). This distinction ties in Loomis's account of sacramentalism with his account of Hopkins's poetic technique: Hopkins's use, not only of 'inscape', but also 'outscape'. 'Outscape' is the contrasting poetic textures of outer 'overthought' and inner 'underthought'; the setting of external experience of the 'affective will' against internal choices of the 'elective will'; the alternating of exuberant 'externalist' natural poetry with poetic monologues on the spiritually-struggling internal soul (Loomis 1988: 9).

Emphasising the importance to Hopkins of his Catholic faith and Jesuit training, Loomis denies the poet was destroyed by an anti-poetic-Jesuit counterpoise, arguing that a poetic vocation destroyed would not produce the highly wrought poetry of Hopkins's last years, poems that are 'such intricate artifacts that they could not result from enforced suppression of energy' (Loomis 1988: 22). Examining Hopkins's poetic development decade by decade, on the basis of the 'husk-kernel' pattern of sacramental revelation, Loomis shapes his exploration through a tripartite sequence: of developing ideas about art; of developing attitudes about nature; and of developing attitudes about human beings' inner spiritual life (Loomis 1988: 32). Considering Hopkins's early poetry, when as an Anglican there were only two sacraments (baptism and the eucharist) and a developed sacramental belief therefore unlikely to be prominent, Loomis has useful discussion of 'Pilate' [**pp. 48–9**] and 'One of the Spies' [**p. 49**], but it is the mature poetry that chiefly benefits from Hopkins's perception of Christ, the Incarnate God, present in his creation, Scotus [**p. 24**] here being a key figure, in the idea of 'the radiance of Christic Presence sacramentally outpouring from nature' (Loomis 1988: 66), even if at times a gap is sensed between things of nature and of God.

In Hopkins's final decade, though, as the world becomes darker externally and in the poet's perception [**pp. 157–8**], description of the natural world becomes an inner landscape, a 'delineation of a saint's inner life' (Loomis 1988: 115), as Hopkins awaits, 'in new silence', the end of all things (Loomis 1988: 115), with nature's signs of devastation in 'The Leaden Echo' [**pp. 105–6**] and 'The Shepherd's Brow' [**p. 121**]. Even in the midst of his personal turmoil, though, Hopkins never lost his poetic power, so that in the 'Terrible' Sonnets, distanced from self-torment, we have not Hillis Miller's 'disappearance of God' [**p. 160**] nor the humanist psyche 'in extremity' of John Robinson (1978) [**pp. 197–8**], but a Christian sacramental biography, where experience can still give grace (Loomis 1988: 135, 142).

CHRIST'S FIGURE AND NATURE

Naturally, as Christian and Catholic, but above all in his devotion and his poetry, paramount for Hopkins was Christ's Incarnation, his dual godhead and humanity. Critics, both humanist and believer, agree, differing on the effect. For Geoffrey Hartman, in *The Unmediated Vision*, consequences follow Hopkins's commitment, as the poet's Christ is 'dangerously near to physical man, while man is still dangerously near to physical beauty' (Hartman, 1966: 60): confusion might therefore arise between religious and sensuous feelings, where the sense of self and the sense of being in Christ 'can no longer be distinguished' (Hartman, 1966: 64).

A more thorough exploration, important, if to be handled cautiously because of the obsession with a 'single thread' to lead us through the labyrinth of poetic interpretation, is James Finn Cotter's *Inscape: The Christology and Poetry of Gerard Manley Hopkins* (1972). A close examination of Hopkins's theological development in relation to the Christ of the gospel, in the Church Fathers, and in Scotus, leads into a detailed reading of the poetry. Cotter, as other studies do, seizes on Hopkins's undergraduate interest in the early Greek philosopher, Parmenides (Barnes 1987: 40, 129–42), and sees his influence in Hopkins's evolution of the idea of 'inscape', since 'being', the essential nature of a thing, is a source of energy from which everything radiates and to which it is drawn back (Cotter 1972: 16): so, as in 'Let Me Be to Thee as the Circling Bird' [**p. 48**], our reflections and desires constantly turn round Christ, the centre of being (Cotter 1972: 17), and Cotter goes on to claim, with reason, that Hopkins's insights into the mystery of the humanity of Christ show a sensitivity unmatched in his time (Cotter 1972: 56–57). From this follows an insistence on the intimacy of divine life, saturating everyday living, permeating Hopkins's poetry, as through his passion and resurrection, 'Christ enters the whole field of man's interests and concerns' (Cotter 1972: 65). Arguing that all martyrdoms are repetitions of Christ's martyrdom, Cotter claims the nun's experience in 'The Wreck' repeats verbally and actually a martyr's death, itself patterned on Christ's: death is 'a choice that answers *yes* in obedience with Christ's great sacrifice' (Cotter 1972: 149).

THE POET AS JESUIT

Hopkins not only became a Catholic, like a number of his Oxford contemporaries, but also a Jesuit and arguments about the results for his religious practice and thought and for his poetry have been fierce and often contradictory. Walter J. Ong's study, *Hopkins, the Self, and God* (1986), explores how no other Victorian quite matched Hopkins in 'the intensity of his passion, his insights, and his theories regarding the importance of being different' (Ong 1986: 3). For Jesuits were different, in discipline, obedience, intellectual culture – different also, in England and elsewhere abroad, in being regarded with suspicion and hostility [**p. 21**]. Himself a Jesuit, Ong traces Hopkins both as a distinctive consciousness and as a Jesuit. The Victorians were fascinated by the interrelationship of external particulars and the interior self, Hopkins typically treating 'the self as face-to-face with itself, confrontationally' (Ong 1986: 22), while the idea of realising oneself in Christ, common to all Christian teaching, 'is particularly highlighted in Jesuit spirituality' (Ong 1986: 25). For Ong there is no doubt about Hopkins's 'workaday' faith and understanding of doctrine, so that in 'Sibyl's Leaves', Ong dismisses Leavis's reading (Leavis 1963: 151) of a 'terrible doubt' at the root of Hopkins's absolutes of 'black, white; right, wrong' in a priest convinced of the 'irreducible seriousness of questions of conscience' (Ong 1986: 105). Central for Ong to the Jesuit experience are the *Spiritual Exercises* of St Ignatius, which focus with intensity 'on the self and on human freedom as centring the self' and which 'penetrated Hopkins' entire life' (Ong 1986: 54–55). Ong lays out well the Jesuit background and many other critics have seized upon the *Spiritual Exercises*, but with surprisingly opposed results.

THE MEDITATIVE TRADITION: IGNATIUS AND THE *EXERCISES*

Critics, aware from early on of Hopkins's Catholic and Jesuit background, touched on forms of meditation and the *Spiritual Exercises* [pp. 22; 88]. Phare glanced at these in her discussion of 'The Wreck', when, obviously thinking of the concrete imagining (the 'composition of place') required by the *Exercises*, she is adversely critical of Hopkins's attempt 'to make himself believe that his feelings ... were more intense than was actually the case', a fault she traces to St Ignatius's method of meditation, in which 'the will is forcing the emotions and forcing them too roughly' (Phare 1933: 109).

Such passing references to the *Exercises* and to the spiritual experiences of Spanish mystics like St John of the Cross [p. 107], lie behind the noted scholar Humphry House's attack (1935) on those who drew an analogy between the 'Terrible' Sonnets and the Dark Night of the Soul. He claimed instead a 'more elementary and universal' experience behind the poetry (Roberts 1987: 308). Against this, in the same year, Christopher Devlin, himself a Jesuit, asserted that the *Exercises* were 'the origin of Hopkins' poetic thought', both in his assimilation of them and in the 'consequent out-pouring of the Holy Spirit', while against House's 'elementary' experience in the 'Terrible' Sonnets, Devlin sees them as no more an 'absolute tragedy ... than there was an absolute tragedy in Gethsemane on Maundy Thursday' (Roberts 1987: 319, 322–23). The *Spiritual Exercises* are touched on in the biographies of Ruggles (1947: 82–686), Kitchen (1978: 118–20), and White (1992: 178–81, 186–87), as well as in Devlin's introduction to Hopkins's writings on the *Exercises*

(*S*, 107–21). The relation of Hopkins to traditions of meditation, of meditative poetry and, in particular, to the *Spiritual Exercises*, continues to be disputed territory.

THE MEDITATIVE TRADITION: THE IGNATIAN SPIRIT

While it is possible to remain sceptical about the extent of the influences of the *Spiritual Exercises* on Hopkins's poetry, it is clear that he is a meditative poet, closely scrutinising nature and God's presence and role in creation. An important study by Louis L. Martz, *The Poetry of Meditation* (1954), focused on the seventeenth century, finds a clear likeness between the earlier meditative tradition and Hopkins's response to the *Spiritual Exercises*. If meditation is a practice according to the 'three powers of the soul' (memory; understanding; will), then there is a likeness to those powers apparent in Hopkins's commentary on the *Exercises*, of identification (seeing what the thing in itself is); memory; and imagination (Martz 1962: xxiii–xxv). So, in 'Spring and Fall' [**pp. 103–4**] (not cited by Martz), Margaret has the power of identification (she grieves over the leaf-fall), but not the other powers, which the speaker *does* have, with the weight of understanding and feeling that memory and imagination bring. In meditation, Martz suggests, the senses, emotions, and intellectual faculties can come together in a moment of 'dramatic, creative experience' (Martz 1962: 1).

The most detailed study of the Ignatian Spirit is David A. Downes's (1959), exploring how the *Exercises* are 'a synthesis and summation of the whole early tradition of meditation' (Downes 1959: 9), taking in therefore not only the concept of Ignatius as a chivalric warrior of Christ, but also the influence on Ignatius and so on Hopkins of earlier meditative writers, notably Thomas à Kempis (1380–1471) in his *Imitation of Christ* (*c.*1440). The first words of the *Exercises* are 'Man was created to praise' and Hopkins's poems praise Christ 'as the prototype pattern of creation' (Downes 1959: 34). Downes examines Hopkins's religious development and then Ignatius and the Ignatian Spirit in the poetry. He traces in 'The Wreck', the two wrecks, of Hopkins and the nun, identical in their spiritual implications, with Hopkins, as a soldier of Christ, being 'on his guard to discern the mysterious actions of God in the affairs of man' (Downes 1959: 52); explores the analogy, rather than the allusion, to Christ's passion in 'The Windhover', its knightly and chivalric terms derived from Ignatius; and reveals the 'Terrible' Sonnets not as Freudian manifestations of frustration, but the revelations of a spiritual plight, 'the result of which God alone knows' (Downes 1959: 145). The poetic rather than the merely autobiographical nature of the 'Terrible' Sonnets is again pursued in Downes's essay, 'The Final Act: Hopkins' Last Sonnets' (Downes 1989: 239–65), which focuses on their biblical subtexts and dramatic contexts.

Experience into technique

How Nature, Science, God, intertwine in Hopkins, and how they cannot be divorced from the poetry and from poetic technique, the concern of the next subsection, is admirably demonstrated by J. Hillis Miller's study, *The Disappearance of God* [p. 160]. For Miller, Hopkins's conversion was 'an attempt to avoid falling into the abyss of the absence of God' (Miller 1975: 312). At the heart of Miller's exploration of Hopkins lies a concern with how nature, science, self, and God tie up together, and the solution found in rhyme and pitch. Pitch, a musical term, was adopted by Hopkins to express the level at which, like musical instruments, we 'perform' in harmony with God or out of it, shared by all, even while our individual selfhood or pitch is shared with no other (Miller 1975: 270; referring to *S*, 122ff). Allied to this technical concept is rhyme, so that all nature is pitched in relationship to the human self and to God, while all things rhyme, in a pattern of chiming. This leads, in a consideration of Parmenides's doctrine of being (Barnes 1987: 40), to an insistence on being as a vital force, a creative energy (Miller 1975: 309), and this being is Christ, so each created thing 'is a version of Christ, and derives its being from the way it expresses Christ's nature in a unique way', and Miller concludes (or rather, seems to conclude) 'All things rhyme in Christ' (Miller 1975: 313). What is found, though, is then snatched away, above all in the 'Terrible' Sonnets, 'the most shattering experience' of any of the Victorians of the disappearance of God.

TECHNIQUE

Miller's linking of Christ and rhyme highlights the essential interaction in Hopkins's poetry between content and style. Hopkins was 'making it new', and while his 'strangeness' was recognised from the first, not all readers and critics took it in the same way. Bridges [p. 132] took the strangeness badly, scorning Hopkins's affectation in metaphor, the 'rude shocks of his purely artistic wantonness', an ambiguous use of language, repellent rhymes, and (capitalised by Bridges) all the 'Oddity and Obscurity' (Jenkins 2006: 50). Other early responses, though, acclaimed 'winged daring, originality, durable texture' (Roberts 1987: 93) or found Hopkins 'full of strange powers' (Roberts 1987: 185). F.R. Leavis, in *New Bearings in English Poetry*

(1932), again stressed difficulty, so much a key term in criticism of Modernist poetry, and claimed 'the difficulty is essential', since 'every word ... is doing a great deal more work than almost any word in a poem by Robert Bridges' (Leavis 1963: 134), while stressing Hopkins's own insistence on the need to read this poetry with the body as well as the eye (Leavis 1963: 140).

Two more recent critics, James Olney and Helen Vendler, are suggestive about Hopkins's technique, if not primarily technical. Olney, considering three 'strange' poets, Emily Dickinson, Walt Whitman, and Hopkins, claims that in poetry it is not a question of *being* strange, but of *making* strange, since the poet's vision will seem strange 'as coming from the extreme bounds – and beyond – of human experience and expression' (Olney 1993: 93). He identifies that vision rather as Hopkins identified Wordsworth's [**p. 28**], the strangeness pointing 'to a mysteriousness or a mysterious something beyond our capacity for rational formulation, but which ... is felt meaning' (Olney 1993: 98). Vendler also talks of strangeness, since when a poet puts off an old style, he 'perpetrates an act of violence ... on the self' (Vendler 1995: 1). She explores Hopkins's use of Sprung Rhythm in the early poetry and through close readings of the mature works. Hopkins, she suggests, found a 'new sense of life' press upon him unbidden, 'making the old style seem unsuitable or even repellent' (Vendler 1995: 1). For Vendler, Hopkins's vision and his technique are intertwined, Sprung Rhythm itself corresponding to his 'most fundamental intuition' that 'the beautiful was dangerous, irregular, and binary' (Vendler 1995: 9). Sprung Rhythm, with its openness on unstressed syllables, is indeed 'irregular' and, citing 'The Windhover' and scrutinising the metrical pattern, in the moment when 'Brute beauty and valour and act ... here | Buckle! AND', Vendler suggests that when 'ecstasy is in question, the "squeezing out" of the interstices between shocks', by the rapid passage over unstressed syllables to stressed, 'is a means of maximising rapture' (Vendler 1995: 18).

TECHNIQUE: FORMAL ANALYSIS

Suggestive, even analytical, as Olney and Vendler are, they do not claim to offer detailed accounts of Hopkins's use of language. That has been the work of two earlier scholars, W.H. Gardner and James Milroy, in studies that overlap and complement each other. Gardner's *Gerard Manley Hopkins: A Study of Poetic Idiosyncrasy in Relation to Poetic Tradition* (2 vols, 1944 & 1949) was a pioneering work, now superseded in its biographical sections, yet still useful on technical exploration and analysis of Sprung Rhythm, literary form, diction and syntax, imagery and theme, while his more critical consideration of the poetry in vol. 2 remains valuable as a matching of acute analysis with critical sense. Milroy's *The Language of Gerard Manley Hopkins* (1977) is more technically focused, though always aware that it is the poetry that justifies the context and analysis of Hopkins's relationship to language. Given each work's organisation, it makes best sense to begin with Milroy and then later run him and Gardner in parallel, with other, related, studies brought in at appropriate points.

Milroy, who overall attempts to show that Hopkins's use of language 'is not a violation, but an extension of *laws* or underlying rules that are already present in the language' (Milroy 1977: 189), begins by placing Hopkins in a fascinating account of Victorian language theory and practice, since Hopkins lived at a time when the investigation of linguistic change and variation was a major scholarly concern. Within this historical survey, Milroy considers how Hopkins sought to hammer out a language proper for poetry, not bound by outworn ideas of correctness or decorum (what Milroy terms 'Continuous Literary Decorum') inherited from the eighteenth century or even the Romantics. It is a language drawing on forms and vocabulary often rejected as 'unpoetic' by Hopkins's contemporaries, whether speech patterns and idioms, or terms appropriate to sailors, ploughmen, blacksmiths. As Wordsworth sought to establish the taste by which he would be judged and as Blake declared that he must either forge his own language or be bound by another man's system, so Hopkins established a language of poetry distinct from the common poetic language of his age.

For Hopkins, the 'obsolete' diction of the Victorians was objectionable since it 'destroyed' earnestness: it blinded one 'to the importance of life around one, suppressed freedom in language and dulled perception' (Milroy 1977: 16–17). Certainly, Hopkins grew up, physically and poetically, in a tradition of Romanticism, of Keats, as in 'A Vision of the Mermaids' [**pp. 45–6**], and of Wordsworth, as in 'The Alchemist in the City' [**pp. 55–6**] or the later 'Cheery Beggar' [**p. 99**]. Phare back in 1933 had explored Hopkins's links to Wordsworth, first because the Romantics were an obvious heritage, second because she perceived that Hopkins was yet different from his assumed immediate predecessor – where Wordsworth submits himself to the arbitrariness of actual experience, Hopkins's mind 'is much more given to the formal and the abstract' (Phare 1933: 55); again, while Wordsworth 'catches the reader up and absorbs him', Hopkins 'keeps him a little aloof, treats him as an audience, does not allow him to take the poet's experience for his own' (Phare 1933: 64). More sympathetic to a tradition stemming from the Romantics, characterised not so much as obvious linguistic likeness as 'continuity of imagination', is Patricia M. Ball's exploration in *The Central Self: A Study in Romantic and Victorian Imagination* (1968), extending the idea of a 'self-conscious Imagination' from the Romantics, through the Victorians, to Modern poetry, claiming for the Victorians, 'participation in the Romantic enterprise' (Ball: 1968 3), so that 'The Ancient Mariner', seen to mark 'the moment when the Miltonic presentation of the supernatural scene gives way to the Romantic investigation of the supernatural experience', leads on to Victorian approaches, including 'The Wreck' (Ball 1968: 96).

Milroy looks at the nineteenth-century excitement in language exploration and argues that while Alison Sulloway may be right about Ruskin's influence on Hopkins's language theories [**p. 152**], it is to the historical and comparative researches of philology that Hopkins owes more. Milroy gives a useful account of the academic, Max Müller, whose idea of language as something 'that must be studied to reveal its inner mysteries' is implicit in Hopkins's Journal entries, for language, 'like nature, has its laws, patterns and inscapes' (Milroy 1977: 52). There was increasing opposition to a centralised standard and to ideas of grammatical 'correctness' – the *Oxford English Dictionary* and the dialect dictionaries of the period attempted to describe, not prescribe language – and this ties in with Hopkins's reverence for the individuality or selfhood of natural objects and scenes, Milroy quoting from 'As Kingfishers Catch Fire' [**p. 97**], as each thing '*myself* it speaks and spells, | Crying *What I do is me: for that I came.*'

The influence of Max Müller more generally upon the later Victorian poets is taken up by Isobel Armstrong in *Victorian Poetry: Poetry, Poetics and Politics* (1993), where in Pt III she considers Müller (pp. 381 ff), before turning to Hopkins in a chapter subtitled 'Agonistic Reactionary – The Grotesque as Conservative Form'. Armstrong notes that Hopkins developed a theory of the structure of language and believed, as a Catholic, in 'the authority of the Word made flesh through the incarnation of Christ' (Armstrong 1993: 420), and she develops her examination through the claim that the strain of holding simultaneously a 'modernist' theory of language and a belief in the incarnate Word 'marks the passionate torsions and desperate ecstasies' of Hopkins's work (Armstrong 1993: 420). A determined student, interested in exploring Hopkins's language, might get something by wrestling with Armstrong, though it is not for the faint-hearted or those without a good dictionary to hand.

After Müller, Milroy turns to 'current' language, insisting that Hopkins's notion of *current language* (or 'ordinary modern language') is much broader than that of his critics. Acutely conscious of the orderliness and pattern of language, Hopkins was drawn to the 'in-earnestness' of speech. He found it in dialect, because he felt that, if he could use it aptly, it would help him capture the inscapes of the world and felt too that specialised and dialect usages could help to build up a new poetic vocabulary to replace the diction of standard models (Milroy 1977: 93). Hopkins was very likely drawn to Richard Chenevix Trench's immensely popular, *On the Study of Words* (1851; 20th edn, 1888), and the reason is obvious when Milroy quotes Trench on the kestrel:

> Any one who has watched the [kestrel] hanging poised in the air, before it swoops upon its prey, will acknowledge the felicity of the name 'windhover', or sometimes 'windfanner', which it popularly bears.
>
> (Milroy 1977: 82).

The potential of 'windhover' is realised alike by Trench (long before Hopkins's poem) and by Hopkins in 'his riding | Of the rolling level underneath him steady air'.

Two other critics, who have taken up issues of Victorian poetic language are Donald Davie and Virginia Ridley Ellis. Davie in *Purity of Diction in English Verse* (1952), seeks to distinguish between the 'diction of verse' and the 'language of poetry', suggesting that Hopkins (like Shakespeare) gives 'no sense of English words thrusting to be let into the poem and held out of it by the poet'. Rather, one 'feels that Hopkins could have found a place for every word in the language' (Davie 1967: 5). Ellis begins from Arnold's dictum, often since disputed, on the purpose of the poet, to see the object as 'in itself it really is'. She insists that 'the object' a critic can 'most validly and usefully examine is the artifact, the made thing, not the maker's psychology, nor the making mind of the reader' (Ellis 1991: xiv). It is a useful corrective to much subjective criticism and if arguably an 'old-fashioned' approach, it yet offers interesting and useful readings of 'The Wreck', 'The Windhover', and the 'Terrible' Sonnets.

TECHNIQUE: DICTION AND SYNTAX

Milroy, having examined the ideas about language and about the language of poetry in the Victorian period, then turns more specifically to Hopkins's practice in the light of the poet's interest in 'current language'. Hopkins himself insisted the diction of poetry, however much drawn from the current language, must be heightened. Gardner more specifically points to Hopkins's own early essay on poetic diction (*J*, 84–85), where Hopkins claims verse necessitates and engenders 'a difference in diction and in thought' (*J*, 84; Gardner 1966: I, 109). For Hopkins, Milroy suggests, heightening is related to inscape – insofar as heightening consists of linguistic devices used to bring about inscape (Milroy 1977: 101) – words as well as the things named have inscape – that makes one word better for poetic purpose rather than another, arguably synonymous, word. In this, Hopkins is not fundamentally different from other poets and Milroy then raises the idea of language as 'game', a concept popularised in the 1960s and 1970s, meaning of course something serious, not childish, since all language-behaviour is rule-governed like a game and 'like a game, language and poetic language would be meaningless without rules' (Milroy 1977: 107). Hopkins delighted in Carroll and Lear [**p. 58**] and Gilbert Highet noted in 1957 that while most lyric poems are predictable – they take a single thought and develop it along a single line – Hopkins, like the Roman poet Horace, and like Dylan Thomas (one of the few genuine successors to Hopkins), is a witty poet, complex and indirect (Highet 1959: 125–26). The shifts and changes in Hopkins's lyric poetry are integral to that witty game, opening out the reader's understanding by unexpected relationships that are yet seen to enlarge understanding and so give poetic pleasure.

Milroy focuses further on Hopkins's vocabulary, looking at his word-systems: doubling of words; coinage; special uses dependent on the relationship contracted by two words in two different dimensions. Not only the choice of words, but their order, is clearly characteristic of Hopkins's poetics. Many of the objections to Hopkins's syntax, from Bridges's onwards, Milroy points out, are really objections to Hopkins's rejection of 'continuous literary decorum', and yet standard Victorian diction itself 'involves considerable exploitation' of a syntax which seems to deviate from ordinary speech – and prose – as much as Hopkins in his 'freedom' (Milroy 1977: 190). All language use is, in a sense, creative. Hopkins's aim was to capture a world full of inscape, in a language he forged, even while he recognised that '"chance left free to act falls into an order as well as a purpose." Language, like nature, has this order and purpose. Hopkins used it with a sense of wonder, and in an orderly and purposeful way' (Milroy 1977: 229).

TECHNIQUE: PATTERNS OF SOUND

Hillis Miller writes of 'chiming' as a crucial effect in Hopkins [**p. 172**] and Milroy and Gardner offer more formal considerations of the device, leading us constantly towards voice and the spoken word. As Francis Berry observes in *Poetry and the Physical Voice*, a quirky but suggestive study, Bridges in reading 'The Wreck' and other poems ought to have been able to hear his absent friend's voice, when the 'right play and positioning of "stress", and the degree and kind of "expression"' would become apparent (Berry 1962: 180).

Gardner and Milroy both deal with Sprung Rhythm, bound up as it is with stress and the spoken voice. Gardner gives a careful analysis of it in 'The Wreck', pursuing the fusion of rhythm and texture, and drawing in issues of alliteration, assonance, interior rhyme, and 'vocalic scales' (Gardner 1966: I, ch. II). Gardner gives also a detailed, highly technical account, tough but illuminating, of Hopkins's rhythmic skills in Vol. II (chs II & III), drawing in Hopkins's interest in earlier poetic forms, both Classical and English. He highlights the movement from quantity to stress, so that strict iambic count is abandoned in favour of carefully regulated patterns, which ties in with the dramatic effects of the speaking voice. Gardner's consideration of earlier forms links up with Walter J. Ong's account, in 'Hopkins's Sprung Rhythm and the Life of English Poetry' (1949), of the 'sense-stress patterning which is so much the bone and sinew of English rhythm' (Ong 1969 [1949]: 167). Ong concludes that even if Hopkins did not know his English forerunners in detail, his rhythmic achievement was not 'of theory but of an extremely keen ear aided by a significantly open and objective mind' (Ong 1969 [1949]: 171).

TECHNIQUE: FORM AND TRADITION

The sonnet is by far Hopkins's preferred form in his mature poetry [**p. 80**]. Gardner notes that he develops variations on the traditional Petrarchan or Italian sonnet form. In English the sonnet takes two main forms: the Shakespearean and the Miltonic. Milton follows the Italian two-part structure in rhyme and division of argument, a form taken up also by Wordsworth, and by Dante Gabriel Rossetti (more directly from the Italian) in his translations and original verse. Gardner considers the constraints of the sonnet and how Hopkins responded to the challenge it presents, with discussion of outriders or hanging feet and of 'counterpointing', noting that 'no other poet has rung so many various and intrinsically beautiful changes' on the form (Gardner 1966: I, 96): Gardner then offers a more critically-focused discussion in Vol. II.

In his useful study, *The Nineteenth-Century Sonnet* (2005), Joseph Phelan sees the sonnet as having an ambiguous position within nineteenth-century poetics, sometimes ephemeral and occasional, yet at others a 'monument' to immortalise poet and subject (Phelan 2005: 2), so that the innovative sonnet-writers, Hopkins chief among them, 'use the form with a full sense of its uneasy relation' to beliefs and assumptions about poetry, aware too of ways in which 'they can exploit the resulting tensions for their own ends' (Phelan 2005:3). Fixing on what he calls 'the sonnet of imperialism', Phelan explores, for example, how Hopkins, a poet who saw the great social and political events, in his own words, 'in a bat-light', yet gave complex expression to the aesthetic and the imperial. Taking 'Harry Ploughman' and 'Tom's Garland' [pp. 116–7] as a pair, Phelan investigates a 'heavily and even grotesque emblematic quality', in which they admit of a variety of 'political discourses' through overt statement and 'underthoughts', activating latent resonances of the sonnet form (Phelan 2005: 75). To move from syntax to metaphorical clusters, removes Harry from the 'very type of honest and productive labour' (Phelan 2005: 76) to architectural qualities, suggesting the stable, hierarchical, organic community of the (imagined) Middle Ages (Phelan 2005: 75–76). Overall, Phelan is useful on Hopkins's sonnet form, on the 'Terrible' Sonnets [pp. 107–14], and finds 'Sibyl's Leaves' a *fin-de-siècle* poem, the motif of 'seize the day', however, transformed into a reminder of the overriding importance of the life to come (Phelan 2005: 150–51).

FORM AND TRADITION: THE CLASSICS

Hopkins's formal education was based in the Classics, which meant an intensive study of Greek and Latin, and the literature, history, and philosophy of those civilisations. From his childhood too and intensively in his theological training Hopkins read and studied the Bible, yet while this is evident everywhere and editors have noted particular references and allusions, there seems to be no extended study of Hopkins and the Bible, though Gardner does consider Hopkins's use of the Bible under Theme and Imagery (Gardner 1966: I, ch.V).

On the Classical side, a number of critics pick up from Hopkins's own notes on the Greek philosopher, Parmenides (*J*, 127–30 [p. 172]), and various attention has been given to Virgil – the 'plough down sillion' of 'The Windhover' (12) seems to echo Virgil's first Georgic as the bull at the 'deep-driven plough' causes 'the share to gleam with the furrow's polishing' (Virgil 1982: 58). On the Greeks, while Alison Sulloway finds a structure in 'The Wreck' based on the unfolding process of Greek tragedy (Sulloway 1976), little interest has been shown in Hopkins's reading of Homer, despite his classroom demonstration of Achilles dragging Hector's body (White 1992: 385) and his never-completed work on Homer [p. 37], though Warren Anderson gives an account of the surviving notes on Homer, concluding negatively, after praising Hopkins's 'superb command of Greek', that he lacked an overview of Homer 'and he lacked the physical and mental energy requisite for [the work's] attainment' (Anderson 1989: 131, 144).

More fruitful has been exploration of Hopkins's relationship to Pindar, the Greek poet (518–438 BC), whose odes, celebrations of rulers and of athletes, were in turn celebrated by the Latin poet, Horace. Pindar is like a swollen river, as the poet 'rides a torrent' where 'new words swirl and headlong | Rhythms defy the rules' (Horace 1964: 223). A flood, sweeping all before it, new rhythms, new words, certainly Hopkins strove for all these.

The Pindaric likeness is explored most extensively by Todd K. Bender in *Gerard Manley Hopkins: The Classical Background and Critical Reception of His Work* (1966), whose focus is on the ideas that helped form the intellectual context in which Hopkins wrote. He devotes ch. 3 to the 'Non-logical Structure' of 'The Wreck', seeking by an examination of the Pindaric ode to illuminate Hopkins's method of composition. He alights upon the 'key word', citing how in Pindar 'bee', for example, becomes for the reader a clue to a whole ode. Similarly, he suggests, 'water' is a key word, the 'underthought', in 'The Wreck', symbolising God's power and mercy. Pendants to Bender's study are Raymond V. Schoder's 'Hopkins and Pindar' (1989), who finds the two poets essentially kindred spirits, their 'inner visions and emotions' producing cognate styles of language (Schoder 1989:113), and Warren Anderson's '"Never Ending Revel": The Wreck and the Ode Tradition' (1976), which declares only Pindar, 'a master of ethical and religious high-mindedness', could give Hopkins 'the example of sustained lyric flight' (Anderson 1976: 140). Wider in its survey and generally useful is Brian Vickers on 'Rhetoric and Formality in Hopkins' (1992), who gives an account of traditional rhetorical theory and practice, and surveys Hopkins's knowledge of rhetoric, as classicist and as practising poet (Vickers 1992: 73 ff).

TECHNIQUE: 'INSTRESS STRESSED'

Hopkins used various technical terms, most notably 'inscape', 'instress', 'self/selving', and 'pitch'. Being for his own use, he never needed to use them consistently. The word 'stress' is taken up by two essays, Anthony Mortimer's 'Hopkins: The Stress and the Self' and Donald Walhout's 'The Instress of Action: Action and Contemplation in Hopkins' Poetry'. Mortimer notes the varying meanings of stress: among them, metrical; emphatic; physical tension; and seeks to unravel 'the whole complex web of stresses' to appreciate the achievements and limits of Hopkins's work (Mortimer 1992: 1). This leads him to the Scotist view, that the world was created after the decree of the Incarnation [p. 134], a world which, created so that Christ might become a creature, 'is permeated by his instress', his distinct nature, which in turn gives creatures their distinctive nature or stress (Mortimer 1992: 20). Walhout takes a different tack, focusing on the human side of instress, rather than on Hopkins's usual way of alluding to the dynamic in nature, so that it has the function of prompting contemplation from action (Walhout 1989: 11). He distinguishes three kinds of action and resulting contemplation: particular but ordinary actions (walking; talking); action by its nature predisposed to contemplation (the call felt by poet and by the nun in 'The Wreck'); and ways of life, their entire action linked closely to contemplation (Duns Scotus; St Alphonsus). 'Instress', then, is both an innate quality and the power that leads to perception.

TECHNIQUE: THEMES AND IMAGERY

With themes and imagery, the emphasis shifts from technical analysis, however essential to understanding meaning and effect, to the more immediately critical effect and response. Gardner emphasises that Hopkins's recurrent themes, as primarily a religious poet, are God, Man, and Nature, while Christian poets have shown 'a marked unanimity in the moral and mystical significance' of such objects as stars, fire, rain, lightning, 'the plough, the soldier and the rod of chastisement' (Gardner 1966: I, 152). While giving attention to the Classical resources at Hopkins's disposal, Gardner also spends rather more time on the Bible, as against, say, the *Spiritual Exercises*, as a store of reference, allusion and imagery.

The dangers of exploring and writing about imagery are exemplified, in very different ways, by a lengthy book and a highly influential essay. Robert Boyle's *Metaphor in Hopkins* (1961), declaring Hopkins's mind found its fullest expression in metaphor, aims to reveal the poet's 'underlying view of divine life flowing into the heart and acts of the just man' (Boyle 1961: xi). Focusing exclusively on metaphor and simile (metre and rhythm are included as 'forms of metaphor'), Boyle offers a detailed examination of significant images in the larger structure of eight poems, such as 'It will flame out, like shining from shook foil' ('God's Grandeur' [p. 83]) and 'My heart in hiding | Stirred for a bird, – the achieve of, the mastery of the thing' ('The Windhover' [pp. 84–6]). The length to which these examinations are taken becomes wearisome: Boyle's analysis of rhythm and of relation of sound to meaning suggests he has difficulty with technical matters; while his lack of understanding in 'The Wreck', stanza 31 [p. 78], of the relationship between Providence and the nun, and of the image of finger and bell – Providence, clearly, both touches and summons – leads him to a disgusting and absurd physical image (Boyle 1961: 11). Elsewhere, Boyle's religious exposition and use of biblical, liturgical, and expository texts (Bede's *A History of the English Church and People*, for example, and hymns) is useful, but only a determined, reasonably advanced student should expend the energy to retrieve what is of use here.

If Boyle's study overwhelms by its dogged quest after metaphor, Yvor Winters's 1949 essay on Hopkins rejects any kind of ambiguity of language, and seems to show no understanding of how imagery works. Winters is baffled by the 'generalization' of 'The mind has mountains, cliffs of fall' ('No Worst' [**pp. 111–2**]) and is uncomprehending of 'shook foil' as an image. Even when he perceptively analyses the rhythm of 'No Worst' and finds it based on 'the principle of violent struggle with its governing measure' or metre, which contributes 'to the violence of feeling in the total poem' (Winters 1966 [1957]: 45), this proves, in Winters's view and to the reader's surprise, to be not a virtue but a fault. Any kind of traditional association or symbolic meaning is also dismissed. In 'The Windhover', Winters says, comparing the kestrel to Christ is ludicrous and even blasphemous, as substituting a dog for the kestrel would be (Winters 1966 [1957]: 54). Winters shows no grasp of association, where the lion as symbol is very different from the (symbolic) meaning of donkey or jackal, and the bird in its masterful flight may show something of the majesty of Christ, as no dog will. And, after all, dogs too (the bulldog, the greyhound, though not Winters's favoured Airedales) can take on symbolic value.

If these two items seem negative in their effect, they can also act by contraries to alert the reader to what Hopkins is doing and achieving and lead us, through particular images and theoretical approaches, to a brief consideration of certain crucial issues raised by a variety of critics in 'The Wreck', 'The Windhover', and the 'Terrible' Sonnets.

Readings

Part II offers a reading of the poetry and prose of Hopkins, but as the present Part will have made clear already, opinions about Hopkins's work, like that of most artists', can be divided, often sharply. The critical diversity underlying those divisions can be demonstrated through selected readings of key poems: 'The Wreck', 'The Windhover', and the 'Terrible' Sonnets. In following these voices, often at odds with one another, remember, as Peter Milward urged, that 'much may be gained by the airing of different, even discordant, opinions [in] the interpretation of a poet like Hopkins' (Milward (ed.) 1976: x).

READING 'THE WRECK': THE ODE

Milward, quoted above, insists also upon the ambiguity and richness of Hopkins's language. From early on, while aware of Bridges's image of 'The Wreck' as the 'dragon in the gate' [p. 132], critics have been prepared to take up the poem's challenges. For Gardner, it was a 'great experiment', yet also and importantly, considerably more (Gardner 1966: I, 40). His analysis of Sprung Rhythm, his identification of a 'vital fusion of the internal rhythm of thought-and-emotion' with 'the external rhythm of sounds' (Gardner 1966: I, 43), and his assured reading of the poem overall remain valuable still. On the technical side, calling to mind this is an ode [p. 66], John E. Keating takes us down to the stanzaic unit in '"A Continuous Structural Parallelism": Stanzaic Pattern in The Wreck', with its bipartite form, the antiphonal effect resulting, in Matthew Arnold's phrase, in 'a dialogue of the mind with itself' (Keating 1976: 160). The poem's two-part structure has been noted, and the inter-relationship of Hopkins and the nun, there being little direct dispute with Leavis's summation: 'the association of inner, spiritual, emotional stress with physical reverberations, nervous and muscular tensions' being explicitly 'elaborated in an account of the storm which is at the same time an account of the inner drama' (Leavis 1963: 143).

Opinions vary on Hopkins's success in presenting feelings, especially his own, in this ode. E.E. Phare, the earliest critic to treat Hopkins at length, found Hopkins at times embarrassing in his exposure of emotion and in 'The Wreck' thought he 'tried to make himself believe that his feelings on the subject ... were more intense than was actually the case' (Phare 1933: 109): her praise is reserved rather for the storm, where Hopkins discovers 'mysterious symbolisms and correspondences which link this small instance of God's dealings with men ... with his dealings as a whole' (Phare 1933: 112). Hopkins's own feelings and the energy of the storm are also linked by Paddy Kitchen, but as proof of that artistic energy, even glee, in the act of creation. For Kitchen, indeed, the wreck, taken with Hopkins's remembrance of his own conversion, 'must have shaken the citadel' of the poet's 'carefully-nurtured selflessness'. Once shaken, Hopkins must include the drama of his submission to God, in parallel to the wreck, itself 'the enactment of God's will' (Kitchen 1978: 162–63). Against Phare and with Kitchen is Alison Sulloway, who approves the excitement ('scarcely controlled') of the ode and suggests Hopkins saw himself and the world 'as fastened to God, yet revolving around Him in a universal charge of motion' (Sulloway 1972: 83). A view dissenting from Kitchen and Sulloway is Boyle's '"Man Jack the Man Is": *The Wreck* from the Perspective of *The Shepherd's Brow*'. In a dense and allusive style recognisable from his book on metaphor [pp. 181–2], Boyle uses a good reading of the late 'Shepherd's Brow' [p. 121] – a poem that has attracted a surprising, though not undeserved degree of attention – to suggest, though, that 'The Wreck' is essentially immature, Hopkins taking himself too seriously, accepting himself 'as an object of heroic stature' in the 'inspired epic of a Catholic Milton' (Boyle 1976: 110). Overall, though, critics recognise the artistry that controls and expresses powerful emotion. Eric Griffiths in an acute study, *The Printed Voice of Victorian Poetry* (1989), after the fine insight of the dreamer and the wreck at the conclusion of the early 'The Nightingale' [p. 60] as parallel to Hopkins and the nun, characterises 'The Wreck' as a 'giant echo-chamber', with its ability 'to leap between levels of English as between levels of fact. Doing two things at once is actually the structural principle' (Griffiths 1989: 347).

Boyle's reference to Hopkins as a 'Catholic Milton' is a sneer, but others take more seriously the placing of the poem within a tradition, whether of Modernism, of Milton, or of the Classical. Edith Sitwell, herself a playfully experimental poet, one of those who hailed Hopkins as a Modern [pp. 137–40], in a still useful and sensitive analysis of the relation of sound to meaning, links his feelings and instinct to such moderns as Ezra Pound, Wilfred Owen, and T.S. Eliot, though Hopkins's rhythmical principles are 'guided by learning' (Roberts 1987: 271). Similarly, though writing later and so choosing a later Modern, Dylan Thomas, Vincent Buckley uses the one successful imitator of Hopkins to initiate a description of God's dealings with the soul, finding something 'provisional, not to be counted on or explained' in those encounters, a kind of 'sensuous initiative': in responding, 'the soul "selves itself" and praises that very initiative' (Buckley 1968: 59). It is Boyle's despised Miltonic model, however, that has proved the most popular point of reference. Loomis, responding to Phare's doubts about the poem's representation of feelings, finds it rich 'in emotional expressions and splendid phrasing', but insists that 'at the core' it is 'an intellectually motivated poem of the Miltonic type', one that jumps with Milton's declared purpose in *Paradise Lost*, for 'The Wreck' attempts 'conceptually to vindicate God's ways … with the cosmos' (Loomis 1988: 76). Milton's declaration is echoed by Hilary Fraser's characterisation: 'a "justification of the ways of God to men" by showing how the storm is symbolic of Christ's crucifixion as the stars are of his beauty' (Fraser

1986: 93). More specifically on Milton, Walter J. Ong offers a parallel consideration of 'The Wreck' and 'Lycidas', itself a poem of wreck and loss, parallelling Milton's own questioning of his (poetic) calling. Ong sees storm and wreck as part of a Pindaric 'underthought' [p. 180] and turns to the crucial element, of understanding what the nun's experience *means* [pp. 77; 187–8], Christ's coming 'in the awful tempest to claim her as his own' (Ong 1986: 47).

Like others, unsurprisingly perhaps, Ong insists upon linking Hopkins and the nun. J. Hillis Miller, less concerned with God's providence, allows that if 'The Wreck' (not unlike 'Lycidas') is 'about both poetic inspiration and grace', yet the theme is not the heroic death of the nun nor is the poem essentially Miltonic: it is Hopkins's response to hearing of the wreck. Hopkins's early experience of the absence of God (Miller's theme [p. 160]) has been 'transformed into what is, in Victorian poetry, an almost unique sense of the immanence of God in nature and in the human soul' (Miller 1975: 319, 323–24). So Hopkins is returned to his own age. Wendell Stacey Johnson finds him combining introspective manner with dramatic matter, the result complex rather than ambiguous, so that the familiar images of the Romantic seascape have now, in Hopkins, come to represent 'not imagined Oneness, but experienced doubleness' (W.S. Johnson 1968: 45, 49), while Patricia Ball, though arguing also for a Romantic continuity in the Victorian age [p. 175], insists 'The Wreck' is double – but in its structure, setting out 'to expose the inner life of emotional conflict and the process of a tense relationship'; the poem's Pt. 2 'reflects the psychological evolution from crisis to insight', the burden of Pt. 1 (Ball 1971: 132–33).

READING 'THE WRECK': CATHOLIC OR JESUIT?

That Hopkins was both a Catholic and a Jesuit was known from earliest publication of the poetry. Hopkins's beliefs did not sit well with the early twentieth century, yet his poetic style was hailed as Modernist, form being valued over content: Paul Turner has noted the oddity that 'modern tastes in poetic style' have been so influenced 'by a man whose ideas were otherwise ... at variance with modern thought' (Turner 1989: 151). Many critics passed over the Catholic meaning of 'The Wreck' or took it at a general level. Herbert Read (1893–1968), an influential Modernist critic and poet, was content in 1933 to proclaim it was a poem 'of contrition, fear, and submission, rather than of the love of God' (quoted Gardner 1966: I, 64), acknowledging its power, but exploring no further, yet against this we can set Gardner's quotation from Matthew Arnold's essay,

'Pagan and Medieval Religious Sentiment', which identifies the success of Christianity in its gladness, not sorrow:

> not in its assigning the spiritual world to Christ, and the material world to the devil, but its drawing from the spiritual world a sense of joy so abundant that it ran over upon the material world and transfigured it.
>
> (Gardner 1966: II, 229)

Hopkins, who read Arnold's essay, might well have written this.

N.F. Lees took up the intellectual milieu in which Hopkins, as a Catholic and Jesuit, found himself. The scientific fatalism of geology and biology, the blind struggle, unguided and unmeaning, part of the Victorian Apocalyptic mode discussed by Alison Sulloway [**pp. 152–3**], was, for Hopkins, to be countered by the witness of martyrs who declared for their faith. So the *Deutschland* impressed him, out of so many wrecks and disasters of the time, since it highlighted the issue of suffering and a loving God. For Hopkins, in 'The Wreck', God's 'purposes are mysterious but not arbitrary' (Lees 1976: 47). Others, too, have examined general Catholic concerns: not least, the question, Who will be saved? Loomis takes up the issue of whether *all* will be saved or whether Christ's 'incarnatory activity' offers but does not guarantee salvation. In the nun's power to *speak* Christ, Hopkins describes her as able also 'to bring Christ to birth in her soul' (Loomis 1988: 74), so that the storm is sacramental, a means of grace for the nun, and a pattern for others, 'a new Christic incarnation ... *and* Christ's baptism of the lost as well' (Loomis 1988: 75), so the people of England, Protestant and unbeliever, can be saved. Similarly, Cotter finds in 'The Wreck' the most complete statement of the living knowledge ('gnosis') of Jesus, which was Hopkins's 'constant aim of perfection' as Hopkins himself *sees* something (Cotter 1972: 145), as indeed Hopkins claimed Wordsworth saw *something* (*L*, 2.147).

More particular yet are those, themselves Jesuits, who see 'The Wreck' as a Jesuit or Ignatian poem, structured on the *Spiritual Exercises* [**pp. 22; 88**]. Schoder relates the 'Ignatian' quality of 'The Wreck' to the aim of the *Exercises*, a 'radical remaking' of one's life into a truly Christian pattern (Schoder 1976: 54) and traces echoes or applications of specific elements in the poem. Most detailed and most specific in his claims is Downes who, offering an analysis of the poem's correspondence to the weeks of the *Exercises*, finds two parallel wrecks in the poem, which both force 'dire spiritual and physical consequences on the stranded', causing 'anguish and suffering analogous to the Passion' (Downes 1959: 55). Both Hopkins and the nun offer to God 'the reenactment of the Incarnation and the Redemption as other Christs' (Downes 1959: 56).

READING 'THE WRECK': THE NUN

The most disturbing figure in readings of 'The Wreck' is the tall nun. What is the nature of her experience and what does it mean? Does Christ appear to her physically or does she have an intense imaginative 'vision', akin to that taught by the *Spiritual Exercises*? Does she want a swift death or does she perceive Christ in a way that proclaims God's providence and renews her to life after (physical) death?

At least three critics, taking up Hopkins's belief in miracles as possible *now*, hold that Christ literally appears in the storm's hurly-burly. Alison Sulloway, referring to Elisabeth Schneider's belief of a real presence, herself suggests that Hopkins hinted to Bridges (*L*, 1.66) that Christ had appeared to him (Sulloway 1972: 184). So in the parallel between the wreck and the apocalyptic coming of Christ in St John's Revelation [**pp. 152–3**], Hopkins has 'translated a contemporary "ordeal of the waters" ... into a mystical event' (Sulloway 1972: 194). Paul Mariani too in his Commentary on the poetry is clear that what the nun saw 'was Christ himself literally walking the waves towards her' (Mariani 1970: 68).

Cotter, rejecting Schneider's miracle, of an actual manifestation, needs to ask *where* is the 'happening' that Hopkins wished to make us see. Heightened language and imagery dramatise 'the moment of inscape', as the nun perceives Providence manifested in the storm, her death not a passive stupor or aggressive rage, but 'the choice that answers *yes* in obedience with Christ's great sacrifice' (Cotter 1972: 148–49). Helen Vendler, decidedly not a Jesuit, suggests the whole poem is Hopkins's act of interpretation of the nun's cry: 'O Christ, Christ come quickly'. Vendler rejects the views that the nun desires a swift death (to end the agony) or the physical coming of Christ. Drawing on the gospel account (Matthew 14: 22–32) of the storm on the sea of Gennesareth, when Christ appears, walking on the water and demands Peter's absolute faith in him, Vendler asserts that God may not rescue the nun from the sea, but unlike Peter, 'she affirmed by her cry that she believed he could ... by the agency of his intervening Son' (Vendler 1992: 41). Walter J. Ong, essentially agreeing with Vendler, takes the nun's cry further, as she conceived 'Christ in faith in her mind' and received him 'for eternity as she met her bodily death' (Ong 1986: 52). The metaphor of 'conception' here may disturb with its physicality, yet linked to the doctrine of an incarnate God it operates as image and natural 'fact'. And Hopkins's perception of the Incarnation, from Duns Scotus [pp. 24; 134], as an act of love rather than ransom, lies within Hilary Fraser's claim that the nun is specifically identified with the Virgin Mary, and seen as conceiving Christ anew (Fraser 1986: 93). The physical and symbolic, material and spiritual, are finely drawn together by Virginia Ellis, who sees the nun not only as 'bride-mother', but also one with God's fire of the Pentecost: 'She is the spiritual beacon more than compensating ... for the physical beacon the *Deutschland* never saw; she is the speaking light of God to all who will see and hear' (Ellis 1991: 115).

READING 'THE WINDHOVER'

'The Windhover' has probably received more attention and provoked wider divergences of critical opinion than any other Hopkins poem. Is it a nature poem or a religious poem? is the bird analogous to Christ — indeed, does the dedication 'to Christ our Lord' tie in with the poem? is the bird divine, natural, or evil? what is the meaning of 'buckle' ('Brute beauty and valour and act ... here | Buckle! AND the fire that breaks from thee then, a billion | Times told lovelier, more dangerous, O my chevalier')? indeed, is it the bird from which the fire breaks or from the poet's 'heart in hiding'?

READING 'THE WINDHOVER': CHRIST, NATURE AND SACRAMENT

The sonnet's dedication is to Christ, though this was added by Hopkins to a later manuscript. Herbert Read in 1933, admiring Hopkins as a poet of nature, but having scant regard for his religion, saw this addition as a subterfuge. Read described the poem as completely objective in its natural description, but the Jesuit, feeling this was insufficient, got 'over his scruples' by the dedication, which therefore 'is a patent deception' and in no way alters the poem's 'naked sensualism' (Roberts 1987: 257). True, Christ is never mentioned in the poem, but a parallel seems obvious, especially given Hopkins's religious nature and his persistent linking of God, above all Christ, with nature, and the inscape or perception of God's creation through the human observer. The falcon as 'dauphin', the son of the king, offers a plain analogy to Christ as the Son.

Eleanor Ruggles insisted in the 1940s that the 'beauty and valour of the winging falcon' are Christ's own qualities 'in an unthinking and finite form', so identifying the one with the other (Ruggles 1947: 123). Others, committed to a religious and indeed Ignatian view of Hopkins, have enforced this. Cotter notes that Christ is present as throughout the other sonnets, in the sun, in 'the dawn drawing the bird to a brilliant expression of itself and hence of its Lord' (Cotter 1972: 177), while Downes explores the linguistic implications of the chivalric terms. Although Downes acknowledges that there is 'no symbol of Christ in the poem, no direct ... allusion to his passion', but an oblique analogy, he enforces his claim by citing Ignatius Loyola's 'autobiography' with its account (Loyola 1996: 20) of the 'knightly' vigil Ignatius underwent before putting off earthly garments and putting on 'the livery of Christ' (Downes 1959: 101, 103).

Is though the poem to be taken as sacramental, a representation of how grace may be given in the sudden, epiphanic understanding of Christ in nature? And given the ending of the poem, the plough-share shining after 'sheer plod', the all-but-extinguished embers revealing brightness, is there also an awareness of different ways that grace may be gained, as in 'The Wreck', where Paul and Augustine (stanza 10) parallel the nun and Hopkins and grace may be by sudden insight (as Paul, 'at a flash') or by a 'long lingering out sweet skill' (as Augustine). The kestrel is sudden in its downward plunge, linking the poet to Christ, yet also the slog of ploughing, the 'galling' of embers, insist that heroic virtue need not be evident to the world, that it can be in the patient carrying out of duty – as did St Alphonsus Rodriguez [**pp. 119–20**].

What might be called the Herbert Read tradition, that this is a nature poem, with nothing about it inherently sacramental, is found in Yvor Winters, while a good example, challenged indeed by Winters, of the full sacramental view is Marshall McLuhan's 1966 [1944]. Winters finds the opening of the bird a fine description, 'but in itself it is merely description' (Winters 1966 [1957]: 49), a slightly odd response to the poem's reverberant language. Hopkins hurls 'miscellaneous images at his subject from all sides, rather than ... develop one of them fully' (Winters 1966 [1957]: 53) and Winters finds remarks about the 'sacramental view of nature' 'merely foolish', concluding it is a poem of 'overwrought emotionalism', carelessly written (Winters 1966 [1957]: 55–56). McLuhan recognises difficulties for the ordinary reader in Hopkins's Catholic beliefs and experiences, yet Hopkins 'does not lay claim to a perception of natural facts hidden from ordinary man'; he is no mystic, as he 'habitually shifts his gaze from the order and perspectives of nature to the analogous but grander scenery of the moral and intellectual order' (McLuhan 1966 [1944]: 82–83), and McLuhan explores in detail the sacramental effect of the poem.

Hilary Fraser, taking a more secular view, yet finds the bird is 'both a unique entity in itself and the carrier of universal and essential truth' (Fraser 1986: 87), and Loomis from a religious perspective,

explores 'The Windhover' as a complex example of '*Jesuit* medita-
tive principles': here 'the true Jesuit Hopkins *tests* his natural vision;
is it from the good or the evil angel?' (Loomis 1988: 27). As the bird
rebuffs the wind do we take it as Christ against the 'powers of the
air that rule [Satan's] world of darkness' or as Satanic scorn for the
'wind' of the Holy Spirit? (Loomis 1988: 27–28).

READING 'THE WINDHOVER': THE KESTREL

The bird itself has provoked diverse responses: a parallel to Christ? a
brute creature? a Satanic figure, even? That there is some element of
conflict in the poem, centred upon the bird, is recognised by many
critics, not least since the bird may be analogous to Christ, but is not
Christ's self. Gardner, while condemning those critics (I.A. Richards,
William Empson, E.E. Phare amongst them) who have used Freudian
analysis to probe the arcana of Hopkins's unconscious mind, none
the less agrees with them that the poem embodies 'a spiritual con-
flict', in two sets of values represented by the windhover and by
Christ (Gardner 1966: I, 181). Hartman sees conflict too, though
placing Hopkins in opposition to both bird and Christ, haunted by
the thought that 'the material world is nearer to Christ's Passion,
Crucifixion and flaming Resurrection' than free-willed man (Hartman
1966: 67).

Gardner's 'psychological' critics produce some odd interpretations.
I.A. Richards takes 'O my chevalier' to refer to the poet, not Christ,
and focusing on the word 'gall' claims the sight of the bird has given
the poet a painful shock which has jarred him into 'unappeased dis-
content' (Robert 1987: 143). The idea of discontent is dealt with more
at length and more suggestively by Phare. Making the poem a very
personal one, she claims that the distress which Hopkins expressed
'was greater than he realised'. She too takes up the galled embers,
meant to symbolise 'an activity ... pleasant to Christ', but the *reader*
realises (for this springs from Hopkins's 'unconscious') that the poet
shows himself in a state of mind close to 'utter defeat' (Phare 1933: 34).

The potential diabolism in the bird is raised by Sulloway, though
she allows a proper balance of possibility. While she finds the falcon
a royal son ('dauphin') of the daylight – Lucifer was identified as 'a
son of the morning' (Isaiah 14:12), not the royal son of a king – yet
it has both diabolic ('brute beauty') and angelic lineaments (Sulloway
1972: 111). The diabolic is opposed by Lichtmann, since it leads to
a 'Manichean mood', which would claim the material world as the
creation of the devil (Lichtmann 1989: 119). The majority view,
though, remains that the 'brute beauty' may be 'dangerous', as all
beauty may be, yet, as W.S. Johnson declares, the bird has three

meanings: a real windhover, which in turn represents Christ, and represents the man who would imitate Christ (W.S. Johnson 1968: 86); while the ecstasy of the bird strains 'outside itself', locked into 'the whole valley, hills and sky which its flight in the direction of the sun concentrates and configures' (Cotter 1972: 179).

The kestrel can be returned to its Victorian context of natural observation and as the focus of the poem through Patricia Ball's fine exploration in *The Science of Aspects*, drawing on Ruskin's description of the windhover, while Hopkins does more, placing the pure fact in a dependent relationship, a context which defines its value, Hopkins showing his ability to integrate fact and feeling, from events in the mind, generating emotion in the heart (Ball 1971: 138–42).

READING 'THE WINDHOVER': 'BUCKLE'

If 'The Windhover' is Hopkins's most discussed poem, one word in it, 'buckle', is possibly the most discussed single word in English poetry – and the problems associated with that word and its discussion come commonly from treating it in isolation. Its meaning in context is clear: the kestrel's qualities come together as the buckle of a knight's armour or the everyday action of snapping or clipping a belt together, and a fire, an imaginative vibrancy, that bursts out for the beholder is a thousand times told lovelier even than the windhover was in his riding of the air [p. 85]. Some, however, take 'buckle' to mean 'warping' or 'crumpling', like metal under pressure, while some complicate the meaning further by taking 'thee', from which the flame breaks, to be the poet's heart.

Hopkins himself, as this study has shown, drew again and again on the multivalent possibility of language, with witty and illuminating results. Unfortunately, in the first half of the twentieth century, both in Modernist poetry and in modern criticism, ambiguity was in high fashion, and this often at the expense of context or that critical tact crucial to poetic understanding. The trouble began with William Empson who, considering types of ambiguity, offers an often perverse reading of the poem. He allows that 'buckle' can relate to a belt, but also pushes it to the buckling of a bicycle wheel (a deliberately prosaic example), which buckled becomes useless. Empson, as his analysis here demonstrates, is in pursuit of Freudian opposites, which for him reveal an unresolved conflict within Hopkins. The poet, Empson insists, if faced by the psychic struggle within himself, revealed yet unresolved in the poem, 'would have denied with anger he meant "like a bicycle wheel," and then ... have suppressed the whole poem' (Empson 1965: 226 fn). An intrusive bicycle wheel has demolished a poem, to Empson's satisfaction. Even Milroy, considering 'buckle' and

Hopkins's use of related words, while pointing to *buck* (applied to the leaping, rolling waves in 'The Wreck'), takes 'collapse' as probably the most nearly correct meaning, though allowing suggestions of 'leaping, thrusting or quick movement' (Milroy 1977:159). Kitchen goes yet further, for this 'buckling' is to crush the sensations aroused by the qualities of brute beauty and valour, 'for only by so doing will [the poet/Hopkins] be ready to receive Christ' (Kitchen 1978: 178). Yet Hopkins constantly sees, as in the night stars [**pp. 25; 60**], the way to Christ through understanding of the creation. And Romano Guardini's landscape is darker still, since 'buckle' must include the meaning 'that what was before free in the heights, surrounded by light ... must now yield to or become a thing that dwells in the lower darkness' (Guardini 1966 [1962]: 78), and even if we pick up the conclusion of that sentence ('yet in truth, greater') and see some analogy to Christ, who came into the world, which being dark did not comprehend the Incarnate Word, the reading of the kestrel's flight as a moral fall seems obtuse, ignorantly dismissive of the very behaviour of such birds.

Happily others can allow a range of possibilities in 'buckle' and integrate them into the whole poem. For W.S. Johnson, the main sense, in a sequence of vision, reflection, and generalising on nature, ending with 'the ploughed-down sillion and gashed embers', is 'to warp or bend under stress' − not to collapse − so that it is 'natural' that brighter fire bursts from a creature buckled under stress 'than from one flying in its freedom, air, and pride' (W.S. Johnson 1968: 93–94). Robert Rehder finds duality in the two-stage process: 'the coming together of the various qualities' of the bird *and* 'the identification of the windhover with Christ'. The verb 'thus conceals a complex transformation' and the failure to note this 'has created much of the confusion in the criticism' (Rehder 1992: 182). If it is a mark of greatness in art to provoke as well as delight, it might be reasonably thought the greatness of 'The Windhover' is assured.

READING THE 'TERRIBLE' SONNETS

The 'Terrible' Sonnets or, for those who feel 'Terrible' a value-judgement rather than a description of the experience they embody, the 'Sonnets of Desolation', have not attracted the contending voices that surround 'The Windhover', partly at least because of a fuller understanding of Hopkins's religious beliefs and artistic tenets. For earlier critics these were Hopkins's last poems, with all the resonance of final statements: Leavis so assumes them to be (1963: 152), but early on Gardner found a very different feeling in the poems of the last two years, and the sonnets are not generally now seen as the necessary climax to the work or to the life. That there is a group of poems linked by theme and the experience they represent is generally agreed, perhaps six [p. 107], but since they are identified by subject and critical interpretation (as well as the time span of their production) other poems may be drawn in or, more fruitfully, discussed as part of the creative sequence. Loomis, for example, quoting from Avrom Fleishman's *Figures of Autobiography* (1983) and Jerome Buckley's *The Turning Key: Autobiography and the Subjective Impulse* (1984), suggests Hopkins the Victorian followed an 'impulse toward self-writing', while able to perceive 'the tyranny of self-awareness' as he located in his personal struggles the 'general plight of mankind' (Loomis 1988: 134–35). This perception, for Loomis, went with a decade of writing, when Hopkins was creating 'an archetypal Christian sacramental biography' (Loomis 1988: 135). Hence Loomis discusses a 'cycle' beginning with 'Andromeda' [pp. 95–6], and taking in 'Peace', while stressing that the 'Terrible' Sonnets proper begin with 'Carrion Comfort'. Downes also prefers a larger view, taking in ten poems which, together, form a remarkable pattern of poetic experience (Downes 1989: 239).

THE 'TERRIBLE' SONNETS: PSYCHOANALYSIS AND RELIGION

Appearing in 1918, Hopkins, through his poems, was subjected to the new 'science' of psychoanalytical criticism, prompted especially by knowledge (and ignorance) of Freud. Gardner saw the appeal to the modern reader of such an approach, rooting it in the sickness of the age, since these sonnets 'crystallize that sense of frustration, of separation from God', which is 'the peculiar psychic disease of the twentieth century' (Gardner 1966: II, 330). I.A. Richards, in 1926, saw Hopkins's religion as a root cause of psychic distress, for 'intellectually he was too stiff, too "cogged and cumbered" with beliefs, those bundles of invested emotional capital, to escape except through appalling tension' (Roberts 1987: 145). But Gardner saw those 'bundles' as crucial to Hopkins, since his faith gave him 'powers of recovery which many of his most sensitive modern readers would lack' (Gardner 1966: II, 332). Gardner's has been the path most followed as studies, directed to Hopkins as Catholic and Jesuit, while accepting strong biographical elements, steer towards the poet as an artist in control, not the helpless victim of a feverish Romantic subjectivity or a Freudian 'disease'.

THE 'TERRIBLE' SONNETS: SUBJECTIVITY AND ARTISTRY

Biography necessarily asks about the subject's nature and Hopkins's biography has often used the poems as keys to his inner world, above all in the Dublin years. Eleanor Ruggles, as noted [p. 145], posed the question raised by this approach: was Hopkins a mystic unanswered? or neurotic unrelieved? though it transpires she was not going to answer. Lahey, in the first biography, himself a Jesuit, writes (over-optimistically) of the Dublin years as a time when Hopkins found the work interesting and consoling, his friends congenial (Lahey 1930: 139–40). He rejects the 'tragic portraits' of exile, loneliness, drudgery and despair (contrast Norman White's tragic emphasis [p. 36]), though not denying Hopkins's sorrows, the most crucial being 'on the black heights of spiritual night with his God' (Lahey 1930: 140, 143).

Others have taken up this sense of a dark night, whether or not they also attribute a smiling day-side to Hopkins. For Hillis Miller, there was a crucial desolation conveyed in these sonnets, a failure of grace and with it the failure, in language, nature, space, and time, of 'all the ways ... in which the self can escape from itself and established connections with nature or with God' (Miller 1975: 355). Miller uses the word 'dryness', linked so often to the spiritual experience of the Dark Night of the Soul [pp. 109–10], yet his secular emphasis appears in his stressing 'sexual impotence' (Hopkins speaks of himself as 'time's eunuch' [p. 37]) as an image for this state. In a direct confrontation, Loomis, Christian though not Catholic, insists these sonnets do not report 'the disappearance of God' as 'Miller would have us believe': rather, Hopkins wants us to see 'a basic Christian biography's extremity, the tormenting pangs of rebirth' (Loomis 1988: 142).

THE 'TERRIBLE' SONNETS: TRAGIC OR COMIC?

Taking Hopkins's poems as elaborated autobiography can give a tragic sense, if that means despair and a lonely premature death in Dublin, with so little achieved, at least in the eyes of the world. Yet taken another way, however uncongenial to the secular perceptions of the twentieth century, the 'Terrible' Sonnets embody a very different progress. Lahey put it emphatically when he insisted that these sonnets are only 'terrible' in the way 'that the beauty of Jesus Christ is terrible', as he invokes both the crucifixion at Golgotha and the Transfiguration, Christ on Mount Tabor revealing his glory (Matthew 17: 1–9): 'Read in this light his poems cease to be tragic' (Lahey 1930: 143).

That there might be periods of dejection, as represented in the sonnets, is not denied by religious commentators. As Downes points out, both Ignatius and Hopkins suffered 'intense dejection which became crucial tests of their spirits' (Downes 1959: 115). In a useful analysis, taking in the pressure of life as a Jesuit, Downes reviews the evidence of Hopkins's 'sorrow' and finds not Freud but St John of the Cross. The sonnets are not Freudian manifestations of frustration, but revelations of a spiritual plight, the result of which God alone knows (Downes 1959: 145). Subsequently, Downes explored the religious and artistic nature of the sonnets, as representing the experience St Ignatius called 'The Discernment of Spirits', 'those forces and powers both within and without the soul that radically reorder its spiritual composure', so the poems, 'in their deepest sense about personal reality', are ways of experiencing the self 'in states of spiritual nakedness, justified and unjustified before the Almighty' (Downes 1989: 239).

Tragedy may explore meaning in events that seem irrational, but Comedy in the higher sense that Dante used it for his *Divine Comedy* rises, as the path Dante represents himself treading, to the Beatific Vision, the certainty of God and of the Divine Order. Hopkins may not see the Vision in the 'Terrible' Sonnets, the way he represents is bleak and frustrating, but he will not feed on Despair, that 'carrion comfort', and the artistry of the sonnets points to a man wrestling with his God, but wrestling too with his art.

Shaping the reputation

From early on, Hopkins was taken seriously as a poet, and claimed as a major figure, first as Modernist, more recently as Victorian. Indeed, the first book-length study, E.E. Phare's *The Poetry of Gerard Manley Hopkins*, appeared in 1933, only fifteen years after the poetry was published. This section, taking representative works of the last eighty years, will suggest how Hopkins, early accepted as a major poet, has been championed and then, most recently, been the subject of specialised investigations of his life and art, the general justificatory study being no longer necessary.

Phare's book, sensitive and stimulating, whatever qualifications may be necessary, sought to establish a way of investigation for this 'bizarre, difficult Modernist-Victorian poet' (Phare 1933: 4) and to offer readings of what were already clearly established as major works, 'The Wreck' and 'The Windhover' amongst them. Influenced by the critical emphases of her time, she starts from the idea of 'tradition', a critical method notably of T.S. Eliot ('Tradition and the Individual Talent', 1920), and F.R. Leavis (*The Great Tradition*, 1948). Yet rather than Hopkins plunged into a poetic maelstrom, the focus is on Hopkins's relationship to Richard Crashaw, as a Catholic poet, and to Wordsworth as a Romantic, a 'primitive' poet (though

Phare could not know Hopkins's own insight into his affinity with Wordsworth [p. 28]), since like other Victorians, Hopkins inherited and was shaped by Romanticism. Phare took Hopkins's Catholicism for granted and rather mocked those suspicious of Jesuitism, who reacted as though 'becoming a Jesuit must involve some unnatural and undesirable deformation or repression' (Phare 1933: 141). Yet she did see a poet divided, between on the one hand intellect and Catholic dogma and, on the other, rejoicing in wild nature, a split between a geometric world and an unruly one (Phare 1933: 56), with little doubt which she favoured. Hopkins is not always in emotional control – she may call 'The Bugler's First Communion' 'uncomfortable', essentially the very effect to be explored in Julia Saville's *A Queer Chivalry* [pp. 200–1]. Overall, though, in 1933, Phare could insist Hopkins is a serious poet, to be taken seriously, a poet dramatic, even witty, and she raises critical issues that continue to exercise us as readers.

MID-CENTURY: THE 1940s

For Phare, Hopkins, a major poet, was a man divided between a geometric world (Catholicism and intellect) and an unruly one (Nature and feeling). Underlying her split may be the dominant Freudian psychology of the 1930s. Two studies of the 1940s, John Pick's *Gerard Manley Hopkins: Priest and Poet* (1942) and W.A.M. Peters's *Gerard Manley Hopkins: A Critical Essay* (1948), take on board Hopkins's Catholicism, Pick sympathetic and Peters himself a Jesuit. For them, Hopkins is a man with two vocations, priest and poet, that were reciprocal rather than at odds.

Pick still stands as a useful and lively introduction to Hopkins, explicatory and explanatory. Pick allows that the poetry can be seen as the result of 'the organic and integral collaboration of the priest and poet, of sensibility and of belief' or indeed of a tension between the two, 'a triumphant and victorious expression' of Hopkins's inner drama (Pick 1966: xii). To clear off misconceptions and misunderstandings of his spiritual life, Pick offers a study of Hopkins's religious thought and development, 'the very inspiration and substance of his poetry as of his life' (Pick 1966: 1), since the undergraduate conflict between sensuous beauty and religious asceticism (a theme much pursued by later critics, notably Julia Saville) was only resolved once he was a Jesuit. Even while Pick stresses that religious significance does not of itself give poetic greatness – the poetry may express a sacramental view of nature and still be inferior as poetry – he emphasises that 'aside from all moral and spiritual considerations', Hopkins's poetry gained qualitatively by his joining the Jesuits (Pick 1966: 127). The importance of the *Spiritual Exercises* [**pp. 22; 88**] and the concept of the Dark Night of the Soul [**pp. 109–10**] is stressed, though Pick (rightly) does not see Hopkins as a mystical poet (Pick 1966: 129–30). Pick is particularly even-handed on the final Dublin years, which provide ammunition for those who see Hopkins's entry to the Jesuits as a destruction of his talent. While not denying misery and depression, Pick insists that those sufferings are not simply attributable to the Society of Jesus. Hopkins made a sacrifice: of fame, of recognition, of acclaim, but this did not prevent him pursuing his vocation as a poet (Pick 1966: ch. 7).

Peters, like Phare and Pick, takes Hopkins seriously, it being no longer possible to pass Hopkins by, his obscurity and oddity not the result of artistic wantonness or bad literary taste, but the logical outcome of his poetical theories (Peters 1970: xv–xvi). The need to make Hopkins more accessible and more intelligible (few would deny the challenges of Hopkins's poetry) determines Peters to investigate Hopkins's mind and then the personal form of his language. In pursuing Hopkins's reflections upon the fact of existence as an individual, as the *self*, an awareness of his body as well as his soul, Peters, more acutely than Pick, highlights the Dublin period and Hopkins's 'Terrible' Sonnets, 'his most personal, his best, and his most harassing poems', creations of a man who had 'earnestly prayed to be raised to a higher degree of grace' and had rather been 'lifted to a higher cross' (Peters 1970: 21, 26, 45, 49). From this, Peters turns to an examination of Hopkins's language, analysing it in detail, even while aware of the need to read the poetry aloud, a poetry often breaking grammar, because grammar limited the possibilities of language as a medium of poetry (Peters 1970: 139). If not all this analysis stands up still, it springs from that conviction, growing stronger as the century progressed, that the greatness of Hopkins could be demonstrated, but not seriously disputed.

MID-CENTURY: 1968 TO 1978

Phare, Pick and Peters are followed by two notable studies, ten years apart: Elisabeth W. Schneider's *The Dragon in the Gate: Studies in the Poetry of Gerard Manley Hopkins* (1968) and John Robinson's *In Extremity: A Study of Gerard Manley Hopkins* (1978). Schneider's book is, as she acknowledges, a series of explorations, while Robinson develops a continuing argument. Both, though, are agreed about Hopkins's greatness, his seriousness as an artist, and the crucial interrelationship rather than opposition of priest and poet. Robinson is explicit that he proposes to claim Hopkins back from the misconceptions, first, that only a priest who should really have given his life to poetry would write like this, or, second, only a religious could

write like this (Robinson 1978: 129). Schneider claims the priesthood
never became 'an unselfconscious, habitual way of life but remained
a conscious striving, accompanied by perpetual awareness of the
choice he had made' (Schneider 1968: 2), Hopkins's artistic sense
being too sure to allow confusion between poem and sermon.
Robinson in turn reinforces the idea of the artist when he admits
Hopkins's unhappiness in Dublin, yet insists that if others too might
have been unhappy, 'the acuteness of both feeling and intelligence
in the poems is Hopkins' own' (Schneider 1968: 105; Robinson
1978: 133).

Asserting the poet's greatness, Schneider and Robinson find it not
least in 'The Wreck', that 'Dragon in the Gate' of Robert Bridges's
opprobrious label and Schneider's title, a poem 'of unique but
indisputable greatness' (Schneider 1968: 40), while for Robinson it is
a poem where death is both certain and unsettling (Robinson 1978:
104). In her detailed explication of 'The Wreck', Schneider tackles
the question of the nun's experience, claiming that it only makes
sense if understood as a miracle, Christ, during 'the night of terror',
appearing to the nun, 'not in a subjective or imagined way but as a
real miraculous presence', a claim in which Robinson thinks her
right (Schneider 1968: 26–27; Robinson 1978: 116).

Such scrutinies (there are hints in Robinson that he was influenced
by Leavis's critical practices) lead to direct, simpler, and therefore
more effective readings of a poem like 'The Windhover'. Schneider
declares earlier critics looked for everything 'except the simple and
the obvious' and while admitting that 'buckle' is the sonnet's structural
centre, she rejects Empson [p. 191], as does Robinson, who finds the
separate ideal categories of beauty, valour, and act, collapse (or are
compressed) in 'buckle' as the falcon, by being wholly itself, 'gives
out the essential truth in things (just as the plough in its activity)'
(Schneider 1968: 146; Robinson 1978: 44). Such revaluations are evi-
dent at a more general level as Robinson, reassessing Hopkins's Irish
experiences, denies they were destructive of his talents and finds a
poetry of conclusions 'or of active engagement to reach them, not a
mood of receptiveness that supposes the will to be in abeyance',
poetic involvement at a high level of imaginative intensity (Robinson
1978: x, 112).

Conclusion: new directions 1992–2008

Critical issues, still of concern, reflecting responses of Hopkins's
earliest readers, include that clash or tension or interrelationship
between the two vocations; Bridges's concerns about rhythm and

poetic language; Catholic doctrine; aesthetics and the whole troubling issue of male desire; and whether Hopkins is a Modern or truly a Victorian. These issues are still apparent in recent studies, though handled differently from earlier critics. Instead of studies covering all the poetry in a general way, particular lines of enquiry are pursued, whether by Daniel Brown through the philosophical and scientific context or Julia Saville through the use of critical theory. Brown seeks to shows Hopkins was shaped by Oxford idealism rather than the Society of Jesus and Julia Saville seeks to reconcile Hopkins's impulses of desire with his love of God: both open up new ways of reading the poetry. Other focused studies of the period include Joseph J. Feeney on Hopkins's playfulness and Catherine Phillips on Hopkins's relationship to the visual world, all indicating how Hopkins studies are active and innovatory.

Daniel Brown's *Hopkins' Idealism: Philosophy, Physics, Poetry* (1997) is not for the faint-hearted or the first reader of Hopkins: it assumes a good basic knowledge of philosophy, certainly of its ter-minology, and some interest in science, but as an enquiry into Hopkins's responses to philosophical and physical (scientific) knowledge at Oxford and so into the development of his ideas of God, Nature, Self and poetry, it is impressive and yields illuminating readings. Brown's wish is to supplement or even supplant the image of Hopkins at Oxford as a conservative High Church ritualist by that 'of the boldly speculative intellectual liberal' which the Oxford writings on philosophy 'allow us to recover' (Brown 1997: viii). The mature poems did not emerge 'almost' from nothing, for the groundwork of ideas on stress, inscape and instress had been laid long before Hopkins read Duns Scotus. The study looks in detail at nineteenth-century Oxford's philosophical studies, in the context of a system of thought (English Idealism) that combined metaphysics, which enquires into what lies beyond the physical world, with personal belief – at Oxford, obviously, a belief in Christianity. Brown relates this encompassing approach, through Hopkins's interest in optics, to energy physics, which provided 'an understanding of the universe in which all things are unified as manifestations of a single constant power', identified with God (Brown 1997: 195).

These strands of thought are then explored in the poetry, 'The Wreck', with its opening threat of dissolution ('almost unmade, what with dread | Thy doing') presented as 'immediate and persistent' in the 'oppositional dynamics' of spirit and matter (Brown 1997: 262). Such a reconciliation of apparent opposites is there also in 'The Windhover', where a catalogue of particular impressions becomes 'caught' as a 'necessary unity', the onlooker thereby recognising not simply 'the objective identity of the creature but the source of all being, including his own' (Brown 1997: 287).

Hopkins, despite some of the early poems, is not generally thought of as a humorous poet. In 1931, Alan Pryce-Jones stated that reading Hopkins necessitated 'a characteristic giving-up of any sense of humour' (Roberts 1987: 219), while Robert Boyle found even the earlier poetry akin to the pedantic and laboured word-play of Holofernes in Shakespeare's *Love's Labours Lost* rather than the robust laughter of Falstaff (Boyle 1976: 102). Since Hopkins, though, is a witty poet, his language constantly making new and unexpected revelations, any investigation along lines of humour and wit is welcome. Joseph F. Feeney's *The Playfulness of Gerard Manley Hopkins* (2008) picks up and develops theories of play from Johan Huizinga's *Homo Ludens* (1938), the human species as an animal that plays. Feeney takes 'playfulness' as fun, and declares Hopkins to have been playful throughout his life (Feeney 2008: xv). The problems here are obvious: all creativity is, anyway, play-full, and Feeney makes his definition far too wide. He also has a disconcerting tendency, exploring particular poems, to overread or misread the text. In 'The Starlight Night' [**pp. 81–2**], not only are the 'fire-folk' envisaged in human form (as 'folk' itself insists), but distractingly pictured as Disney elfs, 'cross-legged, hands clasped around knees'; elsewhere, the opening of 'No Worst' [**pp. 111–2**] is seriously misread, while contrasting stanzas of 'The Wreck' (stanzas 24, 26) are taken as 'irrelevant but delightful digressions', not as part of the contrastive pattern of the ode as form (Feeney 2008: 91, 125, 72).

Suggestive of possible lines of enquiry, rather than successful, Feeney investigates through applying theory, a line pursued more fruitfully by others. Such a work is Julia F. Saville's *A Queer Chivalry: The Homoerotic Asceticism of Gerard Manley Hopkins* (2000). Approaching again the issue of a divided Hopkins, Saville does not consider a conflict between poet and priest, but rather between love for the divine, embodied literally in Christ, and for the masculine. This attachment to the beauty of the incarnate Son, whose outward nature allows us to glimpse the godhead, was for Hopkins, throughout his life, in conflict with his sexual impulses towards men. So Saville examines in detail what Phare in the 1930s had seen, in 'The Bugler's First Communion' [**pp. 138–9**], as 'embarrassment' at the fleshly insistence of 'tender as a pushed peach'. In a language more precisely critical, Saville identifies the same effect as struck Phare, for 'the speaker's act of stalling on a body he figures as beautiful in its chastity is enough to produce queer effects' (Saville 2000: 160). Saville picks up 'queer', a word used by Hopkins himself, to link her exploration primarily to another area of gender politics.

Of two of his sonnets, Hopkins said they were 'not so very queer' (*L*, 3.144), meaning of course 'odd', 'unfamiliar', but necessarily, as Saville suggests, pre-echoing the meaning, from the 1920s onwards, of 'a homosexual man', and so through the 'Queer' theory of the 1960s/1970s, a thread to lead into Hopkins's 'poetics of homoerotic asceticism' (Saville 2000: 1).

Hopkins is 'queer' in that his techniques were distinctive, odd, to achieve his purpose; he also shades over, for the modern reader, into 'queer' in his homoeroticism and the effect that that too has on his poetry and the readers' response to it. As artist, Hopkins strives to express himself, yet his irresolution in how he regards the masculine may be exposed or be part of his success. To exemplify what her theory, which also draws in modern theorists like Michel Foucault and Jacques Lacan and an acute awareness of the social context of Hopkins's life, might achieve, Saville offers a reading of 'The Windhover', placing it within the tradition of Victorian chivalric revival and the Catholic tradition of devotional poetry, where Hopkins develops his own 'queer' brand of chivalry 'to a beloved of his own sex but in a mode associated with the rigorous self-restraint on which a Victorian sense of manliness was predicated' (Saville 2000: 3). In 'The Windhover', as against say 'The Bugler's First Communion', there is a 'finely restrained tension between self-denial as a source of moral betterment and self-punishment as a source of sensual satisfaction, a tension reinforced by strange rhythmic effects' (Saville 2000: 4), a tension between desire and the ascetic.

Looking at each phase of Hopkins's poetic life, Saville notes the intense homosociality of the all-male society of Oxford University and offers a fine reading of 'The Wreck', a celebratory ode, where divine punishment is exhilarating and death a sublime union with Christ. Again, responding to form, Saville is revealing about Hopkins's use of the strategies of courtly love derived from conventions of the Petrarchan sonnet, that respond to but fend off the seductive flower of the visual. At each point in Hopkins's career 'some configuration of ascetic practice is apparent, sometimes enabling and sometimes constraining his capacity to articulate his desire through poetry' (Saville 2000: 8), and the challenge to the critic is 'to gauge whether the erotic charge in any one poem or sequence ... is the product of the poet's conscious calculations or ... the unconscious residue of conscious ascetic practice' (Saville 2000: 21). The reader is constantly turned by Saville back to the poetry, not as biographical or psychological key, not as the bone which theories gnaw, but as art that, however odd or 'queer', constantly justifies itself by its revelations of the physical and spiritual worlds.

While Norman White's biography [**pp. 147–9**] expertly covers the whole life, particular aspects of Hopkins's development, religious, intellectual, and artistic, are open to fuller exploration, as Alfred Thomas [**pp. 145–6**] and Daniel Brown [**p. 199**] and *All My Eyes See* [**pp. 154–5**] have shown. It is the artistic and in particular the visual contact that Catherine Phillips pursues in *Gerard Manley Hopkins and the Victorian Visual World* (2007). Beginning from childhood, she considers the people 'who shaped [Hopkins's] early responses' and 'the vision that grew out of his innate gifts as they were shaped and he learnt to express them artistically' (Phillips 2007: 263). The family background was of an aunt who taught Hopkins to sketch, the two brothers who became professional illustrators, and his father who wrote poetry. Hopkins, Phillips shows, had links to painters of the past and the present: Gainsborough, Landseer, and the Pre-Raphaelites, while various members and connections of his family were photographers, engravers, and lithographers. Hopkins's earliest publication, 'Winter with the Gulf Stream', appeared in *Once a Week*, where his father's verse was published, while his younger brother, Arthur, became an illustrator on the *Illustrated London News*. Phillips illuminatingly discusses Hopkins's 'Andromeda' [**pp. 95–6**], as exemplifying similar interests between father and son, while demonstrating the greater poetic powers of the son (Phillips 2007: 10–12), and prompted by Arthur Hopkins's connection with the *Illustrated London News*, considers 'The Wreck' in terms of accounts in the press, how Hopkins was aware of them and, given widespread public interest in the *Deutschland*, of a possible audience for his poem.

Phillips gives careful consideration to the Sketch books, an important adjunct to Jerome Bump [**pp. 154–5**], and to Hopkins's interest in architecture, not least a review of Oxford buildings based on the interesting (and demanding) tour Hopkins devised for his university visitors. On the art criticism, reviewing the number and diversity of exhibitions Hopkins went to, Phillips, while considering particular pictures in detail, is hampered by the book's lack of adequate and sufficient illustrations, especially of Victorian paintings which few of us have seen, even in reproduction: so in a potentially fascinating discussion of Frederick Walker's *The Bathers* (1866), 'town lads' with the 'bathing qualities of beauty of the antique marble', in various states of undress, clearly likely to have been of great interest to Hopkins, we are only given Walker's own description and a contemporary critic's derisive dismissal (Phillips 2007: 227–28).

Phillips commands a wide range of material and demonstrates not only Hopkins's training, but also how a poet so visually alert, so conscious of the physical world and how it might be represented, developed theories of vision, if 'shaped by social attitudes of his time' (Phillips 2007: 263), that produced the poetry and the prose on which his claim to be a great artist is based.

What these studies, from Daniel Brown to Catherine Phillips, are meant to exemplify are ways in which Hopkins studies have developed. They are not the only ways, but suggest the diversity that follows a confidence that Hopkins no longer needs to be defended as poet, and that he can be treated to specialist consideration as other artists are. Undoubtedly other, equally diverse, studies will follow, some prompted by the Collected Works to be published by Oxford University Press, which will make Hopkins more fully and more generally available than ever before.

FURTHER READING

The critical review in this section should have made clear the various uses of the studies discussed. Useful introductions to Hopkins are Storey (1992) and MacKenzie (1968) and (1981). Roberts (1987) is invaluable for his introduction as well as the range of earlier responses he reproduces; Jenkins (2006) is a sourcebook, with extracts from criticism early and late and a selection of poems, introduced and annotated. Thornton (1973) offers a brief contextual introduction and critical survey of the mature poetry. Dunne (1976) lists books, articles, and reviews up to 1976 and looks (Dunne 1975) at the critical reception. Turner (1989) and Davis (2002) are two literary histories of the Victorian age, both including Hopkins, with different but illuminating approaches to the period. Wheeler (1990), though not concerned specifically with Hopkins, explores concepts of death and immortality, while Zaniello (1989) extends the author's earlier study on Hopkins's relationship to science and miracles. On various aspects of technique, Prince (1962) explores the relationship between Milton and the Italian sonnet, important for Hopkins's use of the form and indeed his relationship to Milton, and Tennyson (1981) the 'devotional mode' of Victorian poetry. On technique and the Classics, Highet (1949) looks at the tradition of the ode (ch.12) from the Greeks to Hopkins; Bonn (1969) at Greco-Roman verse theory; and Badin (1992) at the influence of Plato's dialogues on Hopkins's poetic structures. Three works of 'sexual' critical theory are Morgan (1992), a 'feminist' study and, on masculine desire, Dellamora (1990) and Bristow (1992).

Chronology

1844	Gerard Manley Hopkins (GMH) born, 28 July, in Stratford, East London.
1854	After private schooling, GMH goes to Sir Roger Cholmley's School, Highgate.
1860	Wins school prize for his poem, 'The Escorial'.
1862	GMH's surviving Journals begin.
1863	GMH's first publication, 'Winter with the Gulf Stream', appears in *Once a Week* (February). Wins a place at Oxford (January) and goes (April) to Balliol College, where GMH is influenced variously by his tutors, Benjamin Jowett and Walter Pater, and by H.P. Liddon.
1863–68	GMH writes a wide variety of poems and poetic fragments.
1865	His Oxford friend, Robert Bridges, introduces GMH to Digby Dolben, who deeply impresses him.
1866	GMH determines to become a Catholic (July) and is received into the Church by John Henry Newman (October).
1867	GMH is awarded a first class degree in Classics and Philosophy.
1867–68	Teaches at the Oratory School, Birmingham.
1868	GMH goes to Manresa House, Roehampton, run by the Jesuits, to test his vocation (April); determines to become a priest, to join the Society of Jesus, and to give up poetry (May). Begins his training at Manresa (the Noviciate) (December).
1870–73	GMH takes his preliminary vows and goes to St Mary's College, Stonyhurst, for three years to study philosophy (the Philosophate).
1873	GHM returns to Manresa House, to teach Latin and rhetoric to the novices.
1874	GMH renews his friendship with Robert Bridges.
1874–77	GMH goes to St Beuno's College, North Wales, to study theology (the Theologate).

1875	GMH's surviving Journals break off (February). On the hint that the wreck of the *Deutschland* (December) might be commemorated, GMH writes 'The Wreck of the *Deutschland*' and returns to poetry.
1876–78	GMH writes, besides occasional poetry, sonnets that include 'God's Grandeur', 'The Starlight Night', 'Spring', 'The Sea and the Skylark','The Lantern Out of Doors', and 'The Windhover'.
1877	GMH is ordained priest (September) and sent to teach at Mount St Mary's College, Spinkhill.
1878	GMH is sent to the Church of the Immaculate Conception, Farm Street, London and begins a friendship with R.W. Dixon (June). He is moved to St Aloysius's, Oxford (October).
1878–86	GMH writes, amongst other poems, 'The Loss of the *Eurydice*', 'Duns Scotus's Oxford', 'Henry Purcell', 'The Candle Indoors', 'The Bugler's First Communion', 'Andromeda', 'Felix Randal', 'Spring and Fall', 'The Leaden Echo and the Golden Echo', 'Spelt from Sibyl's Leaves', 'To What Serves Mortal Beauty'. He also works on the uncompleted drama, *St Winefred's Well*.
1879	GMH goes to St Joseph's, Bedford Leigh (Leigh) in Lancashire (October).
1880	GMH is moved to St Francis Xavier's, Liverpool (January).
1881	GMH is transferred to St Joseph's, Glasgow (August–October).
1881–82	GMH returns to Manresa House for the Tertianship, a period of reflection and renewal of vows.
1882–84	GMH teaches Classics to the boys at St Mary's College, Stonyhurst. Begins a friendship with Coventry Patmore.
1884	GMH is elected Professor of Greek at the Catholic University, Dublin (January).
1885–86	Amongst other poems, including 'The Soldier', 'Harry Ploughman', and 'Tom's Garland', GMH writes the sequence called the 'Terrible' Sonnets or Sonnets of Desolation, generally agreed to include 'To Seem the Stranger', 'I Wake and Feel', 'No Worst There is None', 'Carrion Comfort', 'Patience, Hard Thing', and 'My Own Heart'.
1887–89	GMH's last poems include 'That Nature is a Heraclitean Fire', 'St Alphonsus Rodriguez', 'Justus Quidem Tu Es, Domine', 'The Shepherd's Brow', and 'To R.B.'
1889	GMH contracts typhoid fever (May); he dies, 8 June, and is buried in Glasnevin Cemetery, Dublin.

Bibliography

Allen, David Elliston (1978) *The Naturalist in Britain: A Social History*, Harmondsworth: Penguin, 1976.

Allsopp, Michael E. & Sundermeier, Michael W. (eds) (1989) *Gerard Manley Hopkins (1844–1889): New Essays on His Life, Writing, and Place in English Literature*, Lewiston: Edwin Mellen Press.

Anderson, Warren (1976) '"Never Ending Revel": *The Wreck* and the Ode Tradition', in Peter Milward (ed.) *Readings of The Wreck: Essays in Commemoration of the Centenary of G.M. Hopkins' The Wreck of the Deutschland*, Chicago: Loyola University Press.

——(1989) '"Freshness Deep Down Things": Hopkins' Dublin Notes on Homer', in Michael E. Allsopp & Michael W. Sundermeier (eds) *Gerard Manley Hopkins (1844–1889): New Essays on His Life, Writing, and Place in English Literature*, Lewiston: Edwin Mellen Press.

Armstrong, Isobel (1993) *Victorian Poetry: Poetry, Poetics and Politics*, London: Routledge.

Attwater, Donald (1965) *The Penguin Dictionary of Saints*, Harmondsworth: Penguin.

Badin, Donatella Abbate (1992) 'The Dialogic Structure of Hopkins' Poetry', in Anthony Mortimer (ed.) *The Authentic Cadence: Centennial Essays on Gerard Manley Hopkins*, Fribourg: Fribourg University Press.

Ball, Patricia M. (1968) *The Central Self: A Study in Romantic and Victorian Imagination*, London: Athlone Press.

——(1971) *The Science of Aspects: The Changing Role of Fact in the Work of Coleridge, Ruskin and Hopkins*, London: Athlone Press.

Barnes, Jonathan (ed.) (1987) *Early Greek Philosophy*, Harmondsworth: Penguin.

Bede (1968) *A History of the English Church and People*, trans. Leo Sherley-Price, Harmondsworth: Penguin, 1955, rev. 1968.

Bell, Quentin (1963) *Ruskin*, Edinburgh: Oliver & Boyd.

Bender, Todd K. (1966) *Gerard Manley Hopkins: The Classical Background and Critical Reception of His Work*, Baltimore: Johns Hopkins Press.

Bergonzi, Bernard (1977) *Gerard Manley Hopkins*, London & Basingstoke: Macmillan.

Berry, Francis (1962) *Poetry and the Physical Voice*, London: Routledge.

Bible: The Authorized Version (1997), ed. Robert Carroll and Stephen Prickett, Oxford: Oxford University Press.

Bonn, John Louis (1969) [1949] 'Greco-Roman Verse Theory and Gerard Manley Hopkins', in Norman Weyand (ed.) *Immortal Diamond: Studies in Gerard Manley Hopkins*, New York: Octagon Books, 1949; 1969.

Boyle, Robert (1961) *Metaphor in Hopkins*, Chapel Hill: North Carolina University Press.

——(1976) '"Man Jack the Man Is": *The Wreck* from the Perspective of *The Shepherd's Brow*', in Peter Milward (ed.) *Readings of The Wreck: Essays in Commemoration of the Centenary of G.M. Hopkins' The Wreck of the Deutschland*, Chicago: Loyola University Press.

Bridges, Robert (1929) *The Testament of Beauty*, Oxford: Clarendon Press.

Bristow, Joseph (1992) '"Churlsgrace": Gerard Manley Hopkins and the Working-Class Male Body', *English Literary History*, vol. 29.

Brown, Daniel (1997) *Hopkins' Idealism: Philosophy, Physics, Poetry*, Oxford: Clarendon Press.

Buckley, Vincent (1968) *Poetry and the Sacred*, London: Chatto & Windus.

Bump, Jerome (1975) 'Hopkins' Drawings', in R.K.R. Thornton (ed.) *All My Eyes See: The Visual World of Gerard Manley Hopkins*, Sunderland: Coelfrith Press.

Chadwick, Owen (1966 & 1970) *The Victorian Church (An Ecclesiastical History of England)*, London: Adam & Charles Black, 2 vols.

——(1972) *The Reformation (Pelican History of the Church)*, Harmondsworth: Penguin, 1964, rev. 1969, 1972.

——(1990) *The Secularization of the European Mind in the Nineteenth Century*, Cambridge: Cambridge University Press, 1975.

Cotter, James Finn (1972) *Inscape: The Christology and Poetry of Gerard Manley Hopkins*, Pittsburgh: Pittsburgh University Press.

Davie, Donald (1967) *Purity of Diction in English Verse*, London: Routledge & Kegan Paul, 1952, rev. 1967.

Davis, Philip (2002) *The Victorians (Oxford English Literary History)*, Oxford: Oxford University Press.

Dellamora, Richard (1990) *Masculine Desire: The Sexual Politics of Victorian Aestheticism*, Chapel Hill: University of North Carolina Press.

Dolben, Digby Mackworth (1915) *The Poems*, ed. Robert Bridges, London: Humphrey Milford / Oxford University Press.

Donoghue, Denis (1994) 'The Oxford of Pater, Hopkins, and Wilde', in C. George Sandalescu (ed.) *Rediscovering Oscar Wilde*, Gerrards Cross: Colin Smythe.

Downes, David A. (1959) *Gerard Manley Hopkins: A Study of His Ignatian Spirit*, New York: Bookman Associates.

——(1989) 'The Final Act: Hopkins' Last Sonnets', in Michael E. Allsopp & Michael W. Sundermeier (eds) *Gerard Manley Hopkins (1844–1889): New Essays on His Life, Writing, and Place in English Literature*, Lewiston: Edwin Mellen Press.

Dunne, Tom (1975) 'Hopkins' Publications and Their Critical Reception', in R. K. R. Thornton (ed.) *All My Eyes See: The Visual World of Gerard Manley Hopkins*, Sunderland: Coelfrith Press.

——(1976) *Gerard Manley Hopkins: A Comprehensive Bibliography*, Oxford: Clarendon Press.

Ellis, Virginia Ridley (1991) *Gerard Manley Hopkins and the Language of Mystery*, Columbia: Missouri University Press.

Empson, William (1965) *Seven Types of Ambiguity*, Harmondsworth: Penguin, 1930, rev. 1961.

Eusebius (1989) *The History of the Church*, trans. G.A. Williamson, Harmondsworth: Penguin, 1965, rev. 1989.

Faber, Geoffrey (1954) *Oxford Apostles*, Harmondsworth: Penguin, 1933, rev. 1936.

Faverty, Frederic E. (ed.) (1968) *The Victorian Poets: A Guide to Research*, Cambridge, Mass: Harvard University Press.

Feeney, Joseph J. (2008) *The Playfulness of Gerard Manley Hopkins*, Aldershot: Ashgate.

Fraser, Hilary (1986) *Beauty and Belief: Aesthetics and Religion in Victorian Literature*, Cambridge: Cambridge University Press.

Fry, Roger (1972) *Letters of Roger Fry*, ed. Denys Sutton, London: Chatto & Windus, 2 vols.

Gardner, W.H. (1966) *Gerard Manley Hopkins: A Study of Poetic Idiosyncrasy in Relation to Poetic Tradition*, London: Oxford University Press, vol. 1, 1944, rev. 1948; vol. 2, 1949, rev. 1966.

Griffiths, Eric (1989) *The Printed Voice of Victorian Poetry*, Oxford: Clarendon Press.

Guardini, Romano (1966) [1962] 'Aesthetic-Theological Thoughts on "The Windhover"', in Geoffrey H. Hartman (ed.) *Hopkins: A Collection of Critical Essays*, Englewood Cliffs: Prentice-Hall.

Harrison, Anthony H. & Taylor, Beverly (eds.) (1992) *Gender and Discourse in Victorian Literature and Art*, DeKalb: North Illinois Press.

Hartman, Geoffrey H. (1966) *The Unmediated Vision: An Interpretation of Wordsworth, Hopkins, Rilke, and Valéry*, New York: Harcourt, Brace 1954.

——(ed.) (1966) *Hopkins: A Collection of Critical Essays*, Englewood Cliffs: Prentice-Hall.

Hewison, Robert (1976) *John Ruskin: The Argument of the Eye*, Princeton: Princeton University Press.

Highet, Gilbert (1949) *The Classical Tradition: Greek and Roman Influences on Western Literature*, Oxford: The Clarendon Press.

Highet, Gilbert (1959) *Poets in a Landscape*, Harmondsworth: Penguin, 1957.

Hilton, Tim (1985) *John Ruskin: The Early Years*, New Haven & London: Yale University Press.

——(2000) *John Ruskin: The Later Years*, New Haven & London: Yale University Press.

Hopkins, Gerard Manley (1930) *Poems*, 2nd edn, ed. Charles Williams, London: Oxford University Press.

——(1955) *The Letters of Gerard Manley Hopkins to Robert Bridges*, ed. Claude Colleer Abbott, London: Oxford University Press, 1935, rev. 1955.

——(1955) *The Correspondence of Gerard Manley Hopkins and Richard Watson Dixon*, ed. Claude Colleer Abbott, London: Oxford University Press, 1935, rev. 1955.

——(1956) *Further Letters of Gerard Manley Hopkins*, ed. Claude Colleer Abbott, London: Oxford University Press, 1938, rev. 1956.

——(1959) *The Journals and Papers of Gerard Manley Hopkins*, ed. Humphry House and Graham Storey, London: Oxford University Press.

——(1959) *The Sermons and Devotional Writings of Gerard Manley Hopkins*, ed. Christopher Devlin, London: Oxford University Press.

——(2002) *Gerard Manley Hopkins: The Major Works*, ed. Catherine Phillips, Oxford: Oxford University Press, 1986.

Horace (1964) *Odes*, trans. James Michie, Harmondsworth: Penguin.

Hudson, Derek (1949) *Coventry Patmore*, London: Constable.

Jenkins, Alice (ed.) (2006) *The Poems of Gerard Manley Hopkins: A Source-book*, Abingdon: Routledge.

John of the Cross (1960) *Poems*, trans. Roy Campbell, Harmondsworth: Penguin, 1951, 1960.

Johnson, Margaret (1997) *Gerard Manley Hopkins and Tractarian Poetry*, Aldershot: Ashgate.

Johnson, Wendell Stacy (1968) *Gerard Manley Hopkins: The Poet as Victorian*, Ithaca: Cornell University Press.

Keating, John E. (1976) '"A Continuous Structural Parallelism": Stanzaic Pattern in *The Wreck*', in Peter Milward (ed.) *Readings of The Wreck: Essays in Commemoration of the Centenary of G.M.Hopkins' The Wreck of the Deutschland*, Chicago: Loyola University Press.

Ker, Ian (2003) *The Catholic Revival in English Literature, 1845–1961*, Leominster: Gracewing.

Kitchen, Paddy (1978) *Gerard Manley Hopkins*, London: Hamish Hamilton.

Lahey, G.F. (1930) *Gerard Manley Hopkins*, London: Oxford University Press.

Leavis, F.R. (1962) *The Common Pursuit*, Harmondsworth: Penguin, 1952.

——(1963) *New Bearings in English Poetry*, Harmondsworth: Penguin, 1932, rev. 1950.

Leech, Geoffrey N. (1969) *A Linguistic Guide to English Poetry*, London: Longmans.

Lees, Francis Noel (1976) '"The Strong Spur, Live and Lancing": The Motive of Martyrdom in *The Wreck*', in Peter Milward (ed.) *Readings of The Wreck: Essays in Commemoration of the Centenary of G.M. Hopkins' The Wreck of the Deutschland*, Chicago: Loyola University Press.

Lichtmann, Maria R. (1989) *The Contemplative Poetry of Gerard Manley Hopkins*, Princeton: Princeton University Press.

Loomis, Jeffrey B. (1988) *Dayspring in Darkness: Sacrament in Hopkins*, Lewisburg: Bucknell University Press / London: Associated Universities Press.

Loyola (1996) St Ignatius of, *Personal Writings*, trans. Joseph A. Munitiz and Philip Endean, Harmondsworth: Penguin.

Lyons, F.S.L. (1973) *Ireland Since the Famine*, London: Fontana, 1971.

McChesney, Donald (1968) *A Hopkins Commentary*, London: University of London Press.

MacKenzie, Norman H. (1968) *Hopkins*, Edinburgh: Oliver & Boyd.

——(1981) *A Reader's Guide to Gerard Manley Hopkins*, London: Thames & Hudson.

McLuhan, Herbert Marshall (1966) [1944] 'The Analogical Mirrors', in Geoffrey H. Hartman (ed.) *Hopkins: A Collection of Critical Essays*, Englewood Cliffs: Prentice-Hall (1966).

Mariani, Paul L. (1970) *A Commentary on the Complete Poems of Gerard Manley Hopkins*, Ithaca: Cornell University Press.

Martin, Robert (1991) *Gerard Manley Hopkins: A Very Private Life*, London: Collins.

Martz, Louis L. (1962) *The Poetry of Meditation: A Study in English Religious Literature of the Seventeenth Century*, New Haven: Yale University Press, 1954, rev. 1962.

Miles, Alfred H. (ed.) (1906) *The Poets and the Poetry of the Nineteenth Century: Robert Bridges and Contemporary Poets*, London: George Routledge, 1891.

Miller, J. Hillis (1975) *The Disappearance of God: Five Nineteenth-Century Writers*, Cambridge, Mass: Belknap Press / Harvard University Press, 1963, rev. 1965, 1975.

Milroy, James (1977) *The Language of Gerard Manley Hopkins*, London: André Deutsch.

Milward, Peter (1968) *A Commentary on G.M. Hopkins' The Wreck of the Deutschland*, Tokyo: Hokuseido Press.

——(1969) *A Commentary on the Sonnets of G.M. Hopkins*, Tokyo: Hokuseido Press.

——(ed.) (1976) *Readings of The Wreck: Essays in Commemoration of the Centenary of G.M. Hopkins' The Wreck of the Deutschland*, Chicago: Loyola University Press.

Milward, Peter and Schoder, Raymond (1975) *Landscape and Inscape: Vision and Inspiration in Hopkins's Poetry*, London: Paul Elek.

Morgan, Thaïs E. (1992) 'Violence, Creativity and the Feminine: Poetics and Gender Politics in Swinburne and Hopkins', in Anthony H. Harrison & Beverly Taylor (eds) *Gender and Discourse in Victorian Literature and Art*, DeKalb: North Illinois Press.

Mortimer, Anthony (1992) 'Hopkins: The Stress and the Self', in Anthony Mortimer (ed.) *The Authentic Cadence: Centennial Essays on Gerard Manley Hopkins*, Fribourg: Fribourg University Press.

——(ed.) (1992) *The Authentic Cadence: Centennial Essays on Gerard Manley Hopkins*, Fribourg: Fribourg University Press.

Olney, James (1993) *The Language(s) of Poetry: Walt Whitman, Emily Dickinson, Gerard Manley Hopkins*, Athens: Georgia University Press.

Ong, Walter J. (1969) [1949] 'Hopkins' Sprung Rhythm and the Life of English Poetry', in Norman Weyand (ed.) *Immortal Diamond: Studies in Gerard Manley Hopkins*, New York: Octagon Books, 1949; 1969.

——(1986) *Hopkins, the Self, and God*, Toronto: Toronto University Press.

Owen, Wilfred (1963) *The Collected Poems of Wilfred Owen*, ed. C.Day Lewis, London: Chatto & Windus, 1920.

Pater, Walter (1928) *The Renaissance: Studies in Art and Poetry*, London: Jonathan Cape, 1873.

Peters, W.A.M. (1970) *Gerard Manley Hopkins: A Critical Essay towards the Understanding of His Poetry*, Oxford: Basil Blackwell, 1948, rev. 1970.

Phare, Elsie Elizabeth (1933) *The Poetry of Gerard Manley Hopkins: A Survey and Commentary*, Cambridge: Cambridge University Press.

Phelan, Joseph (2005) *The Nineteenth-Century Sonnet*, Basingstoke: Palgrave Macmillan.

Phillips, Catherine (1992) *Robert Bridges: A Biography*, Oxford: Oxford University Press.

——(2007) *Gerard Manley Hopkins and the Victorian Visual World*, Oxford: Oxford University Press.

Pick, John (1966) *Gerard Manley Hopkins: Priest and Poet*, London: Oxford University Press, 1942, rev. 1966.

——(1968) 'Gerard Manley Hopkins', in Frederic E. Faverty (ed.) *The Victorian Poets: A Guide to Research*, Cambridge, Mass: Harvard University Press.

Pinto, Vivian de Sola (1958) *Crisis in English Poetry 1880–1940*, London: Hutchinson, 1951.

Prince, F.T. (1962) *The Italian Element in Milton's Verse*, Oxford: Clarendon Press, 1954, rev. 1962.

Rehder, Robert (1992) 'Inside Out: Omnipotence and the Hidden Heart in "The Windhover"', in Anthony Mortimer (ed.) *The Authentic Cadence: Centennial Essays on Gerard Manley Hopkins*, Fribourg: Fribourg University Press.

Roberts, Gerald (ed.) (1987) *Gerard Manley Hopkins: The Critical Heritage*, London: Routledge.

——(1994) *Gerard Manley Hopkins: A Literary Life*, Basingstoke & London: Macmillan.

Robinson, John (1978) *In Extremity: A Study of Gerard Manley Hopkins*, Cambridge: Cambridge University Press.

Ruggles, Eleanor (1947) *Gerard Manley Hopkins: A Life*, London: John Lane, The Bodley Head, 1944.

Ruskin, John (1897) *Modern Painters*, Orpington & London: George Allen, vol. 1, 1843.

——(1905) *The Two Paths*, London: George Allen, 1859.

——(1907) *The Elements of Drawing*, London: J.M. Dent, 1857.

Sambrook, James (1962) *A Poet Hidden: The Life of Richard Watson Dixon 1833–1900*, London: Athlone Press.

Sandalescu, C. George (ed.) (1994) *Rediscovering Oscar Wilde*, Gerrards Cross: Colin Smythe.

Saville, Julia F. (2000) *A Queer Chivalry: The Homoerotic Asceticism of Gerard Manley Hopkins*, Charlottesville: University of Virginia Press.

Schneider, Elisabeth W. (1968) *The Dragon in the Gate: Studies in the Poetry of G.M. Hopkins*, Berkeley & Los Angeles: University of California Press.

Schoder, Raymond V. (1976) 'The "Carrier-Witted" Heart: The Ignatian Quality of *The Wreck*', in Peter Milward (ed.) *Readings of The Wreck: Essays in Commemoration of the Centenary of G.M. Hopkins' The Wreck of the Deutschland*, Chicago: Loyola University Press.

——(1989) 'Hopkins and Pindar', in Michael E. Allsopp & Michael W. Sundermeier (eds) *Gerard Manley Hopkins (1844–1889): New Essays on His Life, Writing, and Place in English Literature*, Lewiston: Edwin Mellen Press.

Sonstraem, David (1967) 'Making Earnest of Game: G.M. Hopkins and Nonsense Poetry', *Modern Language Quarterly*, XXVIII.

Sterry, Paul (2004) *Complete British Birds*, London: Collins.

Storey, Graham (1992) *A Preface to Hopkins*, London: Longmans, 1981, rev. 1992.

Street, Sean (1992) *The Wreck of the Deutschland*, London: Souvenir Press.

Sulloway, Alison G. (1972) *Gerard Manley Hopkins and the Victorian Temper*, New York: Columbia University Press.

——(1976) '"Strike You the Sight of It?": Intimations of Myth and Tragedy in *The Wreck*', in Peter Milward (ed.) *Readings of The Wreck: Essays in Commemoration of the Centenary of G.M. Hopkins' The Wreck of the Deutschland*, Chicago: Loyola University Press.

——(1989) 'Gerard Manley Hopkins and "Women and Men" as Partners in the Mystery of Redemption', *Texas Studies in Literature and Language*, vol. 32.

Tennyson, G.B. (1981) *Victorian Devotional Poetry: The Tractarian Mode*, Cambridge, Mass: Harvard University Press.

Teresa of Avila (1987) *The Life of Saint Teresa of Avila by Herself*, trans. J. M. Cohen, 1957, Harmondsworth: Penguin.

Thomas, Alfred (1969) *Hopkins the Jesuit: The Years of Training*, London: Oxford University Press.

Thornton, R.K.R (1973), *Gerard Manley Hopkins: The Poems*, London: Edward Arnold.

——(ed.) (1975) *All My Eyes See: The Visual World of Gerard Manley Hopkins*, Sunderland: Coelfrith Press.

Turner, Paul (1989) *English Literature 1832–1890 Excluding the Novel*, Oxford: Clarendon Press.

Vendler, Helen (1992) 'The Wreck of the Deutschland' in Anthony Mortimer (ed.) *The Authentic Cadence Centennial Essays on Gerard Manley Hopkins*, Friborg: Friborg University Press.

Vendler, Helen (1995) *The Breaking of Style: Hopkins, Heaney, Graham*, Cambridge, Mass: Harvard University Press.

Vickers, Brian (1992) 'Rhetoric and Formality in Hopkins', in Anthony Mortimer (ed.) *The Authentic Cadence: Centennial Essays on Gerard Manley Hopkins*, Fribourg: Fribourg University Press.

Vidler, Alec R. (1974) *The Church in an Age of Revolution (The Pelican History of the Church)*, Harmondsworth: Penguin, 1961, rev. 1971, 1974.

Virgil (1982) *The Georgics*, trans. L.P. Wilkinson, Harmondsworth: Penguin.

——(1990) *The Aeneid*, trans. David West, Harmondsworth: Penguin.

Wain, John (1966) [1959] 'An Idiom of Desperation', in Geoffrey H. Hartman (ed.) *Hopkins: A Collection of Critical Essays*, Englewood Cliffs: Prentice-Hall.

Walhout, Donald (1989) 'The Instress of Action: Action and Contemplation in Hopkins' Poetry', in Michael E. Allsopp & Michael W. Sundermeier (eds) *Gerard Manley Hopkins (1844–1889): New Essays on His Life, Writing, and Place in English Literature*, Lewiston: Edwin Mellen Press.

Warren, Austin (1966) [1944] 'Instress of Inscape', in Geoffrey H. Hartman (ed.) *Hopkins: A Collection of Critical Essays*, Englewood Cliffs: Prentice-Hall.

Weyand, Norman, ed. (1969) *Immortal Diamond: Studies in Gerard Manley Hopkins*, New York: Octagon Books, 1949; 1969.

Wheeler, Michael (1990) *Death and the Future Life in Victorian Literature and Theology*, Cambridge: Cambridge University Press.

White, Norman (1975) 'Hopkins as Art Critic', in R.K.R. Thornton (ed.) *All My Eyes See: The Visual World of Gerard Manley Hopkins*, Sunderland: Coelfrith Press.

——(1992) *Hopkins: A Literary Biography*, Oxford: Clarendon Press.

Winters, Yvor (1966) [1957] 'Gerard Manley Hopkins', in Geoffrey H. Hartman (ed.) *Hopkins: A Collection of Critical Essays*, Englewood Cliffs: Prentice-Hall.

Young, G.M. (1937) *Daylight and Champaign: Essays*, London: Jonathan Cape.

Zaniello, Tom (1988) *Hopkins in the Age of Darwin*, Iowa City: Iowa University Press.

——(1989) 'Of Miracles, Martyrs, and Prayer Gauges', in Michael E. Allsopp & Michael W. Sundermeier (eds) *Gerard Manley Hopkins (1844–1889): New Essays on His Life, Writing, and Place in English Literature*, Lewiston: Edwin Mellen Press.

Index

GMH = Gerard Manley Hopkins